Women

who changed the world

Fifty inspirational women who shaped history

Quercus

Quercus Publishing Plc
21 Bloomsbury Square
London
WC1A 2NS

First published 2006
Copyright © Quercus 2006
Reprinted in 2007

A catalogue record for this book is available from the British Library.

ISBN: 1 905204 04 3

Printed in Singapore

Picture Credits
The publishers would like to thank the following for permission to reproduce photographs: akg-images pp. 42, 46, Erich Lessing, p. 26; Giraudon/Bridgeman Art Library p. 10; Bridgeman Art Library p. 34; Corbis/Bettmann pp. 22, 62, 78, 106, 110, 114, 122, 134, 138, 146, 150, 174, Hulton-Deutsch Collection, pp. 98, 170, Reuters, pp. 162, 186, Leif Skoogfors, p. 178, Chris Farina, p. 190, Neal Preston, p. 194; Courtesy of the Library of Congress pp. 54, 66, 70, 94, 182; Dian Fossey Gorilla Fund International/www.gorilliafund.org. p. 166; Glenbow Archives/na-2607-1, na-273-3, na-273-1, na-273-2, na-5395-4, p. 82; Mary Evans Picture Library pp. 6, 14, 18, 30, 38, 50, 58, 74; TopFoto.co.uk, pp. 86, 90, 102, 118, 126, 130, 142, 154, 158, 198, 202.

Cover Photographs:
Chris Farina, top left; TopFoto.co.uk, top right and bottom right; Tim Graham/Corbis, bottom left

Researched, compiled and edited by Cambridge Editorial Partnership, Michael Young Centre, Purbeck Road, Cambridge CB2 2PF, with thanks to Jemma Carter, Martin Hall, Carol Schaessens and Martin Walters. Designed by Zoe Naylor. Picture research by Caroline Thompson.

Introduction

Selecting only 50 women for a place in this book was a daunting and potentially controversial task. Everyone has their own idea of what makes a person great, but all of the women featured here are outstanding individuals who achieved exceptional things in the major fields of human endeavour – politics, literature, art, science, music, social reform, entertainment, sport and adventure.

It would be impossible to consider the influence of the legions of great women throughout our history in a book of this length. No selection of this kind can be comprehensive. Every reader will have his or her ideas about the women included here – and many who have been omitted – but we hope that the choices made by our researchers will prompt thought and discussion. We would welcome suggestions for further volumes.

For the earliest women in this book, their gender – the simple fact that they were women – is a major factor in what made their accomplishments so remarkable. Much of what we know about them is speculative, reported by historic documents of varying reliability, almost all of which were written by men. Many were women of status: queens by birth or marriage, the decisions and alliances they made affected the course of history. Others have been given almost mythical status, important for what they symbolize in enduring legend. Some were spurred to extraordinary action and paid for their convictions with their lives.

Inevitably, an important thread running through this book is women's struggle to make their voices heard in what was, essentially, a man's world. For them to achieve what they did, they first had to fight the limitations imposed on them by society and traditional assumptions about a woman's role. Included here are women who were trying to change the world and confront its inequalities – writers, revolutionaries, scientists, artists and innovators, suffragists, anti-slavery campaigners and feminists. Many lived in times when popular opinion derided their ideas and diminished their femininity.

By the end of World War I, the traditional barriers that women had fought to break down had largely disappeared and the struggles they faced against entrenched ideas and conventions were no longer limited to their sex. Racism, poverty, class and disability were universal issues to be fought, either on their own or on others' behalf. Feminism began to contest discrimination in literature, science, politics, fashion, entertainment and sport.

Many of the women in this book are pioneers, pushing at new frontiers of achievement and showing us how the modern world has been changed and shaped for women, by women.

Contents

Introduction 3

Cleopatra 69 BCE–30 BCE 6

Mary Magdalene c. 4 BCE–CE 40 10

Boudicca early 1st century 14

Hildegard of Bingen 1098–1179 18

Eleanor of Aquitaine 1122–1204 22

Joan of Arc 1412–1431 26

Isabella I of Spain 1451–1504 30

Catherine de Medici 1519–1589 34

Elizabeth I 1533–1603 38

Catherine the Great 1729–1796 42

Mary Wollstonecraft 1759–1797 46

Jane Austen 1775–1817 50

Harriet Beecher Stowe 1811–1896 54

Queen Victoria 1819–1901 58

Florence Nightingale 1820–1910 62

　　Mary Seacole 1805–1881 65

Susan B. Anthony 1820–1906 66

　　Elizabeth Cady Stanton 1815–1902 69

Mary Cassatt 1844–1926 70

Emmeline Pankhurst 1858–1928 74

Marie Curie 1867–1934 78

The Famous Five: Emily Murphy 1868–1933 82

　　Henrietta Muir Edwards 1849–1931

　　Nellie Mooney McClung 1873–1951

　　Louise Crummy McKinney 1868–1931

　　Irene Marryat Parlby 1868–1965

Rosa Luxemburg 1870–1919 86

Helena Rubinstein 1870–1965 90

Helen Keller 1880–1968 94

Virginia Woolf 1882–1941 98

Coco Chanel 1883–1971   102

Eleanor Roosevelt 1884–1962   106

Amelia Earhart 1897–1937   110

    Amy Johnson 1903–1941   113

Margaret Bourke-White 1904–1971   114

Katharine Hepburn 1907–2003   118

Simone de Beauvoir 1908–1986   122

Mother Teresa 1910–1997   126

Dorothy Hodgkin 1910–1994   130

Rosa Parks 1913–2005   134

Jiang Qing (Madame Mao) 1914–1991   138

Billie Holiday 1915–1959   142

Eva Perón 1919–1952   146

Betty Friedan 1921–2006   150

Margaret Thatcher 1925–   154

Marilyn Monroe 1926–1962   158

Anne Frank 1929–1945   162

Dian Fossey 1932–1985   166

Mary Quant 1934–   170

Germaine Greer 1939–   174

Mairead Corrigan 1944– and Betty Williams 1943–   178

Billie Jean King 1943–   182

Benazir Bhutto 1953–   186

Oprah Winfrey 1954–   190

Madonna 1958–   194

Diana, Princess of Wales 1961–1997   198

Ellen MacArthur 1976–   202

Index   206

Cleopatra

Cleopatra VII was the last Ptolemaic ruler of Egypt, holding out against the seemingly relentless spread of the Roman Empire. Her name will always be linked with her two famous lovers, Julius Caesar and Marc Antony, although it is likely that her relationships with them represented strategic political alliances as much as genuine romances.

'Had Cleopatra's nose been shorter, the whole face of the earth would have been different.'

Blaise Pascal

BIOGRAPHY

Name:	Cleopatra Thea Philopator
Lived:	January 69 BCE – August 30 BCE
Place of birth:	Alexandria, Egypt
Place of death:	Alexandria, Egypt
Nationality:	Greek
Famed as:	Queen of Egypt; lover of Julius Caesar and Marc Antony

Cleopatra VII is one of the world's greatest political and romantic heroines. Born in Alexandria in 69 BCE, she was the daughter of Ptolemy XII, also known as Ptolemy Auletes. The Ptolemies were of Macedonian descent, but they ruled Egypt as Pharaohs. Her family was Greek, but she spoke Egyptian and declared herself to be the daughter of the Egyptian Sun God, Ra.

When Cleopatra's father died, in 51 BCE, he left the kingdom to Cleopatra and her younger brother, Ptolemy XIII, and at the age of seventeen Cleopatra ascended the Egyptian throne.

FACTFILE

- Legend has it that Cleopatra was wrapped in a carpet and delivered to Caesar at their first meeting.
- Her supposed beauty has been much debated. Coins bearing her image show a hook-nosed, masculine looking woman.
- Her suicide is likely to have been prompted by her dread of humiliation as a Roman prisoner rather than grief over Marc Antony's death.
- Cleopatra's Needle, which now stands on the Thames Embankment in London, has nothing to do with her. It was erected by Thoumes III, 1500 years before her birth.

Egyptian inheritance was matrilinear so the throne descended through the mother's line. This meant that Cleopatra had to marry one of her brothers in order for him to rule – her own father and mother had been brother and sister. She married Ptolemy, who was then only 12. Although the male ruler was supposed to be the more important, Cleopatra arranged to have only her own name and portrait on Egyptian coins. In this she disregarded the Egyptian Ptolemaic tradition.

When Cleopatra became queen, the Ptolemies had been allied with the Romans for two centuries. However, the Roman Empire, which was constantly growing, had gained more and more control over Egypt. Ptolemy XII had been forced to pay tributes to the Romans in order to keep them out. Egyptian territories including Cyprus, Syria and Cyrenaica had been lost to the Romans and anarchy and famine were threatening the kingdom.

In the period 51–49 BCE, repeated droughts caused the failure of the Egyptian grain crop and the Nile floods, vital for fertilizing and irrigating the soil, did not happen. At this time, supporters of Ptolemy XIII forced Cleopatra to relinquish power and leave Egypt. On his own, Ptolemy banned the export of grain from Alexandria, infuriating the Romans.

In 48 BCE Julius Caesar seized Alexandria. Cleopatra, however, had no intention of being overthrown and smuggled herself through the enemy lines so that she could negotiate directly with Caesar. Her motives are ambiguous and it is impossible to know whether she was trying to save the Ptolemaic dynasty or whether she acted from a personal lust for power. Her aim might simply have been to try to save

TIMELINE

Date	Cleopatra	Related events
69 BCE	Born in Alexandria, Egypt	Roman troops capture Armenia
51 BCE	Ptolemy dies and Cleopatra ascends the Egyptian throne	Civil war in Rome
48 BCE	Cleopatra defeats Ptolemy XIII	Julius Caesar defeats Pompey, who flees to Egypt
		Fire destroys the library at Alexandria
47 BCE	Caesar and Cleopatra's son Caesarion born	Julius Caesar names his nephew Octavian as his heir
45 BCE		Julius Caesar is named dictator for life
44 BCE	Returns to Alexandria	Julius Caesar assassinated. Octavian becomes Emperor
		Marc Antony becomes governor of France and northern Italy
41 BCE		Marc Antony meets Cleopatra in Egypt
36 BCE	Marries Marc Antony	
31 BCE		Egypt defeated at the Battle of Actium
30 BCE	Takes her own life	Marc Antony commits suicide
		Egypt is annexed to the Roman Empire under Octavian

Alexandria. Caesar acted as official arbiter between Cleopatra and Ptolemy but favoured the former. After a short war, Ptolemy XIII was killed and Caesar restored Cleopatra to her throne. In order to secure the dynasty, she then married her even younger brother Ptolemy XIV, but whether from political expediency or real affection – or even both – she also became Caesar's lover.

They had a son whom they called Ptolemy Caesar, popularly known as Caesarion, or little Caesar. However, Caesar refused to recognize Caesarion as his heir, naming his nephew Octavian instead.

In 45 BCE, Cleopatra and Caesarion left Alexandria for Rome and were there when Caesar was assassinated. When they returned to Egypt, Ptolemy XIV unexpectedly died and Caesarion was made co-regent with his mother. It has been suggested that Cleopatra may have murdered her brother to secure the throne for herself.

After Caesar's death, Rome was split between the supporters of leading senator Marcus Antonius (Marc Antony) and Octavian. Marc Antony went to Alexandria to establish Cleopatra's loyalty towards Rome – and fell in love with her. The Roman historian Plutarch described her arrival at their first meeting – the translation is John Dryden's: 'She came sailing up the River Cydnus, in a barge with gilded stern and outspread sails of purple, while oars of silver beat time to the music of flutes and fifes and harps. She herself lay all along under a canopy of cloth of gold, dressed as

Venus in a picture, and beautiful young boys, like painted Cupids, stood on each side to fan her. Her maids were dressed like sea nymphs and graces... The perfumes diffused themselves from the vessel to the shore.' Antony and Cleopatra married in 36 BCE, despite the fact that he had a legal wife in Rome. This development triggered fury in the Roman senate and their anger grew as Marc Antony began giving away parts of the Empire (Crete, Cyprus, Cyrene, Palestine and Tarsus) to Cleopatra and her family. Cleopatra had twins by Marc Antony, who were recognized by him and named Alexander Helios (Sun), and Cleopatra Selene (Moon).

Alexander Helios was crowned King of the Seleucid Empire, and Cleopatra Selene became Queen of Cyrenaica and Crete. Cleopatra later gave birth to another child by Marc Antony, Ptolemy Philadelphos, who was named King of Syria and Asia Minor at the age of two. If Cleopatra had been dreaming of extending her empire, her dream was starting to come true.

In 32 to 31 BCE, Marc Antony divorced his Roman wife Octavia, forcing the wider world and Rome to recognize his relationship with Cleopatra. When Marc Antony had Cleopatra's name put on the Roman coinage, he effectively ended his allegiance to Rome. Octavian declared war. The Egyptians were defeated off the coast of Greece at the famous battle of Actium, in 31 BCE. Arriving a year later in Alexandria, Octavian defeated Marc Antony.

Marc Antony fell on his sword and died in Cleopatra's arms. He was buried as a king. Cleopatra, having been captured by Octavian, decided to take her own life. Most accounts state that her chosen method was snakebite, and the story goes that an asp – probably a cobra – was smuggled to her in a basket of figs. The Egyptians believed that death by snakebite secured immortality, which would explain equally well Cleopatra's choice of means and the enduring legend. She was 39.

Cleopatra was the last ruler of Egypt of the Macedonian dynasty and her death marked the close of an important era of Egyptian history. Alexandria remained the capital of Egypt, which became a Roman province. Caesarion was executed by Octavian but Cleopatra's three children by Marc Antony were spared and taken back to Rome where they were cared for in the household of Octavia, Marc Antony's Roman wife.

Cleopatra's charm, which captivated the two most powerful men in the world, seems to have guaranteed her immortality as an archetypal *femme fatale.* Her story has inspired plays and films for two millennia, including Shakespeare's *Antony and Cleopatra* and Dryden's *The World Well Lost.* Shakespeare's Cleopatra is considered one of the greatest female roles ever written for the theatre.

The epic film *Cleopatra* (1963) cost 20th Century Fox, the studio that made it, $40 million – nearly $300 million in today's terms – and bankrupted the company. Nevertheless, it won five Oscars and brought together another pair of world-famous lovers, Elizabeth Taylor and Richard Burton.

Mary Magdalene

Mary Magdalene is one of the best known and most loved figures in the gospels of the New Testament that recount the ministry of Jesus. While documentary evidence of her life is limited, the image of Mary Magdalene as the sinner who repented and the lone figure who witnessed the Resurrection of Christ has inspired the Christian imagery of two millennia.

'Wheresoever this gospel shall be preached throughout the whole world, this also that she hath done shall be spoken of as a memorial of her.'

Mark 14, 9

BIOGRAPHY

Name:	Mary Magdalene
Lived:	Circa 4 BCE – CE 40
Place of birth:	Palestine
Place of death:	Unknown
Nationality:	Palestinian
Famed as:	Follower of Christ; Christian icon of the redeemed sinner

Mary Magdalene, whose name probably indicates that she came from the town of Magdala on the western shore of the Sea of Galilee, in today's Israel, is described in the gospels as a follower of Jesus and witness of the Resurrection. Both saint and sinner, she has featured in fiction and in film as the lover, even the wife of Christ.

Over the last 2000 years, the figure of Mary Magdalene has been an inspiration. Many churches, chapels, colleges and other institutions have been dedicated to her, perhaps most notably Magdalen College in Oxford and Magdelene College in Cambridge. She has also been widely celebrated in the visual arts. Painters who have depicted her include Corregio, El Greco, Fra Angelico, Giotto, Holman Hunt, Michelangelo, Rembrandt and Titian.

FACTFILE

- The lack of documentary evidence about Mary Magdalene has given commentators and enthusiasts *carte blanche* to speculate on her life. Some suggest that she might be the author of the fourth Gospel (John's), an Egyptian temple priestess, the bearer of the Holy Grail – or even the prototype of an eco-feminist spirit committed to saving the Earth.

- On 22 July 1209, the feast day of St Mary Magdalene, every single inhabitant of the town of Béziers, in the south of France, went willingly to their deaths at the hands of the Pope's men rather than deny their fervently held belief that Mary Magdalene and Jesus were lovers.

- In their 1997 book *The Templar Revelation: Secret Guardians of the True Identity of Christ*, Lynn Picknett and Clive Prince advance the theory that the person to the left of Jesus (to his right) in Leonardo da Vinci's *Last Supper* is actually Mary Magdalene, rather than the apostle John (as most art historians recognize). This theory is a pivotal element of Dan Brown's novel *The Da Vinci Code*.

The mystique surrounding her, and her close, yet uncertain, relationship with Jesus Christ, are probably the reasons why a number of cults have arisen in her name. The Black Madonna stories of medieval Europe and Russia associate Mary Magdalene with a dark-skinned Ethiopian queen, and effigies of this representation can be found in many churches and cathedrals, particularly in Spain and southern France. As the patron saint of the Knights Templar, she is thus closely associated with stories of the Holy Grail. One story is that Mary Magdalene travelled to southern France with the Grail, fleeing persecution of the Christians in CE 42. Another version is that she herself carried the royal bloodline of Christ, perhaps in the form of a young girl, Sarah, who accompanied her on her voyage. Some believe that the union of Jesus and Mary Magdalene produced the bloodline that became the Merovingian lineage of Kings in southern France.

There are few consistent details about Mary Magdalene. Despite the appearance of a 'Mary' in several versions of the life of Jesus in the New Testament – in addition to Mary, mother of Jesus – there is little agreement about whether these are references to one particular Mary.

TIMELINE

Date	Mary Magdalene	Related events
63 BCE		Romans occupy Palestine
c. 4 BCE	Born in Palestine	First century BCE: growth of the Roman Empire
		Birth of Jesus of Nazareth
26		Pontius Pilate is appointed Prefect of Judea
27		Start of Jesus' public ministry
		First miracle – wedding of Cana
28		Jesus preaches the Sermon on the Mount
c. 29	Becomes follower of Jesus	Baptism of Jesus of Nazareth by John the Baptist
		Execution of John the Baptist
c. 30	Witnesses resurrection of Jesus Christ	Crucifixion of Jesus in Jerusalem
c. 35		Conversion of Saul of Tarsus (Paul)
		Christian apostolic missions begin
36		Pontius Pilate recalled to Rome
c. 40	Suggested date of her death	Christianity reaches Egypt

The story of Mary Magdalene as a notorious sinner, possibly a prostitute, appears in the gospels of Mark and Luke. Mary Magdalene may also be the 'woman of the city' who is said by Luke to have washed Jesus' feet, dried them with her hair and rubbed them with expensive perfume. Jesus said: 'Do you see this woman? I entered your house; you gave me no water for my feet, but she has wet my feet with her tears and wiped them with her hair. You gave me no kiss, but from the time I came in she has not ceased to kiss my feet. You did not anoint my head with oil, but she has anointed my feet with ointment. Therefore I tell you, her sins, which are many, are forgiven, for she loved much.' It is Christ's attitude towards the fallen woman showing repentance that makes Mary Magdalene a pivotal figure in the story of Christian forgiveness.

Some modern fiction, notably the best-selling novel *The Da Vinci Code* (Dan Brown, 2003) holds that Mary Magdalene was actually the wife of Jesus, using non-Biblical manuscripts to support the argument. While sources like the Gospel of Philip depict Mary Magdalene as being closer to Jesus than any other disciple, there is no authentic ancient document that claims she was his wife. There is also a Gospel of Mary Magdalene, which survives in two third-century Greek fragments and as a longer fifth-century Coptic translation. In this manuscript, Mary Magdalene appears as a teacher of the apostles and is beloved by Jesus above the disciples, and, according to this source, after the Resurrection Mary Magdalene describes to the disciples a vision of the Saviour Christ.

Whatever the truth of the various stories, the New Testament gospels seem to agree that Mary Magdalene, freed from sin and overwhelmed with gratitude, became Jesus' ardent follower. Another Mary, sister of Martha, occurs in Jesus' visit to the town of Bethany. John alone identifies this Mary with Mary Magdalene; later scholars have disputed the attribution. In the account, Mary sits at Jesus' feet and listens to his words while her distracted sister serves food and complains that Mary should be helping her; but Jesus praises Mary for doing the right thing.

According to Matthew, Mark and Luke, Mary Magdalene accompanied Jesus on his last journey to Jerusalem. At Jesus' crucifixion she stood near the cross until the body was taken down and laid in a tomb in a nearby garden. Later the tomb was found empty, and although the gospels differ in their accounts of exactly what occurred, Mary Magdalene was the first recorded witness of the Resurrection, seeing a vision of the risen Christ, who spoke to her. According to the gospel of John:

> Jesus said, 'Do not hold on to me, for I have not yet returned to the Father. Go instead to my brothers and tell them, I am returning to my Father and your Father, to my God and your God.' Mary Magdalene went to the disciples with the news: 'I have seen the Lord!' And she told them what he had said.

There are two theories about Mary Magdalene's final resting place: one, that she went to Ephesus, in modern-day Turkey and was buried in Constantinople; the other that she was cast adrift in a boat which finally floated to rest in southern France, where she lived as a hermit in a cave and died at the age of 72. Following the latter tradition, Roman Catholics venerate her relics at Saint Maximin la Sainte-Baume near Marseilles, where a great Gothic basilica was erected from the mid-thirteenth century. Though the bones were scattered during the French Revolution, the head remains in a shrine in a cave at La Sainte-Baume.

Mary Magdalene has had various afterlives. While her name became a symbol of repentance for the vanities of the world, unfortunately it was also used for the infamous Magdalen asylums in Ireland, where supposedly fallen women were treated as slaves. A non-Biblical tradition says that she was a woman of some wealth and social standing. Following Jesus' death and resurrection, she was invited to a banquet given by Emperor Tiberius Caesar. When she met him, she held a plain egg in her hand and exclaimed 'Christ is risen!' Caesar laughed, and said that Christ rising from the dead was as likely as the egg in her hand turning red. Before he finished speaking, the egg in her hand turned bright red, and Mary Magdalene continued proclaiming the gospel to the imperial household. Today, many Eastern Orthodox Christians end the Easter service by sharing bright red eggs and proclaiming, 'Christ is risen!' The eggs represent new life, and Christ bursting forth from the tomb. Thus began the tradition of colouring Easter eggs.

Boudicca

Boudicca, warrior queen of the Celtic Iceni tribe, had the courage to take on the Roman Empire. Widely regarded as a heroine in her own time, her fame resounds to this day.

'If you weigh well the strength of the armies, and the causes of the war, you will see that in this battle you must conquer or die. This is a woman's resolve; as for men, they may live and be slaves.'

BIOGRAPHY

Name:	Boudicca, also known as Boadicea
Lived:	Early first century (dates uncertain)
Place of birth:	East Anglia, England
Place of death:	East Anglia, England
Nationality:	Icenian
Famed as:	Warrior chieftain; resistance fighter

Boudicca was a famous queen of ancient Britain, probably born about CE 30. She also appears in Roman annals under the name Boadicea Victoria. The name may have been given to her by her people and have come from the Celtic goddess of victory, Boudiga. She lived in southeast Britain and married, around CE 48, Prasutagus, King of the Iceni tribe, becoming queen of the region which is now centred on Norfolk. Boudicca struck a fine figure – tall and imposing, with long red hair flowing down to her hips. The Roman writer Cassius Dio described her as 'very tall. Her eyes seemed to stab you. Her voice was harsh and loud. Her thick, reddish-brown hair hung down below her waist. She always wore a great golden torc around her neck and a flowing tartan cloak fastened with a brooch.'

FACTFILE

- The site of Boudicca's last battle is unknown. It is reputed to be on the site of King's Cross station in London and Boudicca herself is supposed to be buried under one of the platforms.

- It was Prince Albert, husband of Queen Victoria, who commissioned Thomas Thorneycroft to make the statue of Boudicca that stands outside the Houses of Parliament in London. He shared the Victorians' voguish passion for Boudicca's story.

- Thorneycroft sculpted blades on the chariot wheels in his statue. There is no evidence that the Iceni used weapons of this kind – and a close inspection of Thorneycroft's chariot shows that it would not have been able to move.

This period in British history was very troubled. The Romans had invaded under Julius Caesar in 55 and 54 BCE and succeeded in subduing the indigenous tribes, including the Iceni. Caesar left in 54 BCE to deal with uprisings in Gaul, and for a period the local people were able to live under relative freedom. However, the Romans returned to Britain in CE 43, this time under Claudius. They struck a deal with Prasutagus, allowing him to continue as King of the Iceni but under the dominion of Rome. Although Roman rule brought benefits like protection, education and jobs, there were many disadvantages, including slavery. The Iceni, like other tribal communities, suffered from the heavy taxes levied by Rome, conscription and many other indignities.

Boudicca came to prominence as leader of the Iceni on the death of Prasutagus in CE 60 or 61. Roman law decreed that most of Prasutagus's possessions were left to the Emperor, now Nero, and little was inherited by his wife and their two daughters. Rome however, used the fact of his having left money and goods to his daughters as a pretext to seize all of his assets. Armed struggle ensued, with Iceni chiefs evicted from their lands, homes plundered and many Iceni sold into slavery. Boudicca was unable to pay the debts demanded and she was taken, stripped and beaten in public, while her daughters were raped by Roman soldiers. Other subdued tribes, such as the Trinobantes, were subjected to similar treatment, and rebellious feelings against the occupying forces of Rome were never far from the surface.

TIMELINE

Date	Boudicca	Related events
30	Approximate date of birth of Boudicca	First century CE: spread of Christianity and growth of the Roman Empire
41		Claudius becomes Roman Emperor (until 54)
48	Boudicca marries Prasutagus of the Iceni	Paul of Tarsus begins his first mission
60	Death of Prasutagus Boudicca leads revolt against the occupying Romans	Gospels of Matthew, Mark and Luke are being written
61	Defeat of the Iceni and their allies by the Romans Dies, possibly in London	British govenor Suetonius replaced by the more lenient Publius Petronius Turpilianus.
63		Joseph of Arimathea comes to Glastonbury on the first Christian mission to Britain
75–77		Roman conquest of Britain complete
79		Pompeii and Herculaneum destroyed in the eruption of Mount Vesuvius

These outrages were the stimulus for an uprising against Rome, and Boudicca united various quarrelling tribes into a focused force directed against the Roman oppressors. At this stage the Roman governor of Britain, Suetonius Paulinus, was distracted by a military campaign against rebels who had sought safety on the island of Anglesey, and this gave Boudicca her chance to attack. She is alleged to have gathered an army some 100,000 strong and attacked Camulodunum Colonia (Colchester), with hostilities lasting some days. Her army spared no one and the city was razed to the ground. The Britons even desecrated Roman cemeteries, defacing statues and shattering tombstones. Examples of some of these mutilated statues can be seen today in Colchester Museum. They also dealt mercilessly with a detachment of Roman soldiers ordered to assist from the north, ambushing the troops and killing all the infantry. News spread to the Procurator Decianus in London, who fled.

Suetonius meanwhile had marched his troops back from Anglesey to a position close to London and, having assessed the military situation, he decided to abandon the town, deeming it impossible to defend. In due course Boudicca's forces arrived and destroyed London, setting much of it ablaze. Cassius Dio records that 'those who were taken captive by the Britons were subjected to every known outrage. The worst most bestial atrocity committed by their captors was the following. They hung up naked the noblest and most distinguished women and then cut off their breasts and sewed them to their mouths, in order to make the victims appear to be eating them. Afterwards they impaled the women on sharp skewers run lengthwise through their entire body.'

But Boudicca was not finished. She turned her army, now estimated at more than 200,000, northwards to Verulamium (St Albans). Suetonius gathered his troops together, but could only raise about 10,000. Most of Verulamium's inhabitants fled and Boudicca's army burned the town and killed any of those who had stayed behind.

Yet it was inevitable that, with their potentially superior forces and organization, Rome would eventually prevail, and so it proved, in CE 61. The site of this final battle is thought to have been near Nuneaton, in the West Midlands. Suetonius positioned his troops at the top of an incline with a thick forest to one side. Boudicca and her followers must have been a formidable sight, some clad in tartans, some naked, with their skin painted blue, and all spurred on and encouraged by drums, pipes and shouts, and armed mainly with swords and spears.

Boudicca and her daughters drove round in her chariot to all her people before battle commenced, rallying her forces. The Roman historian Tacitus wrote that she must have realized that the battle could not be won when she addressed her troops: 'It is not as a woman descended from noble ancestry, but as one of the people that I am avenging lost freedom, my scourged body, the outraged chastity of my daughters. Roman lust has gone so far that not our very persons, nor even age or virginity, are left unpolluted. But heaven is on the side of a righteous vengeance; a legion which dared to fight has perished; the rest are hiding themselves in their camp, or are thinking anxiously of flight. If you weigh well the strength of the armies, and the causes of the war, you will see that in this battle you must conquer or die. This is a woman's resolve; as for men, they may live and be slaves.'

As the Britons charged, the Romans held their ground, protecting themselves with their shields. Then they hurled their javelins as the enemy came within range, and followed this with wave after wave of infantry, before finally trapping the remaining Britons by pincer-like cavalry charges from the sides. The victory was very one-sided: nearly 80,000 Britons died while Roman losses were about 400.

Although there is no reliable record of the fate of Boudicca, legend has it that she survived the battle, returned to her home and killed herself by taking poison. We do know, however, that the British, by whom she was regarded as a heroine and a symbol of independence, gave her a grand burial. In the aftermath of the battles, the Romans resumed persecution of the Iceni, destroyed many of their farms, and took large numbers of slaves.

As a woman of unusual courage, Boudicca features strongly in the folk history of Britain, and she is commemorated in a fine bronze statue commissioned by Queen Victoria's husband, Prince Albert and executed by Thomas Thorneycroft. It was completed in 1905 and stands on the Thames embankment near the Houses of Parliament in London. It is something of an irony that this anti-imperialist rebel should have come to be identified with the figurehead of the British Empire.

Hildegard of Bingen

Hildegard of Bingen lived in convents, withdrawn from the world for most of her life, yet wrote books and music that influenced the intelligensia of Europe. Consulted by bishops, popes and kings, at a time when women had no role in public life and were accorded little respect, she became known as 'the sibyl of the Rhine'.

'With nature's help, humankind can set into creation all that is necessary and life sustaining.'

BIOGRAPHY

Name:	Hildegard von Bingen
Lived:	16 September 1098 – 17 September 1179
Place of birth:	Bermersheim, Germany
Place of death:	Disibodenberg, Germany
Nationality:	German
Famed as:	Abbess, mystic, author, composer

Hildegard of Bingen was an unusual and remarkably gifted woman. She was the tenth child of a noble family and, as was often then the custom with 'extra' children, she was dedicated at birth to the church, thus setting the tone for what was to be a long life centred around religion. As early as the age of three she apparently started to have visions, for which she would later become famous, and this ability remained with her for years.

Her father served as a knight to a count, and when Hildegard reached the age of eight she was sent away to live with Jutta, the count's sister, who had dedicated her life to God, so that Hildegard could receive a thorough religious education. Jutta became an anchoress (from the Greek *anakhoreo*, meaning 'retire'), a sort of religious hermit and ascetic who spent most of her days in devout prayer or quiet handworking, living in a cell. In these early years, it was mainly from Jutta that Hildegard received what education she could, such as reading religious texts in Latin. Jutta's anchorage was close to a Benedictine monastery at Disibodenberg, so Hildegard would have had many opportunities to listen to religious music, an influence on her own compositions in years to come. Jutta died when Hildegard was 38, and by then the anchorage and its students had formed the basis of a convent with at least 20 nuns, to which Hildegard was elected prioress.

FACTFILE

- Hildegard had a strange childhood: the helpless victim of disturbing and inexplicable visions, she was separated from her family and spent her early years attending the eccentric anchoress Jutta.

- Anchorites and anchoresses withdrew so completely from the world that they were given the last rites before they entered their cell. Nevertheless, they retained some contact with others, who brought them food or came to them for instruction.

- Hildegard identified phenomena associated with cancer and prescribed natural treatments for the disease.

- Nowadays, her music and medicine are very popular with New Age movements, whose members are drawn to her ethereal melodies and herbal remedies, now regarded as alternative therapies.

The year 1141 marked an important event in Hildegard's life: she had a vivid vision of God which seems to have blessed her with an understanding of the meanings of religious texts and decreed that she should write down and record those things that she observed in her visions. Hildegard was in no doubt that this and her other visions came to her directly from God and were therefore of immense importance, not just to her, but to all people. She wrote: 'And it came to pass…when I was 42 years and 7 months old, that the heavens were opened and a blinding light of exceptional brilliance flowed through my entire brain. And so it kindled my whole heart and breast like a flame, not burning, but warming…and suddenly I understood of the meaning of expositions of the books…'

TIMELINE

Date	Hildegard of Bingen	Related events
1098	Born in Bermersheim	Christians on the First Crusade (1096–99) advance into Turkey and Syria
1133		Durham Cathedral completed; Exeter cathedral begun
1136	Elected prioress of her convent	Peter Abelard writes *Historia Calamitatum* ('The Story of My Misfortunes'), in which he details his relationship with Heloise
1141	A vision of God moves her to begin to write religious texts	Death of mystic philosopher Hugh St Victor
1147–1149		The Second Crusade
1150	Relocates her convent to Bingen in Germany and begins to write religious music	The first English scientist, Adelard of Bath, dies after translating Arabic alegbra book into Latin
1154		Monks discontinue Anglo-Saxon Chronicle after 183 years
1158	Completes her 'symphony' of 77 songs	
1163	Starts work on her *Liber divinorum operum* – takes ten years to complete	
1170		Murder of Archbishop Thomas Becket in Canterbury Cathedral, at the instigation of Henry II
1179	Dies at age of 81	The Third Lateran Council in Rome authorizes the first ghettoes for Jews

Yet she was too modest and humble to write down her visions at this stage, and also mindful and in awe of the male-dominated world in which she lived. Another factor was probably her wish to avoid encouraging any schism or faction within the Catholic church, and her desire to gain the church's approval for anything she might offer. Eventually she wrote to Bernard, the Abbot of the Cistercian monastery at Vézelay in Burgundy, who was encouraging. In due course her predicament came to the attention of Pope Eugenius (1145–53). The Pope was sympathetic to Hildegard and encouraged her to write about her visions. This led to her producing her first visionary work, *Scivias* ('Know the ways of the Lord'), which took her ten years to write and which is a summary of Christian doctrine based on many of her visions. With this she gradually became widely known throughout Germany and also abroad.

Hildegard's convent at Disibodenberg grew in fame and in numbers and in about 1150 she moved it some 30 km to the north, close to Bingen on the Rhine, and later founded another convent on the other side of the river, at Eibingen. Now she was able to write more and also to compose religious music.

Her writings cover a surprisingly wide range of subjects, including plays, a medical encyclopedia and a medical handbook, as well as a work of moral instruction, and eventually her last major work of divinity, *Liber divinorum operum*, which deals with the relationship between God and humankind.

As was typical of the age, her scientific views were based on ancient Greek teachings of the four elements: earth, air, fire and water and their corresponding humours of the body – melancholy (black bile), blood, choler (yellow bile) and phlegm. Bodily sicknesses could be treated by using plant or animal products that restored the missing quality as related to these humours.

Remarkably perhaps for a nun, Hildegard also wrote about human sexual relations and dealt probably for the first time with the importance of pleasure and orgasm to the female partner: 'When a woman is making love with a man, a sense of heat in her brain, which brings with it sensual delight, communicates the taste of that delight during the act and summons forth the emission of the man's seed. And when the seed has fallen into its place, that vehement heat descending from her brain draws the seed to itself and holds it, and soon the woman's sexual organs contract, and all the parts that are ready to open up during the time of menstruation now close, in the same way as a strong man can hold something enclosed in his fist.'

Although perhaps best known for her religious and other texts, Hildegard is also very important as a composer. She wrote music and words to songs, mostly religious liturgical plainchant in honour of saints and the Virgin Mary, some of which are still popular and studied to this day. She regarded music as a means of recapturing the original state of paradise, with its joy and beauty. She believed that, in the Garden of Eden, Adam had a pure voice and sang God's praises with the angels, but that after the Fall the task of praising God came through the invention of music and musical instruments. Arguably, her compositions were an attempt to recreate her ideas of heavenly choirs.

Recently it has been conjectured that Hildegard's visions might have been caused by migraines, and some of her descriptions fit quite closely with the symptoms of this condition. She spoke of intense light, stars and temporary blindness, followed by sickness and sometimes a state of euphoria. Whatever the truth of this theory, visions or migraines, this remarkable woman left a large body of fascinating writings and music to future generations.

We know little of Hildegard's final years, but she visited and preached at various monasteries, completing her final tour around 1171 at the age of 73, and she continued to write until at least 1175.

After her death, Hildegard was beatified and four attempts were made to have her canonized, although none was completed. However, she was popularly referred to as Saint Hildegard for so long that she seems to have become a Saint almost by default. Hildegard has an official feast day (17 September).

Eleanor of Aquitaine

Eleanor, born in the Aquitaine region of France in 1122, became first queen of France and later queen of England. Two of her sons, Richard and John, also became kings of England. She was renowned for her beauty, personality and power, and for her tempestuous marriages, particularly to her second husband, King Henry II, founder of the Plantagenet dynasty in England.

'I thought that I had married a king, but I find that I have married a monk.'

Of her husband, Louis VII

BIOGRAPHY

Name:	Éléonore d'Aquitaine, Aliénor d'Aquitaine, or Eleanor of Guyenne
Lived:	1122 (date uncertain) – 31 March 1204
Place of birth:	Bordeaux, France
Place of death:	Fontevrault, Anjou
Nationality:	French
Famed as:	Queen of England, Queen of France, Duchess of Aquitaine; mother of two English kings (Richard I, John)

Eleanor was a granddaughter of Guillaume IX of Aquitaine (1070–1127), who was one of the first and most famous troubadours – French lyrical poets, mostly from the south, who accompanied their verse with music. In 1137, after her baby brother and both her parents had died, Eleanor inherited the French Duchy of Aquitaine, a vast territory that stretched from the River Loire to the Pyrenees in the south, the largest and richest of the provinces that would become modern France. This inheritance made her the richest woman in Europe.

Unlike many men and most women at that time, Eleanor had been carefully educated and was an excellent student, able to read and speak Latin, and well versed in music and literature. She enjoyed riding, hawking and hunting. In the same year that her father died, she was married at the age of 15 to the dull and severe Louis VII, King of France. He was a weak and pious man and a poor match for the lively Eleanor, but although he never understood his young wife, he adored and admired her. Eleanor's court set a trend for luxury and sophistication in the medieval world, known for its patronage of poets and troubadours, some of whom were believed to be in love with the beautiful Eleanor. It is said that in her effort to civilize her unruly knights she would conduct mock trials, judged by ladies who sat on an elevated platform and listened to the knights, the latter with long hair and dressed in flowing garments, as they read out poems of homage to women and acted out courtship rituals.

FACTFILE

- Distressed as she was by Henry's infidelity, Eleanor was nevertheless no angel herself. One of her reputed lovers was Henry's father, Geoffroi d'Anjou, who warned his son against marrying her.

- While regent in Richard I's absence, Eleanor successfully thwarted her son John's traitorous alliance with Philip Augustus of France.

- Eleanor became known as the 'grandmother of Europe'. Her daughter Matilda married Henry the Lion, Duke of Saxony and Bavaria; Eleanor married Alfonso VIII, King of Castile and Joan married first William II, King of Sicily and then Raymond VI, Count of Toulouse. Her granddaughter Blanche married the King of France.

- Living into her eighties – extraordinary for that time – Eleanor outlived both her husbands and eight of her ten children.

- Eleanor and Henry II are the main characters in the play *The Lion in Winter*, by James Goldman, which was made into a film starring Peter O'Toole and Katharine Hepburn, and remade for television in 2003 with Patrick Stewart and Glenn Close.

This was the era of the great crusades against the Saracens and Turks in the Holy Land. At 19, Eleanor famously offered thousands of her knights to join the Second Crusade. There is a story that she appeared to the Abbé Bernard at Vézelay dressed like an Amazon, galloping through the crowds on a white horse, urging them to join the crusades. Dressed in armour and carrying lances, the women went, but never

TIMELINE

Date	Eleanor of Aquitaine	Related events
1122	Born in Bordeaux	Concordat of Worms ends, investiture controversy between Pope Calixtus II and Holy Roman Emperor Henry V
1137	Inherits Duchy of Aquitaine and becomes the richest woman in Europe Marries Louis VII of France	
1147	Accompanies her husband on the Second Crusade	Beginning of Second Crusade (1147–49)
1152	Annulment of her marriage to Louis on grounds of consanguinity Marries Henri d'Anjou – as close a blood relative as her former husband	Frederick Barbarossa (Redbeard) accedes as Holy Roman Emperor
1154	Henri d'Anjou accedes to the English throne as Henry II	Nicholas Breakspear, the only English pope, is elected as Pope Adrian IV
1169	Returns to run the Duchy of Aquitaine Runs court in romantic tradition of courtly love	Saladin becomes sultan of conquered Islamic territories
1170		Murder of Archbishop Thomas Becket in Canterbury Cathedral, on the orders of Henry II
1172	Leads unsuccessful rebellion against Henry II and is confined to house arrest for the next 15 years	Pope Gregory absolves Henry II for the sin of murdering Thomas Becket
1189	Death of Henry II and accession of Richard I (Lionheart) Becomes regent	Beginning of Third Crusade (1189–92)
1204	Dies at Fontevrault and is buried there with Henry II	End of the Fourth Crusade (1201–04)

fought. On the Crusade, Eleanor, tired of her husband, became involved in a relationship with young, handsome Raymond, newly appointed Prince of Antioch and her own uncle. She supported Raymond's strategy of recapturing Edessa, in order to protect the Western presence in the Holy Land, rather than going to Jerusalem, as Louis determined. The King demanded that Eleanor follow him to Jerusalem. Eleanor, furious, denounced their marriage but was forced to go with Louis. The Jerusalem expedition failed and the defeated pair returned to France in separate ships. Raymond was killed in battle. Eleanor and Louis had asked the Pope for a divorce, but he refused. Although Eleanor's marriage to Louis continued for a time, and they had a second daughter, the relationship was over. In 1152 the marriage was annulled on a technicality and Eleanor's vast estates reverted to her control. She left her two daughters to be raised within the French court. Within a year she married 20-year-old Henri d'Anjou, 11 years her junior, who two years later became King

Henry II of England. This time Eleanor's temperament as well as her wealth found its match. Her lands passed to the English crown, which, when combined with his English possessions, made King Henry much more powerful than King Louis, a cause of hostility between the two countries.

In the next 13 years Eleanor and Henry had five sons and three daughters. Through their alliances and warfare they created an impressive empire. But their relationship grew stormier as their children grew older, provoked partly by Henry's succession of mistresses during Eleanor's years of childbearing.

In 1169 Henry sent Eleanor to Aquitaine to restore order as its duchess. She resolved to establish her own domain there, refusing to be the pawn of a feudal king. She set up her own law court, dispensed her own justice and patronage and established her favourite son Richard in Aquitaine. Once again the ducal palace at Poitou became a centre of refinement and civilization, where troubadours, musicians and scholars were welcomed. There, in 1170, Eleanor and her first daughter Marie of France, had a 'code of love' written down in 31 articles describing feminist ideals that moved far beyond the twelfth-century cult of chivalry. In addition, Eleanor sponsored the 'courts of love' where men having problems with love suits could bring their questions before a tribunal of ladies for judgement.

As her children grew older and dynastic squabbles broke out, Eleanor led three of her sons in rebellion against their father. The rebellion was put down, however, and Eleanor, now 50 years old, was imprisoned by Henry in various fortified English buildings over the following 15 years. In 1189, Henry died. By then three of their sons had also died and Henry's successor was Eleanor's favourite, Richard I, known as Lionheart (1157–99).

When Richard left on the Third Crusade, Eleanor became regent. In his absence, she arranged Richard's marriage to Berengaria of Navarre. Eleanor risked her life to bring Berengaria to Greece for the wedding, surviving shipwreck on the way. She was over 70 when she made the journey. She also frustrated her son John's attempt to take the throne from his older brother. John was made to remain in Aquitaine during Richard's absence.

In 1192, Richard was captured on his return to England and held to ransom by the Holy Roman Emperor Henry VI. An extortionate sum of 70,000 marks (some sources say even more) was demanded for his release. Eleanor worked ceaselessly to raise the money, which was amassed through taxes, the confiscation of 25 per cent of personal property across the kingdom and gold and silver church treasure. Richard was released on 4 February 1194. When he heard the news, Phillip of France wrote warningly to John, 'Look to yourself, the devil is loose.'

Eleanor lived into her eighties, surviving her son Richard and seeing John, her youngest son, become king of England. One of the great political leaders of medieval Europe, she died in 1204 at the Abbey of Fontevrault, a retreat that she had visited for brief periods of rest during her hectic life.

Joan of Arc

Joan of Arc was the daughter of peasants who farmed in the Champagne region of France, an unlikely beginning for a military leader who believed herself to be on a God-given mission to liberate northern France from the English. Her fame is the stuff of legend, so much so that it is difficult to distinguish fact from fiction. Her trial for heresy and witchcraft, however, is well documented and her status as a national heroine, established soon after her death, is as great now as it was then.

'I am not afraid. I was born to do this.'

BIOGRAPHY

Name:	Jeanne d'Arc; also known as the Maid of Orléans
Lived:	6 January 1412 – 30 May 1431
Place of birth:	Domrémy, France
Place of death:	Rouen, France
Nationality:	French
Famed as:	French national heroine; Catholic saint (1920)

Joan of Arc was destined to become an iconic figure in French history. Many portents are said to have been associated with her birth, including the pre-dawn crowing of the village cockerels, heralding a joyous time.

During this period, the political situation in France was very unstable. Charles VI was the monarch, but he suffered periods of delusion and was in effect incapable of ruling. Various members of the royal family controlled the country on his behalf, including Queen Isabel and the Dukes of Orléans, Burgundy, Berry and Bourbon. In 1407, Duke Louis of Orléans was assassinated on the orders of his cousin Duke Jean-sans-Peur, 'the fearless'. France was then plunged into a civil war and became divided between the Armagnacs (Orléanists) and the Burgundians. In May 1413, the conflict led to the Cabochien Revolt in Paris, led by Simon Caboche and inspired by the Burgundian Pierre Cauchon. The latter was to feature significantly in Joan's later life.

FACTFILE

- Joan's famous white armour was not white at all. 'White armour' simply meant armour with no decoration.

- Equally apocryphal is the story of her immediately identifying the heavily disguised Dauphin at the French court when she was introduced there in 1428. This was interpreted in legend as divine confirmation of his disputed claim to the throne.

- When she was sentenced to be burned at the stake on 24 May 1431, Joan broke down in fear and recanted. However, a week later she had regained her courage, withdrew her recantation and faced death bravely.

- The dunce's cap has its origins in the paper cone that was placed on the heads of women accused of witchcraft during the Middle Ages. When Joan was martyred, she was wearing one on which were inscribed the words 'Heretic, Apostate, Relapsed, Idolator.'

- Joan is the patron saint of France.

France was therefore in turmoil as Joan was growing up in the picturesque, peaceful countryside of the Meuse valley, and in 1415, when she was three, King Henry V of England invaded Normandy, claiming his family's historic right to the French throne. Henry famously defeated the French army close to the village of Agincourt (modern Azincourt, about 50 kilometres south of Calais), on 25 October 1415. This fragmented the French aristocracy and also weakened the Armagnac faction.

Meanwhile, the d'Arc family worked their 50 acres of land in the Meuse valley. By all accounts, Joan was a good, dutiful child who, along with her three older brothers and her sister, helped with the various tasks involved in running the family farm. She was later variously described as a 'good, simple, sweet-natured girl' who 'went to church gladly and often' and was 'greatly committed to the service of God and the Blessed Mary'. One Simonin Musnier recalled that 'she helped those who were ill and gave alms to the poor, as I saw, because I was ill when I was a boy and Joan consoled me'.

TIMELINE

Date	Joan of Arc	Related events
1412	Born in Domrémy, France	
1415	English army under the command of Henry V defeat the French at the Battle of Agincourt – the worst defeat for France in the 100 Years' War	Religious thinker and reformer Jan Hus burned at the stake in Constance, Southern Bohemia
1420		Treaty of Troyes
1424	Joan first experiences her visions	
1428	Voices urge her to speak to the Dauphin. In October the English begin the siege of Orléans	
1429	Granted command of an army 29 April leads French troops to victory over the English at Orléans 17 July the Dauphin, son of Charles VI, crowned King of France	Death of French mystical theologian Jean Gerson
1430	Captured by the Burgundians and sold to the English	French poet, philosopher and feminist writer Christine de Pizan dies
1431	Condemned as a heretic and burned at the stake in Rouen	

At around this time, a new figure began to emerge on the French political landscape, one who was to have a decisive influence on events, and whose career is closely bound up with that of Joan of Arc. He was the Dauphin (claimant to the throne) Charles de Ponthieu, a young man now allied to the Armagnac faction, although his mother, the queen, was linked with the Burgundians.

In 1419, Duke Jean-sans-Peur of Burgundy was killed by the Armagnacs, and was succeeded by Philippe-le-Bon who allied himself with the English. In 1420 Henry V of England was granted title to the kingdom of France through his marriage to Catherine de Valois, the daughter of King Charles VI and the Dauphin's sister. This resulted in the Dauphin Charles being disinherited, and the country being divided between the Duke of Burgundy and Henry V, the treaty being negotiated by the ferociously pro-English Pierre Cauchon, who was appointed Bishop of Beauvais. The year 1422 saw the deaths of both Henry V and Charles VI, leaving Henry VI, then an infant, as the ruler of England and France.

Around the summer of 1424, Joan announced that she had begun to experience visions, and this development changed the course of her life, propelling her to eventual fame. 'I was in my thirteenth year when I heard a voice from God to help me govern my conduct. And the first time I was very much afraid. And this voice came, about the hour of noon, in the summer time, in my father's garden…'. The voices were sometimes accompanied by a blaze of light and she was able to recognize some of the visions as, among others, St Michael, St Margaret and St Catherine. Although she never boasted of her visions, they seem to have been very real to her, prompting her to say, at her later trial, 'I saw them with these very eyes, as well as I see you.' Joan believed that the saints were telling her to drive the English away from Orléans and out of the country and then to take the Dauphin to Reims to be crowned. Throughout her life she never entertained a moment's uncertainty that she was in the company of the divine. This conviction gave her the superhuman courage and certainty in her own authority that she demonstrated later in her life.

There came a point in Joan's life when her family and friends began to notice that she was becoming increasingly devout. If she was in the fields and heard the bell ringing for mass, she would immediately run to the church to hear the service. The frequency with which Joan went to confession increased too – so much so that people began to comment on it.

By May 1428 Joan was no longer in any doubt about her mission, and her voices urged her to seek the attention of the court. In due course she was brought before the Dauphin, Charles de Ponthieu. The effect that Joan had on the weak and indecisive Charles was immediate. Like its leader, the realm was demoralized and divided against itself. Suddenly, an energetic young girl with an appetite for action appeared, her way prepared by prophecy. She had no doubts or hesitation so Charles, who had nothing to lose, sought the approval of church scholars at Poitiers and granted Joan command of an army. Her army went on to lift the siege of Orléans on 8 May 1429, defeated the English army at Patay on 18 June, and forced various towns, including Troyes, to surrender. This was followed by the triumphal entry of the Dauphin into Reims for his coronation on 17 July as King Charles VII. Joan and her family were granted noble status by the king on 29 December 1429.

On 23 May 1430 Joan was captured by the Burgundians at Compiègne and sold to the English, after which she was put on trial by the English and the pro-English French clergy in Rouen. She was accused, among other things, of witchcraft and convicted in highly dubious circumstances, largely orchestrated by her arch-enemy Pierre Cauchon, whose violent partisanship for the English made a fair trial impossible. Charles made no attempt to come to her rescue. Joan was burned at the stake on 30 May 1431, her end witnessed by over 10,000 people drawn from the town and surrounding countryside. Her charred body was held up for all to examine, then returned to the fire where it was burned to ashes and her ashes scattered over the Seine. It is said, however, that her heart would not be consumed.

A later inquisition on 7 July 1456 was to declare her innocent, after the English were eventually driven from Rouen, and Joan was officially designated a martyr. According to Mark Twain she was 'easily and by far the most remarkable person the human race has ever produced.' She was beatified in 1909 and canonized a saint in 1920.

Joan of Arc remains France's best-known heroine, responsible for rebuilding the spirit of French nationalism. She represents a possibly unique combination of humility, religious devotion, patriotism and bravery.

Isabella I of Spain

Queen Isabella I, 'The Catholic', was the joint ruler of Spain with her husband, Ferdinand of Aragon, the patron of Christopher Columbus (pictured above presenting samples of his discoveries to Isabella) and mother of Catherine of Aragon, the first wife of the English king Henry VIII. Isabella was remarkable for her political astuteness, her intelligence and the skill with which she negotiated her difficult succession to the throne.

'Tanto monta, monta tanto – Isabel como Fernando.'

Official motto: 'Isabella and Ferdinand are one and the same.'

BIOGRAPHY

Name:	Isabella of Castile
Lived:	22 April 1451 – 26 November 1504
Place of birth:	Madrigal de las Altas Torras, Spain
Place of death:	Medina del Compo, Spain
Nationality:	Castilian
Famed as:	Co-ruler of Spain with her husband Ferdinand V; patron of Christopher Columbus; instituted the Spanish Inquisition

Born in 1451, Isabella was the second child and only daughter of John II of Spain and his wife Isabella of Portugal. She had a younger brother, Alfonso, the expected heir to the throne, and a half-brother, Henry. In 1454, John II died and it was Henry who took the throne as Henry IV. At the age of three, Isabella moved to Arévalo with her mother and younger brother. In 1457, Henry IV, well aware that his siblings would be political targets for noblemen opposed to his reign, had both Alfonso and Isabella brought to court where they could be under his eye.

Henry IV, also known as Henry the Impotent, was not successful at marriage – his first ending childless and in divorce and the second tinged by scandal because of his second wife, Joan of Portugal's, relations with Henry's favourite Beltran de la Cueva. When Joan bore a daughter, Juana, the child became known as 'La Beltraneja' – implying that Beltran was her real father. Juana was to become an important rival in Isabella's later struggles for the crown.

FACTFILE

- Queen Isabella gave Columbus 90 sailors and a sum of money for his voyage to discover a new route to the Indies.

- Isabella and Ferdinand were given the title *Reyes Católicos* by Pope Alexander VI for their religious devotion in 'cleansing' Spain and making it a solely Christian nation.

- The style of the period is called 'isabelino' after the queen; it combines Gothic, Moorish and Renaissance features.

- Isabella was the first named woman to appear on a US coin. In 1893 a commemorative quarter was struck, marking the 400th anniversary of Christopher Columbus's first voyage.

Powerful noblemen opposed to Henry failed to have him replaced by Alfonso, who died from poisoning. The noblemen then attempted to have Isabella made queen. She showed early signs of her strength of personality, high moral standards and political understanding by refusing the title while her brother lived. In acknowledgement of this, and possibly the doubtful parentage of Juana, Henry recognized Isabella as his heiress at the Accord of Toros de Guisando on 19 September 1468.

Henry then sought to arrange a suitable marriage for Isabella, now heiress to Castile. Possible husbands from Portugal, Aragon, England and France were variously proposed by Henry. However, once again Isabella exercised her considerable willpower. After several years of successfully avoiding Henry's preferred suitors, in 1469 she married the husband of her choice, Ferdinand of Aragon, without Henry's approval.

As a result, Henry withdrew his recognition of Isabella as his heir, restoring Juana to favour. When he died in 1474 there followed a five-year civil war over the succession. Forces ranged against Isabella included Alfonso V of Portugal, Juana's prospective husband. The war eventually ended in 1479 with Juana abandoning her

TIMELINE

Date	Isabella I of Spain	Related events
1451	Born in Madrigal de las Torras	Birth of Christopher Columbus (Cristoforo Colombo) in Genoa, Italy
1469	Marries Ferdinand, heir to the throne of Aragon	Birth of Niccolò Machiavelli, Italian historian and political author
1473	Crowned Queen of Castile and Léon	Copernicus born
1474–79	War of Succession	
1479–1504	Queen of Aragon	
1478	Isabella and Ferdinand institute the Spanish Inquisition. It lasts until 1820	Succession of Bayazid II, Sultan of the Ottoman Empire
1482	Beginning of the reconquest (*Reconquista*) of Granada	
1485	Birth of Isabella's daughter Catherine, later to marry Crown Prince Arthur of England and then his brother, King Henry VIII	
1492	Isabella sponsors Columbus on his voyage to discover a new route to the Indies	Columbus lands in the Caribbean, believing he has reached Asia
	Spanish Jews who refuse to convert to Christianity are expelled	Sultan Bayazid II's Empire dispatches the Ottoman navy to rescue Jews expelled from Spain
	Muslim Kingdom of Granada falls to Isabella and Ferdinand	
1504	Dies in Medina del Compo, Spain	France cedes Naples to Aragon. Ferdinand becomes King Ferdinand III of Naples

claim and retreating to a nunnery. Isabella was recognized as queen of Castile.

In the same year, following the death of John II of Aragon, Ferdinand became king of Aragon. Through Isabella and Ferdinand's joint rule the kingdoms of Castile and Aragon came together, creating the foundations of modern Spain. With domestic policy for Spain largely in Isabella's hands and foreign policy in Ferdinand's, the joint sovereigns blended their personal strengths and interests – beginning their reign by introducing reforms to reduce the power of the nobility in favour of the crown.

There is no doubt that Isabella was extremely pious. However, she also used the church as a means to achieve political goals and centralize her own power. In 1478 she and Ferdinand set in motion the infamous Spanish Inquisition, aimed at exposing heretics, Jews and Muslims who, although apparently converted to Christianity, were suspected of practising their faiths secretly. Although jointly honoured with Ferdinand in receiving the title 'The Catholic Kings' from Pope Alexander VI in recognition of their purifying of the faith, Isabella was not afraid to ignore or challenge papal appointments if she felt these did not best serve the interests of her country.

Isabella and Ferdinand were also determined to achieve the long-sought goal of *Reconquista*, the retaking of the last Muslim stronghold in Spain, the kingdom of Granada. Their attempt began in 1482 and was a protracted and difficult struggle, straining the finances of Castile until 1492. Isabella took an active part in the war and was apparently responsible for improving the methods of supply and setting up a military hospital.

It was during the *Reconquista* that Isabella and Ferdinand were visited by Christopher Columbus, who was seeking support for his voyage to discover a new route to the Indies. Isabella was quick to grasp the financial and religious opportunities the voyage represented. Terms were agreed in 1492 and when Columbus discovered the New World, it came under the power of Castile and the influence of Christianity. Laws were established to regulate the treatment of the indigenous population of the New World and Spaniards who ill-treated natives of the conquered territories were punished. However, slavery was the norm for those who did not convert to Christianity and, as much as the early Spanish settlers affirmed their determination to 'do God's work', they also intended to become rich.

Although it is hard to identify precisely the personal achievements of Isabella during her reign with Ferdinand, she was clearly a woman of great influence who understood how to use her power. Characterized by enormous energy and enthusiasm, piety and high moral standards, she was able to secure popularity with Castilians resistant to female rule by promoting carefully certain aspects of her personality and femininity.

Isabella was likely to have presented a striking figure with her blue eyes, luxuriant hair and magnificent dress. She made much of her personal devotion to Ferdinand: her public displays of affection created a lasting legend of a love match. She ensured that all her daughters were skilled in feminine arts such as spinning and sewing, while also educating them to a level beyond that of most women at the time. She herself became fluent in Latin after the age of 30 and also set up a school in the palace for the sons of the nobility. Many important literary works of the time were dedicated to Isabella and she was also an important patron of the arts. Parts of her extensive collection of Spanish and Flemish works of art still exist.

Perhaps Isabella's most significant legacies as a ruler were the conquest of Granada, which established civil peace in Spain, and her foresight in supporting Columbus. Nevertheless, she will always be associated with the cruelties of the Spanish Inquisition. Isabella became one of the most popular monarchs of her time and one widely venerated since. Her ardent Catholicism was to live on through her daughter, Catherine and thence, and most significantly, in her granddaughter Mary Tudor, the Catholic queen of England known as 'Bloody Mary'.

Catherine de Medici

Married to the French king Henri II at the age of 14, Catherine exercised enormous power as Queen Mother to his sons, the last three Valois kings of France. Although she became a woman of great influence, much of Catherine's life was spent in complex political manoeuvring and plotting, as well as in vain attempts to temper the strategic follies of her sons.

'In France, and at the most important period of our history, Catherine de Medici has suffered more from popular error than any other woman.'

Honoré de Balzac

BIOGRAPHY

Name:	Caterina Maria Romola di Lorenzo de Medici
Lived:	13 April 1519 – 5 January 1589
Place of birth:	Florence, Italy
Place of death:	Blois, France
Nationality:	Italian
Famed as:	Queen consort and regent of France; wife of Henri II of France; mother of three French kings

The daughter of the Duke of Lorenzo II de Medici and French princess Madeleine de la Tour d'Auvergne, Catherine was born into the richest non-royal family in Europe and was related to two popes. However, both her parents died while she was still young and she was sent to Rome by Pope Leo X to live with a family with papal connections. At the age of six she returned to Florence, where she was brought up by the wealthy Medicis, whose rule of the city was characterized by violence and intrigue. When their enemies forced them to flee, Catherine was taken in by the nuns from the convent at Murate where she was trained, disciplined and educated, becoming fluent in Greek and Latin.

FACTFILE

- Catherine regularly consulted Nostradamus who, when Catherine was 23 and still childless, predicted the death of Henri II in an accident and that Catherine would become the mother of three kings.

- Catherine's son François II was married as a child to Mary Stuart, later Queen of Scots. Although François was badly deformed, in poor health and certain to die young, he and Mary were said to love one another dearly.

- Catherine notoriously failed to complete any major building project she undertook. This was attributed to another of Nostradamus's predictions that she would die when she completed her palaces.

- The financial affairs of the French court were so dire that towards the end of her life Catherine began to pawn the crown jewels in order to pay bills. Henri III issued orders that she should not be allowed anywhere near the vaults in which the jewels were stored.

In 1533, at the age of 14, Catherine was sent to France to marry Henri duc d'Orléans, the future King Henri II. He was only 14 himself and had been a hostage for two years in a Madrid prison. He was uncouth and wild and his father sought the help of Diane de Poitiers to guide his courtly manners. Although she was 20 years his senior, Diane became Henri's mistress and completely dominated him during his marriage. As a young and powerless foreigner, Catherine was forced to endure Diane's domination right up until her husband's death. Although appointed regent in 1552 during Henri's absence at the Siege of Metz, for the most part Catherine lacked any political or personal influence during her marriage.

To make matters worse, Catherine remained childless for ten years and, as Henri was keen to perpetuate the Valois line, rumours of divorce spread through the French court. However, Catherine eventually bore Henri ten children, seven of whom survived – and three became kings of France: François II, Charles IX and Henri III. It was through her children that Catherine gained the political power she had lacked as queen consort.

In 1559 Henri II died suddenly in a jousting accident. Catherine then became Queen Mother. François II, the first of her sons to reign, had been a sickly child and died in 1560 after just a year on the throne.

TIMELINE

Date	Catherine de Medici	Related events
1519	Born in Florence	Ferdinand Magellan sails from Spain in search of western passage to Indonesia Leonardo da Vinci dies in Amboise, France
1521	Goes to Rome to live with the Papal family	Excommunication of Martin Luther
1533	Marries Henri duc d'Orléans, the future King Henri II	Henry VIII marries Anne Boleyn Birth of Elizabeth I
1559	Death of Henri II	
1560	Death of Francois II Catherine becomes regent	French diplomat Jean Nicot brings tobacco to France – hence 'nicotine'
1561	Outbreak of Wars of Religion	
1563	Accession of Charles IX	Church of England (Protestant) established at Convocation of Canterbury
1572	St Bartholomew's Day Massacre	
1574	Death of Charles IX Henri III succeeds to throne	
1589	Dies in Blois. Assassination of Henri III. Protestant Henri IV succeeds to the throne and converts to Catholicism	

Catherine's second son, Charles IX, was only ten when his brother died, so Catherine became regent – sovereign in all but name. Significant disputes between the warring Catholic and Huguenot factions now became apparent in France. Catherine tried to appease leaders of both religious factions through the Conference of Poissy in 1561, but was unable to prevent the outbreak of civil war. The Wars of Religion lasted for ten years and dominated her life and reputation. Although some held her responsible for the start of the wars, the reasons for the continuing conflict were complex. Throughout, Catherine alternated in her support for Catholic and Huguenot forces and used various strategies in her attempts to put the interests of her own dynasty above all else – ranging from compromise, concession and conciliation to swift action, including assassination. In one particular project, however, she was notably unsuccessful: trying to marry one or other of her sons to Elizabeth I, the Protestant queen of England.

In 1563 Charles IX reached majority and, although now king, assured his mother that she would continue to govern. At 41 Catherine was still active and ambitious. However, during Charles's reign an event occurred that was to ensure Catherine's lasting notoriety: the 1572 St Bartholomew's Day Massacre in Paris. The roots of this crime against humanity lay in Catherine's fear of the excessive influence on

Charles IX of the Huguenot Admiral of France, Gaspard de Châtillon, comte de Coligny.

In August 1572 there was a large gathering of Huguenots in Paris, a Catholic city, to celebrate the marriage of Catherine's daughter and Henri de Navarre, leader of the Huguenots. On 22 August there was a failed assassination attempt on Coligny, in which Catherine was said to be involved. When an investigation seemed likely to expose her role, Catherine allegedly persuaded Charles IX to order the death of Huguenot leaders, including Coligny, in anticipation of a supposed plot. This triggered the massacre of 24 August that was said to have claimed over 50,000 lives.

In 1574 Charles IX died at the age of 24 and Catherine's third and favourite son, Henri, duc d'Anjou, became King Henri III. Although very fond of her son, Catherine had limited influence over him and recognized the weakness of his character. She actively tried to restrain his dangerous activities, which looked likely to involve France in hostilities with Spain, right up to the time of her death. Catherine struggled to prevent France sinking into chaos under Henri's rule. The given cause of her death in 1589 was pneumonia, but it was thought that she would probably have been strong enough to overcome the illness if she had not been weakened by shock and despair over her son's assassination of his enemy in the powerful Catholic Holy League, Henri duc de Guise. Six months later, Henri was himself murdered. This marked the end of the rule of the House of Valois.

Apart from her political involvement and ceaseless efforts to influence her children, Catherine was notable for her cultural influence. Although disliked by some at court for following Italian practices, Catherine always retained a love for her cultural origins. She is credited with establishing ballet as a popular art form. Very fond of Italian dance and Italian pageants, Catherine made daily dance classes part of French court life. She commissioned the Italian violinist Balthasar de Beaujoyeux to compose the *Ballet Comique de La Reine* to celebrate the marriage of Henri's favourite. This was de Beaujoyeux's most important work and is regarded as the first ballet.

Catherine took after the Medicis in her love of luxury and art. She was famous for the sumptuous banquets she held at the Palais de Fontainebleau and was a patron of letters and the arts. She was particularly interested in architecture, in which she also had a taste for pomp and magnificence. She ordered the building of a new wing of the Louvre and initiated work on the palace's famous Tuileries gardens. Her personal library, one of the most noted in Renaissance Europe, contained many rare manuscripts.

Despite being a political realist, Catherine was very superstitious and relied on the advice of astrologers. Although essentially pacifist herself, Catherine's machinations on behalf of her royal family probably aggravated religious conflict in Europe. She lacked any religious faith: her interest in the Catholic church extended only to its advantages to the crown. In all things, and above all else, she acted as a mother intent on securing the perpetuation of her sons' rule.

Elizabeth I

Queen Elizabeth I of England oversaw a glorious period of creativity and stability in England. She bravely and skilfully negotiated her difficult succession to the crown. She knew how to use her femininity to advantage – at a time when the people of England had just lived through the reign of her unpopular sister, Mary.

'I have already joined myself in marriage to a husband, namely the Kingdom of England.'

BIOGRAPHY

Name:	Elizabeth Tudor
Lived:	7 September 1533 – 24 March 1603
Place of birth:	Greenwich, England
Place of death:	Richmond, England
Nationality:	English
Famed as:	Queen of England and final Tudor monarch; established the Protestant faith in England

Elizabeth was the daughter of Henry VIII and Anne Boleyn, whom Henry had married after divorcing his first wife, Catherine of Aragon, thereby breaking with the Catholic Church. With only one daughter from his first marriage, Mary Tudor, Henry desperately needed a male heir. However, Anne was only able to bear him a daughter. Falling out of favour with Henry, Anne was executed in 1535 when Elizabeth was aged just two.

Henry then remarried Jane Seymour who bore him a son, Edward, in 1537. Henry's Act of Succession meant that the crown would pass from Edward, through Mary and to Elizabeth. In the event, Elizabeth's ascension to the throne was fraught with danger as she struggled to survive her Catholic sister's suspicions of her as focus of Protestant opposition to the throne.

FACTFILE

- During her reign, Elizabeth was variously known as 'Good Queen Bess', 'The Virgin Queen' and 'Gloriana'.

- Sensitivity to unwashed bodies and bad smells is falsely supposed to be the reason for Elizabeth's frequent removal from one house to another. In fact, these progressions around the country were part of Elizabeth's policy of being visible to the people.

- She whitened her face with a mixture of egg, powdered eggshells, poppy seeds, white lead (a lethal ingredient), borax and alum. When her hair began to thin, probably because of this poisonous mixture, she wore a large red wig.

Elizabeth was highly intelligent, industrious and had a remarkable memory. Brought up by governesses and tutors at Hatfield House in Hertfordshire, she easily grasped languages and the classics while very young and, as she grew up, became a skilled player of the virginals, as well as excelling at riding, archery and dancing. Early pictures show her to be a serious, pale-faced young girl with auburn hair. She was devoted to her father though she saw little of him until he married his last wife, Catherine Parr, who was a concerned and kindly stepmother and ensured that Henry's children spent more time at court. Catherine arranged for Elizabeth to be taught the art of public speaking. This was to serve her well throughout her reign, enabling her to address ministers in Parliament and troops on the battlefield and contributing to her widespread popularity as queen.

After Edward's death, and a brief period while a distant claimant for the throne, Lady Jane Grey, was queen, Mary became queen and set about re-establishing Catholicism, the faith of her mother and Spanish relations, in England. Protestant opponents to Mary and her proposed husband Philip of Spain tried to make use of Elizabeth, who had to step carefully to avoid being implicated in their schemes. However, Mary's fears that Elizabeth was involved in various plots against her led to Elizabeth being incarcerated – first, and most terrifyingly, in the Tower of London, and then under house arrest in Woodstock, Oxfordshire. She was eventually reconciled with Mary after negotiating her imprisonment with a mixture of strategic

TIMELINE

Date	Elizabeth I	Related events
1533	Marriage of Henry VIII and Anne Boleyn Born in Greenwich	Ivan IV (The Terrible) accedes to Russian throne
1535	Henry VIII declares himself Head of the English Church	Thomas More refuses to renounce the Catholic Church and is executed for treason
1538		Pope Paul III excommunicates Henry VIII
1558	Death of Mary I Elizabeth ascends to the throne	French soldiers take Calais, England's last remaining continental possession
1559	Coronation The Act of Supremacy declares Elizabeth the supreme governor of the Protestant Church of England	Henri II of France dies in a jousting accident
1569	Catholic uprising in the north of England	Phillip II of Spain institutes the Inquisition in South America
1577		Francis Drake sails around the world
1587	Execution of Mary Queen of Scots	
1588	Defeat of the Spanish Armada and prevention of invasion by Spain	Thomas Hobbes, English philosopher born (d. 1679)
1603	Dies at Greenwich, London	James VI of Scotland, son of Mary Queen of Scots, becomes James I of England

circumspection, passive resistance and protestations of her innocence. Eventually the sisters were reconciled, and when Mary was dying she named Elizabeth as her only successor and wrote begging her to keep the Catholic faith alive in England.

Elizabeth knew that settling religious issues was a priority. However, she disliked the religious extremes of both Edward's and Mary's reigns and favoured a climate of moderation. In the year following her coronation, she introduced acts that returned England to the Protestant faith, ruled that public worship and religious books and prayers were to be used in English rather than Latin and introduced a new Book of Common Prayer. Despite Parliament's desire for stronger measures, with characteristic pragmatism, Elizabeth argued that 'she wanted no windows into men's souls': allegiance to the Crown was more important than religious loyalties, and citizens were English first and foremost.

Although there was continued discontent in both Catholic and Puritan quarters, the establishment of the Protestant church helped accomplish the civil stability that characterized Elizabeth's reign. However, tougher measures were later passed against Catholics, following Catholic plots to assassinate Elizabeth after Mary Queen of Scots' arrival in England in 1568 and a Papal bull in 1570 absolving Catholics from allegiance to Elizabeth as queen.

Although she never met her, Mary Queen of Scots was a source of anxiety to Elizabeth. Mary had been forced to abdicate by the Scots after a series of scandals connected with her various husbands, and fled to England. Aware that her presence could lead to a Catholic uprising, Elizabeth ordered her imprisonment. As feared, Mary was found to be corresponding with Catholic plotters. After much prevarication by Elizabeth, Mary was executed in 1587.

Following Mary's death, growing Catholic opposition to England was encouraged by the Pope and Philip II of Spain, who wanted to depose Elizabeth and reinstate a Catholic monarch in England. In the late summer of 1588 the Spanish Armada (naval fleet) approached England, intending to challenge the English navy and provide cover for invasion by the Spanish Army. Elizabeth gave a famous speech to her troops at Tilbury near London, assembled to fight the expected invasion: 'I know I have the body but of a weak and feeble woman; but I have the heart and stomach of a king, and of a king of England too.' One of the most significant naval battles in history then followed, in which the Spanish Armada was unexpectedly defeated by the superior seamanship of the English, the use of fire ships and the direction of the 'Protestant wind' that favoured the English fleet.

Throughout her reign, Parliament was deeply concerned by Elizabeth's reluctance to marry – even refusing to grant her funds at one point until she settled the matter. Elizabeth cleverly argued that the country's welfare was her priority and that she would marry when it was convenient. However, throughout her reign she was involved in various flirtatious and possible alliances with several foreign princes. She also enjoyed the company of men and had several favourites including Robert Dudley, Earl of Leicester, Sir Walter Raleigh and, at the end of her life, the Earl of Essex who was eventually executed for treason.

Elizabeth ruled England for over half a century, a time when the country flourished politically, economically and in the arts, especially literature. She chose highly competent advisers and was a skilled leader in bringing together rival groups in her council. However, she failed to settle the question of succession before she died, though some thought she indicated at the very end that her heir should be James I of Scotland, son of Mary Queen of Scots.

Elizabeth embodied many excellent qualities as well as human frailties. She was extremely clever, skilled, quick witted, enigmatic and articulate. She was also susceptible to flattery, vain, indecisive and at times ruthless. One of her main achievements during her reign – both in her own view and that of many historians – was her popularity, maintained by an understanding of public relations that was ahead of her time and supported by widespread public appearances. Throughout her reign she made continued avowals of her dedication to the well-being of her people and, near the end of her life in 1601 said, 'This I account the glory of my crown, that I have reigned with your loves'.

Catherine the Great

The Empress Catherine II of Russia was one of the most powerful figures of the eighteenth century. Considered by many to be an enlightened monarch, she instituted reforms that transformed the world's view of her country and helped to position Russia as a leading world power. Her patronage of the arts in Russia exceeded that of any monarch before or since.

'I leave it to posterity to judge impartially what I have done.'

BIOGRAPHY

Name:	Sophia Augusta Frederika von Anhalt-Zerbst
Lived:	21 April 1729 – 17 November 1796
Place of birth:	Stettin (then Germany, now Poland)
Place of death:	St Petersburg, Russia
Nationality:	German
Famed as:	Empress of Russia; patron of the arts and education

Catherine the Great, as she came to be widely known, was born a German princess, Sophie Augusta Frederika, in Stettin, now Szczecin, Poland, on 21 April 1729. Her parents were Johanna Elizabeth of Holstein and Christian Augustus, Prince of Anhalt-Zerbst.

On 21 August 1744 she married Peter III, Grand Duke of Holstein and heir to the Russian throne. Sophie changed her name to Catherine – in Russian Ekaterina or Yekaterina – and also accepted the Russian Orthodox faith. However, this arranged marriage proved very unsuccessful, and Catherine became closely involved with other members of the court, not least several who were opposed to Peter. She also educated herself, reading the classics and corresponding with leading figures of the time, such as Voltaire and Diderot, and generally kept herself well informed about politics and current affairs throughout Russia and Europe.

FACTFILE

- The infamous 'horse' story associated with Catherine's death is entirely fictional. So, too, is the version that suggests she died on her commode. She died of a stroke.

- Catherine is rumoured to have had as many as 300 lovers. It is only really possible to substantiate the fact that she had two husbands and eleven 'favourites'.

- In 1754, Catherine gave birth to Paul, future emperor of Russia. Paul's father was reputed to be Serge Saltykov, a Russian army officer and Catherine's first lover.

Catherine found her husband, who was weak from various illnesses, unattractive and a creature of pity. She wrote: 'I should have loved my new husband, if only he had been willing or able to be in the least lovable. But in the first days of my marriage, I made some cruel reflections about him. I said to myself: If you love this man, you will be the most wretched creature on Earth. Watch your step, so far as affection for this gentleman is concerned, think of yourself, Madame.'

In 1762 Peter succeeded to the Russian throne, as Tsar Peter III, and the royal couple lived in the Winter Palace in St Petersburg. However, the rift between Peter and Catherine grew wider and the two cultivated different supporters and contacts. Peter signed a treaty with Prussia, restoring all occupied territories to Russia's enemy, and in the process alienated the Russian Army by imposing Prussian discipline and uniforms. In due course, Catherine took Grigori Orlov as her lover and he became the leader of a conspiracy that ousted Peter from the throne, installing Catherine as Empress Catherine II, in a bloodless coup. On 17 July 1762 Peter died, perhaps from illness, but possibly killed by his wife's supporters. Peter was buried at Alexander Nevsky Monastery and Catherine did not attend his funeral.

At this time a manifesto was printed and circulated that included the words: 'the State of Russia has been exposed to supreme danger by the course of recent events…we have found ourselves compelled, with the help of God, and in accordance with the manifest and sincere desire of our faithful subjects, to ascend

TIMELINE

Date	Catherine the Great	Related events
1729	Born in Stettin	1700–1800: period of social and political unrest in Europe and US
1745	Marries Peter Feodorovich, heir to the Russian throne in St Petersburg	
1754	Catherine gives birth to Paul, future emperor of Russia	Architect Bartolomeo Rastrelli starts to build the Winter Palace
1756–63		Seven Years' War – pitted Prussia, Hanover and Great Britain against France, Austria, Russia, Sweden and Saxony
1762	Overthrows her husband and becomes Catherine II	Peace treaty between Russia and Prussia
1764–75		Construction of the Small Hermitage
1788		Imposes protectorate on Poland War with Sweden
1789	Fearing that the revolution in France might spread, Catherine begins to reverse her liberal reforms	
1796	Dies in St Petersburg	Edward Jenner discovers that vaccination with cowpox gives immunity to smallpox

the throne as sole and absolute sovereign, whereupon our loyal subjects have solemnly sworn us an oath of allegiance.'

On Sunday 22 September 1762 Catherine was crowned Empress in the old Cathedral of the Assumption in the Kremlin in Moscow, with the Archbishop of Novgorod celebrating mass.

On returning to St Petersburg, Catherine worked hard to understand the state of Russia and to find ways of improving the economy and infrastructure, beginning with agricultural reforms. Studies were made of Russia's soils, and experts brought in to advise on the best crops to cultivate. Agricultural technology was also improved and machines were imported from England to improve efficiency. Dockyards were founded and expanded and warships constructed. Geologists were sent out to prospect for valuable ores and silver mines were excavated. Other industries that developed under her encouragement included the Siberian fur trade and the production of linen, leather goods, pottery and furniture. Much of this development was based upon expertise imported from abroad, including England. The Imperial porcelain works were improved by German, French and Austrian craftsmen. There was active trade with the east, with camel caravans plying the routes to Manchuria. Russia took leather, furs and linen to China, importing cotton, silk, silver, tobacco and tea in return. By 1765 the Russian economy had been transformed and was thriving, improving the lot of most of Russia's citizens.

The masses of the Russian population were poorly educated, and Catherine began a programme of establishing schools in every provincial town. She also converted a convent in St Petersburg into a boarding school for girls – the Smolny Institute.

Another key area with which Catherine was concerned was medicine. At that time, smallpox was a major killer and left thousands disabled and disfigured. Catherine promoted the new practice of inoculation against contagious disease, and was herself inoculated by Dr Thomas Dimsdale whom she brought from Scotland to St Petersburg for the purpose. Special inoculation hospitals were established with Dimsdale's help, and in 1763 Catherine founded Russia's first College of Medicine, which trained doctors, surgeons and apothecaries.

Catherine was also a great lover and promoter of the arts, adding to the Imperial collections and commissioning the building of special palaces, including the famous Hermitage. She had a theatre built for performing both plays and operas. She purchased the libraries of Diderot and Voltaire, and increased the Imperial library from just a few hundred to 38,000 volumes. During her reign, St Petersburg became one of the leading cultural centres of Europe. Catherine became renowned as a patron of the arts, of education and literature, and she herself wrote memoirs, fiction and comedies.

The aristocrats of the age depended upon serfdom, of which Catherine apparently disapproved, but while she did not abolish it for fear of alienating the nobility, she did issue decrees for the humane treatment of the serfs. Nevertheless, the power of the nobility increased under her regime, the system of serfdom was strengthened, and although the common people benefited from some of her reforms, they remained in essence an exploited working class. She reformed the legal system, and in 1785 issued a charter that freed the nobles from taxes and from service to the state. She also granted the nobility hereditary status, and gave them full control over their own lands and serfs.

In due course, Catherine transferred her affections to another important Russian figure, Gregory Potemkin, and with his assistance Russia annexed the Crimea from the Turks, thus expanding the size and wealth of the realm. She made Potemkin a Prince of the Empire.

Catherine was a popular empress and ruled for 34 years. When she died on 17 November 1796 she was widely mourned. Although popularly known as Catherine the Great, she rejected the designation when it was officially proposed, stating modestly: 'I leave it to posterity to judge impartially what I have done.'

Her reputation has been partly sullied by rumours implying a life of debauchery and sexual excess. Certainly she took several lovers, had an active sex life and maintained a secret room decorated with erotic paintings and sculptures. But the more exotic tales surrounding her seem to have been invented by French writers soon after her death, at a time when France was fighting against a coalition that included Russia.

Mary Wollstonecraft

Mary Wollstonecraft was an early political feminist, who courageously rejected the restrictions and values imposed on the lives of women in eighteenth-century British society. While her writing and behaviour outraged her contemporaries, she is regarded as a pioneer in the struggle for women's rights.

'If the abstract rights of man will bear discussion and explanation, those of women, by a parity of reasoning, will not shrink from the same test: though a different opinion prevails in this country.'

BIOGRAPHY

Name:	Mary Wollstonecraft
Lived:	27 April 1759 – 10 September 1797
Place of birth:	London
Place of death:	London
Nationality:	British
Famed as:	Author and radical political feminist

From difficult beginnings, as one of seven children of an abusive and drunken father, and as part of a nomadic Anglo-Irish family, Mary Wollstonecraft rose to become a highly influential thinker and writer, to many the first political feminist in Britain.

There had been money in Mary's family, but it was lost through her father's fecklessness. Her radicalism probably had its roots in the misery she endured in her early home life, where she suffered from her parents' overt preference for her older brother and the constant threat of violence from her father. Throughout her life she had to deal with the consequences of a damaged emotional life and was subject to periods of rage and despair.

Mary worked as a lady's companion and governess after leaving home, and was often privy to the intimacies of unhappy marriages. She nursed her mother through her last illness and shouldered the domestic and financial responsibilities of the whole family for a while. Her later writings propose practical methods for change, all based on ideas of education. She insisted that in order to be equal, women needed to be educated exactly like men.

FACTFILE

- For a considerable period, Mary supported her father, brothers and sisters with the money she earned from writing.
- The critic Horace Walpole, reviewing *A Vindication of the Rights of Woman*, called Mary 'a hyena in petticoats'.
- Mary went to Paris in 1792 to distance herself from John Henry Fuseli, a Romantic painter and married man with whom she had become obsessed.
- Her daughter, Mary, later married the poet Percy Bysshe Shelley and wrote the Gothic masterpiece *Frankenstein*.

Mary set up a school with her close friend Fanny Blood in Newington Green, near London, where a number of leading intellectuals had settled. Here she met Richard Price and Joseph Priestly, Dissenters who rejected Christian ideas of original sin and eternal punishment and supported American independence. It was through the Dissenters that she met her future publisher, Joseph Johnson. Their meeting saw Mary through a difficult time. Fanny Blood had married and gone to live in Lisbon, Portugal, but was fatally ill with consumption and expecting her first child. Mary left the school and reached her friend in time to witness her death and that of her child. The loss of her friend triggered a profound depression. Returning to England, she continued to teach but her school failed. When she confided her intention to write for her living to Joseph Johnson, he supported her and took her into his home.

Mary's first publication, commissioned by Johnson, was *Thoughts on the Education of Daughters* (1787). This was a treatise aimed at the emerging middle class of girls who needed improved instruction. It offered alternative teaching methods and suggested entirely new areas of study for young women. The works that followed

TIMELINE

Date	Mary Wollstonecraft	Related events
1759	Born in London	
1778	Leaves home to work as a lady's companion in Bath	Jean-Jacques Rousseau writes *Emile*, stating that women should be entirely subordinate and dependent on their husbands
1783	Sets up a school in London	
1785	Leaves England for Lisbon to nurse Fanny Blood	Death of Fanny Blood
1787	Writes *Thoughts on the Education of Daughters*	
1789		Start of the French Revolution American Declaration of the Rights of Man
1790	Writes *A Vindication of the Rights of Men*	Society of Friends petitions the American Congress for the abolition of slavery
1792	Writes *A Vindication of the Rights of Woman* Moves to France	Divorce law passed in France, giving the grounds for divorce that women as well as men could use
1793	Meets American writer Gilbert Imlay in Paris	Louis XVI of France found guilty of treason and guillotined
1795	Mary returns to London and attempts suicide	Royalist riots in Paris are crushed by Napoleon Bonaparte
1796	Meets William Godwin again and they become lovers	
1797	Marries William Godwin Dies in childbirth	Death of Edmund Burke

this first book, *Mary: A Fiction* (1788) and *Original Stories, From Real Life* (1788), were less theoretical, incorporating both biographical and fictional elements, but nonetheless attacked the *status quo* from a similar standpoint.

Mary now emerged as a formidable intellectual presence and had a powerful ally in Richard Price. A rhetorical spat between Price and Edmund Burke over the implications of the French Revolution led her to write a defence of Price's humanistic viewpoint. This was the pamphlet entitled *A Vindication of the Rights of Men*, in which Mary demonstrated her rational and anti-sentimental style of argument. She was now making intellectual enemies, but radical ears were pricking up. Thomas Paine, John Cartwright, John Horne Tooke, William Godwin and William Blake became interested in her work. Their thinking would shape the entire Romantic Movement into the nineteenth century.

Mary followed the *Rights of Men* with *A Vindication of the Rights of Woman*, her most famous work. In this she challenged aspects of married life and the ways in which women were educated. The ideas she presented were highly controversial and provoked some negative reactions, most remarkably among her fellow radicals. Mary advocated the destruction of all forms of patriarchy, including the military, the Church and even the monarchy.

The backlash against Mary and her British contemporaries began in 1793, with Edmund Burke describing them as 'loathsome insects that might, if they were allowed, grow into giant spiders as large as oxen'. King George III felt it was time to assert his authority too and threatened serious punishment of any writer or politician who continued to condemn the monarchy.

In 1792 Mary, a supporter of the French Revolution, moved to Paris, where she met Gilbert Imlay, an American entrepreneur. They had an illegitimate daughter, named Fanny after Mary's friend, in 1794. The facts about this period of Mary's life were unknown until after her death. Her relationship with Imlay was one-sided and in 1795 his infidelities pushed her to attempt suicide. When she recovered she travelled to Scandinavia and there wrote the book that allegedly made William Godwin fall in love with her: *Letters Written During a Short Residence in Sweden, Norway and Denmark.* The book started a vogue for personal, entertaining travelogues. Mary returned to London after the trip, where the reality of Imlay's abandonment made her miserable enough to attempt suicide once again by throwing herself in the Thames. She was rescued and shortly afterwards reintroduced to William Godwin. They had met previously in 1791 but not taken to one another. Now they became lovers and married – despite their public resolve not to – in March 1797. Mary was expecting their child. Complications arose during delivery and she died of blood poisoning on 10 September 1797.

At the time of her death, Mary had been working on another book, *Maria, or the Wrongs of Woman*, which was to appear posthumously in Godwin's dedicatory work, *Memoirs of the Author of the Vindication of the Rights of Woman* (1798), in which her relationship with Gilbert Imlay, and the birth of Fanny, were first revealed. *The Wrongs of Woman* charts the mistreatment of Maria, its heroine, following her husband's decision to confine her to a mental institution. This publication provoked still more contemptuous responses and it was a long time before Mary's opinions on marriage, sex and education were considered rationally.

Mary Wollstonecraft's contribution to feminism has only been appreciated in recent years. In *A Vindication of the Rights of Woman* she insisted on the essential spiritual equality of men and women, and this revolutionary conviction was what inspired her to become a radical among radicals. She is distinguished by the measured, reasoned presentation of her views. Readers today would find it hard to understand how they could incite such vitriol from her opponents.

Jane Austen

Jane Austen established the English novel as a medium for entertainment, amusement and social comment. Her stories about the lives of middle-class people in rural England, untouched by the political unrest and wars redefining Europe at the time, are still widely read and discussed today.

'That young lady has a talent for describing the involvements of feelings and characters of ordinary life which is to me the most wonderful I ever met with.'

Sir Walter Scott

BIOGRAPHY

Name:	Jane Austen
Lived:	16 December 1775 – 18 July 1817
Place of birth:	Steventon, Hampshire
Place of death:	Winchester
Nationality:	British
Famed as:	Author of enduringly popular novels of English country life and manners

For the first 25 years of her life, Jane Austen's home was the rectory at Steventon where her father George Austen was vicar. She was brought up with her five brothers and her older sister, Cassandra, from whom she was inseparable. Jane was educated mainly at home, apart from a brief period when she and her sister attended a boarding school, and never lived independently from her family. Her life was circumscribed. She left home only to holiday in places and with people the Austens knew well. While two of her brothers joined the navy, fought in the Napoleonic Wars and eventually became admirals, change in Jane's life was marked by moves from one country house to another. In 1801 the Austens moved to Bath, and lived there until George Austen died in 1805.

After her father's death, Jane and her mother and sister returned to Hampshire, settling in Southampton. In 1809, her older brother Edward invited his mother and sisters to make their home with him. As a boy, Edward had been adopted by a wealthy childless couple, the Knights, and Edward inherited their estate at Chawton. Many of Jane's major works were created or completed at Chawton, in a cottage on Edward's estate, and in the seven and a half years she lived there she enjoyed a period of steady productivity.

FACTFILE

- Jane was affectionately referred to as 'Jenny' by her family.

- In 1802, Jane agreed to marry Harris Bigg-Wither, a younger man and the brother of a friend. However, she changed her mind overnight and broke the engagement. She never married.

- For her family and friends, Jane would speculate on what became of her characters after the end of the novels.

- In 2005, *Pride and Prejudice* was voted the best British novel of all time in a BBC poll. It has inspired numerous films and television adaptations worldwide, including *Bridget Jones's Diary* (2001) and *Bride and Prejudice* (2004).

Jane had a lifelong love of literature and began to write as a child, initially to amuse herself and her family. She also wrote and performed plays with her brothers and sister. The access she had to her father's extensive library provided her with inspiration for short, satirical sketches and some early novels, in which she explored and parodied existing genres of story telling.

In her early twenties Jane wrote the narratives that were to be published as *Pride and Prejudice*, *Sense and Sensibility* and *Northanger Abbey*. The first, entitled *Elinor and Marianne* and drafted in 1795, explores the question of proper feminine conduct through the portrayal of two contrasting sisters, the rational Elinor and her romantic sister Marianne who falls hopelessly in love only to have her heart broken. Jane later reworked this novel as *Sense and Sensibility*, a title reflecting the novel's concern with the limitations of romantic liberty for women in contemporary

TIMELINE

Date	Jane Austen	Related events
1775	Born in Steventon, Hampshire	
1800		William Wordsworth writes *Lyrical Ballads*
1801	Jane's family moves to Bath	
1805	Jane's father dies and the family moves to Southampton	Sir Walter Scott's epic ballad *The Lay of the Last Minstrel* is published
1807		Washington Irving writes his short story *Rip Van Winkle*
1809	Settles at her brother's estate at Chawton	Robert Southey, English Poet Laureate, joins the staff of the *Quarterly Review*
1811	Publication of *Sense and Sensibility*	Luddite Movement born
1812		Beethoven writes his 7th and 8th Symphonies
1813	Publication of *Pride and Prejudice*	Publication of Percy Bysshe Shelley's *Queen Mab*
1814	Publication of *Mansfield Park*	Francis Scott Key writes *The Star-Spangled Banner*
1815	Publication of *Emma*	Battle of Waterloo and exile of Napoleon on Elba
1816	Contracts Addison's disease and begins work on *Sanditon*	Publication of Samuel Taylor Coleridge's *Kubla Khan*
1817	Dies in Winchester and is buried in the Cathedral	John Keats publishes *Poems* and begins *Endymion*
1818	Posthumous publication of *Persuasion* and *Northanger Abbey*	Publication of Lord Byron's *Don Juan* and Mary Shelley's *Frankenstein*

society. Jane's literature, as well as providing witty accounts of daily life in regency England, illuminates contemporary concerns for women. It is this aspect of her writing that has always engaged feminist interest in her work, despite frequent criticism of her novels' parochialism. This was quite deliberate: she once asserted that 'three or four families in a country village is the very thing to work on'.

Pride and Prejudice, Jane's best known and probably best loved novel, was drafted as *First Impressions* between October 1796 and August 1797. The story, which typically focuses on the expectations, desires and loves of her characters, explores the effects on a country family of the stationing of a militia regiment in the local town. The novel's prime concern is with the romances and fates of the five sisters of the Bennett family who stand to lose their inheritance on the death of their father. Their mother's sole ambition, to marry off her daughters to maximum social and pecuniary advantage, is ridiculed by her husband, Mr Bennett, who delights in mocking his silly wife. Elizabeth Bennett, her father's lively and independent-minded favourite daughter, initially has too much pride to admit her love for the haughty, misunderstood – and extremely rich – Mr Darcy. *Pride and Prejudice* tracks the ups and downs of the family, and the social and love life of Elizabeth Bennett, culminating in her marriage to Mr Darcy. It was not published until 1813, two years after the publication of *Sense and Sensibility*.

Jane's other novels, *Mansfield Park*, *Emma*, *Persuasion* and *Northanger Abbey* were published between 1811 and 1818. During her lifetime, all the novels were published anonymously, bearing only the inscription 'By a Lady'. *Persuasion* and *Northanger Abbey*, which was probably the first novel she drafted, were published posthumously in 1818, when Jane's brother revealed her authorship.

In her novels, Jane depicts with sympathetic irony her well-bred young heroines' and heroes' preoccupation with courtship and marriage. The focus is without exception the daily dilemmas faced by her characters, all from families of varying economic circumstances but all fundamentally middle-class and relatively well-to-do, landed gentry, country clergymen and families desperate to maintain or enhance their social positions. She had no rivals and no predecessors in this literary genre and the limited actions and settings that characterize her work were carefully planned. When it was suggested that she should turn her talent to other styles of writing, she wrote, 'I could no more write a [historical] romance than an epic poem. I could not sit seriously down to write a serious romance under any other motive than to save my life; and if it were indispensable for me to keep it up and never relax into laughing at myself or other people, I am sure I should be hung before I had finished the first chapter.' More soberly, she acknowledged that her skills were best expressed by the limits she set herself: 'the little bit (two-inches wide) of ivory on which I work with so fine a brush, as to produce little effect, after much labour.'

The novels were hugely popular in Jane's lifetime. Her most famous enthusiast was the Prince of Wales, later King George IV, whom Jane disliked. Nevertheless, *Emma* is dedicated to him, at his request. More satisfactory admiration came from the poets Samuel Taylor Coleridge and Robert Southey, the famed wit Sydney Smith and Sir Walter Scott.

In the winter of 1816 Jane contracted Addison's disease, a rare disorder of the adrenal glands. At this time she began work on what was to be her final incomplete novel, *Sanditon*. The disease prevented Jane from being able to walk far, a pursuit that she, like many of her heroines, loved. Instead she used to drive out in a little donkey carriage, which can be seen at the Jane Austen Museum at Chawton. By May 1817 Jane was so ill that Cassandra rented rooms in Winchester so that Jane could be near the doctor who was caring for her. At that time, there was no known cure for her illness and Jane Austen died on 18 July 1817 at the age of 41. She is buried in Winchester Cathedral.

Harriet Beecher Stowe

Harriet Beecher Stowe was a journalist, novelist and lifelong anti-slavery campaigner. Her novel *Uncle Tom's Cabin* exposed the atrocities of the slave system in the United States to a population largely ignorant of what was happening in their own country. The book fuelled the tensions that led to the Civil War and the eventual success of the emancipation movement.

'Does not every American Christian owe to the African race some effort at reparation for the wrongs that the American nation has brought upon them?'

Uncle Tom's Cabin

BIOGRAPHY

Name:	Harriet Beecher Stowe
Lived:	14 June 1811 – 1 July 1896
Place of birth:	Litchfield, Connecticut
Place of death:	Hartford, Connecticut
Nationality:	American
Famed as:	Abolitionist, journalist and novelist; author of anti-slavery novel *Uncle Tom's Cabin*

Harriet Beecher Stowe was born Harriet Beecher in Litchfield, Connecticut, one of several children of Lyman Beecher, a Protestant preacher. Her mother died when Harriet was five years old. The Beecher children were brought up in a puritan tradition of high moral standards and Christian piety, but were also encouraged by their father to practise religious tolerance and debate the issues of the day. Harriet was a student and later teacher at her sister Catherine's seminary for girls in Hartford, one of a small number of schools that took female education seriously. The school emphasized writing skills as well as the complexities of household management.

The Beechers moved to Cincinnati, Ohio, in 1832, when Lyman was appointed president of the Lane Theological Seminary. This move gave Harriet her first opportunity to see the effects of the slave trade in the neighbour state Kentucky, just across the Ohio River. In 1836 she married Calvin Stowe, a professor of biblical literature at Lane, and they eventually had seven children. Calvin always encouraged Harriet in her literary work.

FACTFILE

- *Uncle Tom's Cabin* was the first American book to sell a million copies and was also the best selling book of the nineteenth century.

- Harriet produced a book a year and, through her writing, supplemented her husband's modest income.

- She received hate mail, including one letter enclosing the ear of a slave and the threat that more would happen to the slave if she continued writing.

- At a reception held in her honour in London, the Duchess of Sutherland presented her with a gold bracelet made of ten oval links in imitation of slave fetters.

- It has been alleged that Harriet read many of the works cited in *The Key to Uncle Tom's Cabin* only after the original novel was published.

The years in Cincinnati were marked by poverty and isolation, and by a cholera epidemic that claimed the life of the Stowes' 18-month-old son. Harriet later said that her grief enabled her to empathize with the plight of a slave mother forced to give up her child. Harriet's family shared her abolitionist views, and helped to hide runaway slaves.

During a writing career of over 50 years, Harriet published 30 books, including novels for adults and children, short stories, poems, magazine articles, theological works, travel books and practical household manuals. Her informal, conversational style, in which she presented herself as an ordinary wife and mother, partly accounts for her popularity. Her first book was a selection of short stories under the title *The Mayflower: Sketches and Scenes and Characters among the Descendants of the Puritans* (1843).

In 1850 Calvin was appointed professor at Bowdoin College in Brunswick, Maine. At the time, there was public uproar over the newly established Fugitive Slave Law,

TIMELINE

Date	Harriet Beecher Stowe	Related events
1811	Born in Litchfield, Connecticut	
1836	Marries Calvin Stowe. They shelter fugitive slaves until their move to Brunswick	Ralph Waldo Emerson's Essay on Nature signals the start of the Transcendentalist movement
1850	Calvin Stowe is offered a professorship at Bowdoin and the couple move to Brunswick, Maine	Fugitive Slave Law passed by Congress – helping an escaped slave becomes a crime
1851	*Uncle Tom's Cabin* serialized	Herman Melville writes *Moby Dick*
1853	Writes *The Key to Uncle Tom's Cabin* Makes the first of three visits to Europe	Nathanial Hawthorne writes *Tanglewood Tales for Girls and Boys* and is appointed to the Consulship of Liverpool, England
1856	Writes *Dred: A Tale of the Great Dismal Swamp*	
1861		Start of The Civil War
1862	Introduced to Abraham Lincoln	
1863	Writes *A Reply to the Address of the Women of England* and *Sojourner Truth, the Libyan Sibyl*	President Abraham Lincoln delivers the Gettysburg Address
1865		End of The Civil War Slavery abolished by the 13th Amendment to the US Constitution
1876		Mark Twain writes *The Adventures of Tom Sawyer*
1896	Dies in Hartford, Connecticut	

which made it a criminal act to harbour slaves who had escaped north from the southern states. It was in Brunswick, amid her growing family and household chores, that Harriet wrote *Uncle Tom's Cabin*, to show the nation the cruelty of the slave system. The novel was published in 40 instalments, starting in 1851, in *The National Era*, an abolitionist newspaper. Families throughout the country read the episodes, full of suspense and sentiment. Although the slave trade was mostly confined to the south, and northerners did not consider themselves responsible for its evils, *Uncle Tom's Cabin* became a sensation everywhere. In 1852 the entire book was published in two volumes and became an instant bestseller, both in America and abroad. By 1857 half a million copies had been sold.

The story tells of Uncle Tom, a loyal and saintly slave to the Shelby family, who is separated from his wife and children and sold to a slave trader when the Shelbys lose their money. Taken south, he saves the life of little Eva, whose grateful father buys Tom. In New Orleans Tom is happy in his friendship with Eva and her friend Topsy, until Eva and her father die and Tom is sold to a cruel Yankee, who has Tom beaten to death when he refuses to betray two female slaves. George Shelby, the son of Tom's original owner, arrives too late to save Tom, but vows to fight for the abolitionist cause.

Many incidents in the novel became famous, including the plight of the fugitive slave Eliza, who carries her baby across the icy river to avoid separation, and the highly sentimental death of little Eva. Stowe once said that God wrote the book – 'I just took his dictation' – but it was the combination of exciting incident, personal conviction and homely style that ensured its appeal. Anti-slavery literature was by no means unusual before *Uncle Tom's Cabin* was published, but Harriet's human, sentimental story put the issue under the spotlight. The Civil War, the devastating regional conflict between northern and southern states, grew out of a mixture of causes, including humanitarian concern for slaves. Abraham Lincoln, who was introduced to Harriet at a White House reception, is said to have exclaimed, 'So you're the little woman who wrote the book that started this great war'.

Harriet was an innovator in terms of the novel. Not only did she succeed in her goal of translating polemic into fiction, but also she led the way for later novelists by her commitment to realism, particularly in the imitation of local dialect, in which she predated Mark Twain. She only received royalties on the American edition of *Uncle Tom's Cabin*, although the book was translated into over 60 languages. Countless unauthorized 'Tom' shows based on the novel continued to be performed in theatres in the US, London, Berlin and Paris until the end of the century.

Harriet made three triumphal tours of Europe (1853, 1856 and 1859) where she developed friendships with contemporary writers like George Eliot and Elizabeth Barrett Browning. She received harsh criticism from those who claimed that her novel was prejudiced and inaccurate and that she could not know at first hand what life in the south was like. This prompted Harriet to publish *The Key to Uncle Tom's Cabin* (1853), a collection of source material that documented the reality behind the book. However, the controversy surrounding *Uncle Tom's Cabin* has never abated, with critics denouncing its sentimental portraits of African-Americans, and arguing that Harriet's romantic ideas of slavery reveal a basic racism. Harriet published a second anti-slavery novel, *Dred: A Tale of the Great Dismal Swamp* in 1856.

Harriet wrote a column in the New York newspaper, *The Independent*, urging American women to campaign against slavery through petitions, lectures and the spread of information. Later, she turned away from political writing and produced novels on a variety of themes, including love and marriage and New York society, which display her moral views about matters like divorce. Harriet's practical instructions about domestic matters (including the 'servant problem') in *The American Woman's Home*, co-written with her sister Catherine (1869), were highly influential.

In the 1860s the Stowes built a winter home in Mandarin, Florida. There, Harriet helped establish schools for African-American children and was instrumental in creating an ecumenical church for people of all denominations. She died on 1 July 1896 in Hartford, Connecticut, where she had returned in 1873, and where she had become a neighbour and friend of Mark Twain.

Queen Victoria

Queen Victoria has given her name to an age of extraordinary economic, social and technological progress, when British global power and influence reached its peak. She defined the role of the constitutional monarchy in a democratic nation.

'She was a part of the establishment – an essential part as it seemed – a fixture – a magnificent, immovable sideboard in the huge saloon of state.'

Lytton Strachey, Queen Victoria

BIOGRAPHY

Name:	Alexandrina Victoria Hanover, Princess Victoria of Kent
Lived:	24 May 1819 – 22 January 1901
Place of birth:	Kensington Palace, London
Place of death:	Osborne House, Isle of Wight
Nationality:	British
Famed as:	Longest reigning British monarch; Empress of India; matriarch of several European royal families

Born in May 1819 at Kensington Palace, Victoria became Britain's longest reigning monarch and gave her name to an entire era in history, becoming head of an empire that stretched right around the globe.

Victoria was the only child of Edward, Duke of Kent, who was the fourth son of King George III. Edward had married Victoria Maria Louisa of Saxe-Coburg-Gotha, but he died when his daughter was only eight months old. Victoria was brought up in seclusion by her German mother. She was a warm-hearted, diligent child, with an aptitude for drawing and painting, and was educated at home by a governess.

FACTFILE

- As a child, Victoria spoke only German but learned to speak English without a trace of an accent.

- After Albert's death, she insisted that his rooms were kept just as they had been during his life and that his clothes should be laid on the bed every evening.

- Victoria survived eight assassination attempts, all by shooting. These attempts were unconnected, although conspiracy theories were popular. She was injured only once, in 1872. Prince Albert was instrumental in commuting the punishment for threatening the monarch from death to seven years' imprisonment and flogging. Most of the would-be assassins were judged insane, most served shorter terms and not one was flogged.

Victoria became heir to the throne because none of her three uncles, who preceded her in the succession, had a surviving child. At the age of 18 she became Queen on the death of William IV. Her dismissal of her overbearing mother and governess from the court signalled her determination to rule without their influence, and at a time when the monarchy was unpopular, made it clear that she wished to be active in politics. For the first few years of her reign Victoria developed a close relationship with the Whig Prime Minister, Lord Melbourne, who protected and nurtured her political interests, influencing her with his conservative values. He advised her on how to rule within a constitutional monarchy, where she would have little power but could exert considerable influence.

In 1839 Victoria's German cousin, Albert of Saxe-Coburg-Gotha, visited London and she fell in love with him. They married in 1840, and over 18 years Victoria bore nine children, several of whom married into the royal families of Europe, forming a web of dynastic alliances that were later to prove valuable for Britain. Despite his sponsorship of the arts and sciences, Albert met with indifference from the English, and he was only granted the title of Prince Consort after 17 years as Victoria's husband. But the couple were devoted: Victoria adored and admired Albert and relied on his judgement. For the next 21 years Albert was her chief adviser, replacing Melbourne. Albert's wide-ranging interests led to his hosting the Great Exhibition at Crystal Palace in 1851, an event that fuelled a sense of national pride that grew during the century and reflected glory on the monarchy. Several museums in

TIMELINE

Date	Queen Victoria	Related events
1819	Born in Kensington Palace, London	
1837	Accedes to the throne	Charles Dickens publishes *The Pickwick Papers*
1840	Marries Albert of Saxe-Coburg-Gotha First assassination attempt	Penny post starts – stamps sold for the first time
1841	Birth of Albert Edward, Prince of Wales and later King Edward VII	Conservative Robert Peel becomes Prime Minister
1842	Survives three assassination attempts (further attempts in 1849, 1850, 1872 and 1882)	Alfred Lord Tennyson writes *The Morte d'Arthur* Chartist Riots
1848	Takes out lease on Balmoral Estate	The Public Health Act institutes a Central Board of Health to supervise street cleaning, refuse collection, water supply and sewage disposal
1849	John Brown becomes Prince Albert's ghillie	
1851		The Great Exhibition opens at Crystal Palace
1853	Purchases Balmoral for £31,500	
1854		Start of the Crimean War (ends 1856)
1861	Prince Albert dies of typhoid	Start of the American Civil War
1877	Victoria is made Empress of India	
1887	Golden Jubilee	Sir Arthur Conan Doyle publishes his first Sherlock Holmes story, *A Study in Scarlet*
1897	Diamond Jubilee	
1901	Dies at Osborne House, Isle of Wight	

Kensington were built with the money raised by the Exhibition, including the Victoria and Albert Museum.

Victoria worked well with her next two Prime Ministers, Sir Robert Peel and Lord John Russell, but disapproved of Lord Palmerston, who was Foreign Secretary. Palmerston wanted to increase Britain's power at a time when the Queen and Prince Albert wished to strengthen alliances against republicanism among European royalty. Relations between the Queen and Palmerston improved after the latter became Prime Minister in 1855.

When Albert died of typhoid fever in 1861 Victoria never fully recovered from her loss. She wore black mourning clothes for the rest of her life. Initially her depression was so engulfing that she retired from public life for several years, doing damage to the reputation of the monarchy and encouraging republican sentiments. She was rescued partly by the care and attention of her servant John Brown at her Balmoral estate and later by the friendship and flattering attention of the Tory Prime Minister, Benjamin Disraeli. It was several years before she agreed to appear in public once again, but in 1866 she was persuaded to open Parliament.

After her return to London and resumption of royal duties, Victoria's popularity steadily grew. One of the many achievements of her long reign was constitutional reform and the removal of direct political power from the monarch to a broader electorate.

Although in private Victoria was often stubborn, opinionated and wilful, in public she recognized that the key to the monarch's continuing influence lay in being above party political issues. Although she did not support votes for women, she was keen to see improvements in standards of housing, health and education. She supported the work of Florence Nightingale during the Crimean War, instituted the Victoria Cross for bravery, and was involved in many charities.

Victoria was a very visible monarch. The Queen and her family took advantage of transport innovations and journeyed frequently between her favourite estates, Osborne House on the Isle of Wight, which was built with Albert, and Balmoral in Scotland. She was the first monarch to use the train. Always a prolific letter writer on both domestic and political matters, she also raised her public profile by publishing two books about Scotland, *Leaves from the Journal of our Life in the Highlands* (1868) and *More Leaves* (1884).

The Queen's friendship with Disraeli continued during his term of office, but relations with Gladstone, who was Liberal Prime Minister intermittently from 1868–94, were correspondingly strained and she opposed many of his foreign policies, in particular Irish Home Rule. When Disraeli died in 1881 Victoria was devastated.

In her middle years, apart from the Crimean War, which began in 1853, Victoria supported peace and reconciliation. She persuaded her government not to intervene in the Prussia-Austria-Denmark war, and her dynastic alliances also helped to avoid a second Franco-German war. Later in her reign, Britain's imperial ambitions increased and the Empire doubled in size. After the Indian Mutiny, the government of India was transferred to the Crown, and Victoria was made Empress of India in 1877. During her long reign, Australia, Canada, and parts of Africa and the South Pacific were also added to the Empire. Imperial support brought the Queen close to her last Prime Minster, Lord Salisbury. She was delighted when General Kitchener was victorious in the Sudan (1898) and was enthusiastic in support of the British war against the Boers in South Africa.

Victoria died at Osborne House on 22 January 1901 after a reign of nearly 64 years. She was buried beside her beloved Albert at Frogmore near Windsor.

The term 'Victorian England' is characterized by the Queen's morality and taste, which tended to reflect middle-class habits. She also presided over an unprecedented expansion of industry and economic progress. In her later years, she symbolized the British Empire.

Florence Nightingale

Florence Nightingale revolutionized nursing in England, helping to found institutions that continue to train medical personnel today. The fame she won for her intervention in the management and care of the wounded in the Crimean War ensured respect for a previously denigrated and undervalued profession.

'And so is the world put back by the death of every one who has to sacrifice the development of his or her peculiar gifts to conventionality.'

BIOGRAPHY

Name:	Florence Nightingale
Lived:	12 May 1820 – 13 August 1910
Place of birth:	Florence, Italy
Place of death:	London
Nationality:	British
Famed as:	Pioneer of nursing; reformer of hospital sanitation

Florence was born in 1820 to Frances and William Nightingale. Her parents toured Europe for the first two years of their married life, and she was named after the city where she was born – Florence in Italy. Florence and her sister Parthenope (named after the Greek for Naples, her birthplace) were educated by governesses, and by their father who taught them classics and politics. Florence loved learning, and was extremely bright, with a particular talent for mathematics.

She was expected to fulfil the conventional role of a daughter to wealthy parents, that is, to make a good marriage and live a conservative life. But this did not suit Florence, who developed an early interest in social issues, visiting the sick at home and in local hospitals. Florence was a devout Christian, and she later came to believe that God was directing her thoughts towards social issues and nursing.

FACTFILE

- Florence was the first woman to be elected a fellow of the Statistical Society.
- She repeatedly refused marriage proposals from Richard Monckton Milnes, Lord Houghton, and never married.
- 12 May (the date of her birth) is International Nurses Day.
- After her return from the Crimean War she never again appeared in public, attended a public function or issued a public statement.
- She kept 60 cats, including three Persians called Bismarck, Disraeli and Gladstone.
- Her favourite pet was on owl named Athena. The owl was with her for four years prior to the Crimean War, often travelling in her pocket.

Less acceptable to her family was her enthusiasm for mathematics. Her father wanted Florence to study subjects thought more suitable for women. But Florence eventually persuaded them to let her study with James Joseph Sylvester, who described her as his most accomplished pupil. Florence was attracted to the application of mathematics, not just the subject itself. Her interest in statistics played almost as important a part in her life as nursing, and in due course she was able to combine the two.

In the mid-nineteenth century, nursing was considered an unsuitable profession for most women, and out of the question for educated, well-to-do ladies. The stereotype of nurses at the time was of poorly-trained, ignorant and promiscuous women. In 1845, when Florence declared that she wanted to work in a hospital, her parents opposed her strongly. Her only recourse was to study abroad.

In 1850 she started to train as a nurse at the Catholic-run Institute of St Vincent de Paul in Alexandria, Egypt. She also trained in Düsseldorf, Germany and in Paris. In 1853 she returned to London, where she secured a voluntary position as superintendent of the women's hospital, the Establishment for Gentlewomen during Illness, with the prestigious address of 1 Harley Street.

TIMELINE

Date	Florence Nightingale	Related events
1820	Born in Florence, Italy	
1837		Queen Victoria ascends the throne
1851	Florence trains as a nurse	
1853	Appointed Superintendent of a women's hospital	Start of the Crimean War
1854	Goes to the Barrack Hospital in Turkey with a party of 38 nurses	England and France declare war on Russia Mary Seacole sails to the Crimea
1855	Becomes ill with Crimean Fever	January – death rate of soldiers in the Crimea increases dramatically; by April it has begun to fall
1856	Returns to England	End of the Crimean War
1860	Establishes training institutions at St Thomas's and King's College Hospitals in London	
1863	Completes Sanitary Commission Report (The Red Book)	Cholera epidemic in England Abraham Lincoln makes his Gettysburg Address
1865		Salvation Army founded by William Booth
1881		Mary Seacole dies
1883	Awarded the Royal Red Cross	
1907	Receives the Order of Merit	
1910	Dies in London	King George V accedes to the throne

In March 1854, Britain, France and Turkey declared war on Russia, marking the start of the Crimean War. British medical facilities were heavily criticized during this conflict. Sidney Herbert, the British Secretary for War and a friend of Florence, responded by asking her to undertake the role of nursing administrator, a position that involved overseeing the nursing in military hospitals. Florence's official, wordy title was Superintendent of the Female Nursing Establishment of the English General Hospitals in Turkey.

Taking specialist nursing staff into the field for the first time, she organized a team of 38 nurses at the Barrack Hospital in Scutari, an Asian suburb of Constantinople (now Istanbul). When she arrived in Turkey, conditions were dire. In the unhygienic surroundings, injured soldiers were more likely to die from disease in hospital than they were on the battlefield. Cholera and typhus pervaded. Florence set about improving conditions. She ensured that fresh water, fruit, vegetables and adequate hospital equipment were made available. She also collected data and organized a record-keeping system that enabled her to calculate mortality rates. By February 1855 the death rate had dropped dramatically.

During her time in the Crimea, reports of her skills and devotion to duty reached England, and she became famously known as the 'Lady with the Lamp', a romantic reference to her evening rounds, visiting injured soldiers. However, years of single-minded struggle to establish her career and the demands of Scutari began to take their toll on her physical and emotional health. When she returned to London in August 1856, Florence was herself an invalid.

Nevertheless, her career prospered. From her bed she produced statistical evidence to support the improvement of sanitary conditions in all military hospitals. She came to the attention of Queen Victoria, Prince Albert and the Prime Minister, Lord Palmerston, and in May 1857 a formal investigation was launched into her concerns.

In 1860, Florence established training institutions at St Thomas's and King's College Hospitals in London with money from the Nightingale Fund, public contributions made during her time in the Crimea. Her training schools functioned on two principles: nurses would have practical training in purpose-built institutions and live moral and disciplined lives. Her innovations transformed the negative image that nursing and nurses had previously suffered.

In 1883 she was awarded the Royal Red Cross by Queen Victoria and was the first woman to receive the Order of Merit in 1907.

Despite her ill health, Florence published 200 books, reports and pamphlets, mainly on sanitation, military health and hospital organization. Her *Notes on Nursing*, published in 1860, is still widely influential. She died on 13 August 1910 aged 90, and is buried at St Margaret's Church, near Embley Park in Hampshire. The Crimean Monument in London was erected in 1915 and honours the contributions she made to the Crimean War and to the health of the forces.

Mary Seacole 1805 (date uncertain) – 14 May 1881

Mary Seacole, a Jamaican woman married to an English merchant, was taught nursing by her mother. She volunteered her services as an army nurse to the British but despite letters of recommendation from doctors in Jamaica was repeatedly refused, something she attributed to her colour. Travelling to the Crimea at her own expense, with quantities of medication, she established the British Hotel for convalescent soldiers at Sebastopol and frequently treated the wounded under fire. Florence Nightingale was disparaging about the British Hotel and although Mary visited her at Scutari, they did not work together. Like Florence, Mary returned to England with her health broken, but unlike her, did not receive the same degree of recognition and fame. For a time her position was very difficult, but the publication of her autobiography and the patronage of grateful soldiers brought her financial security. She died in London, where she is buried in the Roman Catholic cemetery at Kensal Green. Although she was awarded the Crimean Medal and the French Légion d'Honneur in her lifetime, she remained a historically neglected figure until late twentieth-century interest in her story re-established her significance.

Susan B. Anthony

Susan B. Anthony, above right, was an anti-slavery campaigner as well as an educational reformer, labour activist, temperance worker and, above all, a dedicated activist for women's suffrage. Together with Elizabeth Cady Stanton, above left, she campaigned for the vote for US women by organizing groups, running a newspaper, writing a history of women's suffrage and travelling the length and breadth of the United States to give speeches.

'There will never be complete equality until women themselves help to make laws and elect lawmakers.'

BIOGRAPHY

Name:	Susan Brownell Anthony
Lived:	15 February 1820 – 13 March 1906
Place of birth:	Adams, Massachusetts
Place of death:	Rochester, New York
Nationality:	American
Occupation:	Woman's suffrage campaigner and political activist; abolitionist

Susan Brownell Anthony was the daughter of a Quaker cotton manufacturer and the second of eight children. Daniel Anthony was a strict believer and did not allow his children to indulge in childish pastimes. Instead he encouraged self-discipline, high principles and a belief in one's own self-worth. An intelligent child, Susan was literate by the age of three. At six she was educated at a home school established by her father – unusually for the time under the leadership of a woman, Mary Perkins. Mary was educated and independent and provided an early role model for Susan. Other important influences on Susan's later career were the weekly meetings of prominent members of the anti-slavery movement at the family farm.

Susan trained as a teacher and in 1846, aged 26, she became head of the girls' department at Canajoharie Academy. At this time she became involved with the temperance movement, which was one of the first outlets for feminist activity in the United States. Susan helped establish the pioneering Woman's State Temperance Society in New York.

FACTFILE

- Susan B. Anthony appeared before every Congress from 1869 to 1906 to ask for passage of a suffrage amendment.

- She toured the United States tirelessly. In one year alone, she managed to cover 13,000 miles and gave over 170 speeches.

- In 1979, her image was chosen for the new dollar coin, making her the first woman ever to be depicted on US currency.

- Susan initially supported Amelia Bloomer's dress reform by wearing 'bloomers' (a knee-length undergarment). However, she found that her audiences were paying more attention to her clothes than her words and in 1854 she reverted to conventional dress.

Her work in the temperance movement convinced Susan that women needed the vote in order to play a role in public affairs. In 1852 she met Elizabeth Cady Stanton, a leader of the women's rights movement, with whom she struck up a strong friendship and a highly productive intellectual partnership. Susan and Elizabeth hoped the Republicans would reward women for their work in building support for the 13th Amendment, abolishing slavery in the United States, by giving them the vote and were shocked and angry when this did not happen.

From 1856 until the outbreak of the American Civil War in 1861, Susan worked as an agent for the Anti-Slavery Society in New York, often meeting hostility and violence in mobs attending her meetings. Her effigy was hanged, and in Syracuse her image was dragged through the streets. Willing to speak out against many other injustices, she was especially committed to women's rights. In 1860 she and Elizabeth successfully petitioned the New York legislature for property rights for women, winning them control over their wages and guardianship of their children. She also urged women teachers to demand higher wages.

TIMELINE

Date	Susan B. Anthony	Related events
1820	Born in Adams, Massachusetts	Joseph Smith, 14, claims to have a vision of God and Christ. He will found the Church of Latter Day Saints (Mormons)
1846	Gains position as head of the girls' department at Canajoharie Academy	Brigham Young leads the Mormons to the Great Salt Lake
1852	Joins the women's rights movement	
1856	Becomes an agent for the American Anti-Slavery Society	Pro-slavery forces raze the town of Lawrence, Kansas
1861		Outbreak of the American Civil War (ends 1865)
1863	Organizes a Women's National Loyal League to support and petition for the 13th Amendment outlawing slavery	Abraham Lincoln signs the Emancipation Proclamation
1868	Susan's newspaper *The Revolution* first appears	Louisa May Alcott publishes *Little Women*
1870	Formed and was elected president of the Workingwomen's Central Association	The 15th Amendment of the US Constitution gives US citizens (but not women) the right to vote
1872	Susan and other women arrested for trying to vote in local elections	Brigham Young arrested for bigamy (he had 25 wives) Victoria Woodhull becomes first woman to be nominated for US Presidency
1900	Raises $50,000 in pledges to ensure the admittance of female students to the University of Rochester	
1904	Helps found the International Women's Suffrage Alliance	Joseph Smith condemns polygamy
1906	Dies in Rochester, New York	

From 1868 to 1870 Susan and Elizabeth published a weekly paper in New York – *The Revolution* – arguing the case for equal pay for women. It eventually went bankrupt. Susan gave lectures throughout the country for six years in order to pay off the $10,000 debt. This was characteristic of someone who once said: 'There is not the woman born who desires to eat the bread of dependence, no matter whether it be from the hand of father, husband, or brother; for any one who does so eat her bread places herself in the power of the person from whom she takes it.'

Susan strongly believed that proposals to grant the vote to male African-Americans in the 14th and 15th Amendments should also apply to women. On the grounds that she was entitled to vote as a citizen, she led a group of women in trying to vote at the Rochester city elections in 1872. She was then arrested, tried, freed and given a fine, which she refused to pay. For the rest of her life she continued to campaign ceaselessly for a federal female suffrage amendment through a variety of organizations that she established and by lecturing throughout the country.

In 1870, aware of the almost complete omission of women in historical literature, she set to work with Elizabeth and other colleagues on a four-volume *History of Women's Suffrage*. She used a personal legacy to buy most of the first edition for college libraries. Later, she helped a biographer to work on a three-volume book about herself that drew on her own scrapbooks, diaries and letters and is now in the Library of Congress.

In her late sixties and into her seventies Susan travelled abroad promoting her cause, visiting London and Berlin and in 1904 forming the International Women's Suffrage Alliance. At home, in 1900, she persuaded the University of Rochester (her home town) to admit women and in 1905 made a personal visit to President Theodore Roosevelt to urge his support for women's suffrage.

She carried on her activities into her eighties. A month before her death she attended her last suffrage convention and 86th birthday celebration. Yet when she died on 13 March 1906 female suffrage had been won in only four US states, New Zealand and Australia. However, there is no doubt that her work paved the way for the adoption of the 19th (women's suffrage) Amendment in 1920.

Although Susan received many proposals into middle age, she never married. Her talents lay in organizing, travelling and speaking. By nature she was both aggressive and compassionate and her keen intellect was inspirational, but she often attracted antagonistic public opinion. In her memoirs, Elizabeth recalled Susan as a young woman in her thirties: 'Whenever I saw that stately Quaker girl coming across the lawn, I knew some happy convocation of the sons of Adam was about to be set by the ears.'

Elizabeth Cady Stanton 12 November 1815 – 26 October 1902

Elizabeth Cady Stanton was an early campaigner for women's rights and suffrage in the United States. The daughter of a judge, she met her husband, journalist and anti-slavery campaigner Henry Stanton, through her abolition and temperance work. They had seven children. Elizabeth and Susan Anthony became lifelong friends after they were introduced by Amelia Bloomer in 1851. In 1869 Elizabeth became the first president of the National Women's Suffrage Association, which she founded with Susan. She campaigned internationally and in 1888 helped to found the International Council of Women. Elizabeth was an outspoken critic of racism and organized religion, particularly Christianity.

Mary Cassatt

Mary Cassatt is one of the most important American painters. Never entirely an Impressionist, her later paintings show that she understood very well the importance of line and drawing, as well as use of colour. She influenced the spread of Impressionism in America, guiding wealthy patrons to purchase paintings, many of which can now be seen in the Metropolitan Museum of Art in New York.

'She has succeeded in expressing, as none of our own painters have managed to do, the joyful peace, the tranquil friendliness of the domestic interior.'

Joris-Karl Huysmans

BIOGRAPHY

Name:	Mary Stevenson Cassatt
Lived:	22 May 1844 – 14 June 1926
Place of birth:	Pennsylvania, USA
Place of death:	Beaufresne, France
Nationality:	American
Famed as:	Painter and etcher; sponsor and promoter of Impressionist art

Robert Cassatt, Mary's father, was a wealthy American investment banker of Huguenot descent living in Pennsylvania. He and his wife, Katherine Kelso Cassatt, had five children, to whom they gave extensive opportunities for education, including exposure to European culture. By the time Mary was ten she had visited most of the capitals of Europe with her family and learned to speak German and French.

Although her family did not want her to become a professional artist, in 1860, when she was 16, Mary enrolled at the Pennsylvania Academy of the Fine Arts. At the time regarded as progressive in allowing women to access its entire curriculum, Mary came to view it as stifling. She found the course too theoretical and often escaped with other students to the Academy's galleries where they learned by making their own copies of pictures. She said later, 'Museums are all the teachers one needs.'

FACTFILE

- Mary was commissioned to paint a 58 x 12 foot mural for the Women's Building of the 1893 World's Columbian Exposition in Chicago. After the Women's Building was pulled down, the mural, entitled *Modern Woman*, was lost although numerous prints and paintings using motifs from it remain.

- Although she never married, fearing that it would distract her from her career, Mary doted on her nephews and nieces and on the children of her friends.

- Cassatt detested modern artists such as Matisse and Picasso, referring to their 'dreadful paintings'.

Mary had set her sights on going to Paris, then considered the art capital of the world, but had to wait until the end of the Civil War and find a female travelling companion in order to embark on her trip. Once in Paris, she had private instruction from a professor at the École des Beaux-Arts and attended classes for women in the studio of the painter Charles Joshua Chaplin. She continued to tutor herself by copying old masters in the Louvre – a common practice for women since they were not allowed to attend classes at the École itself.

In 1867 Mary entered a work for the annual Salon, the showcase for contemporary art and a stepping stone to becoming established as a professional artist. Although rejected that year, in 1868 Mary's *La Mandoline* was accepted, a portrait of a peasant woman in traditional costume. After having another picture accepted in 1870, she returned to America when the Franco-Prussian war was threatening, intending to continue her career as an artist there.

Mary quickly found Philadelphia restrictive and moved away to find buyers for her work in Pittsburgh and Chicago. After losing her paintings in a fire in Chicago she became anxious to return to Europe but could not finance the journey. However, by a stroke of luck she received a commission from the Bishop of Pittsburgh to copy some works of Correggio in Italy and by December 1871 she had once again left America.

TIMELINE

Dates	Mary Cassatt	Related events
1844	Born in Pennsylvania	Thomas Eakins, America's greatest realist painter, born
1860	Enters the Pennsylvania Academy of the Fine Arts	Alphonse Mucha, printmaker and painter of the Art Nouveau movement, born
1863		Edouard Manet exhibits *Déjeuner sur l'herbe* in the Salon des Réfusés in Paris
1866	Goes to Paris where she begins four years of study and travel	Jules Chéret popularizes the technique of colour lithography. His designs influence Henri de Toulouse-Lautrec
1868	First picture accepted by the Salon	Opening of the Académie Julian, the first Parisian art school to admit women
1874	Settles permanently in Paris and meets Degas	American painter John Singer Sargent begins work in Paris
1879	Exhibits with the Impressionists	Paul Klee, German Expressionist painter, born
1891	First solo exhibition	Les Nabis hold their first exhibition
1893	*Modern Woman* mural by Mary Cassatt displayed at Columbian Exposition, Chicago	Aubrey Beardsley produces illustrations for his first commission, *Le Morte d'Arthur* for publisher J. M. Dent
1904	Awarded the Légion d'honneur	Rodin's sculpture *Le Penseur* (*The Thinker*) displayed in public for the first time
1914	Forced by failing eyesight to stop painting	World War I breaks out in Europe
1926	Dies in Beaufresne, France	Death of Claude Monet

After travels in Italy, Spain, Holland and Belgium, Mary returned to Paris where she set up home in a flat with her sister Lydia. In an attempt to establish herself in the Parisian art world, Mary began with the secure option of painting portraits of Americans living abroad. Meanwhile, a picture she submitted to the Salon in 1875 was rejected and she began to feel disillusioned with what she felt were arbitrary choices on the part of the Salon jury.

Mary's paintings were now increasingly reflecting the world in which women lived – taking tea, doing needlework or reading and dressing. The immediacy of these paintings and her depiction of modern women brought her in touch with the Impressionists, an independent circle of painters who, frustrated by constant rejections by the Salon, had set up their own annual exhibition. Having encountered the work of Degas in 1872, Mary was extremely excited by the style. In turn, Degas so admired a portrait of Mary's shown in 1877 that he commented: 'Here is someone who feels as I do' and invited her to join the Impressionists. As she said: 'I accepted with joy. I hated conventional art. I began to live.' In 1879 she exhibited 11 works with them.

Although much of the Impressionists' work was unfavourably received by the conservative art newspapers, Mary's works were praised for their harmonious colour and pleasing subject matter. Degas and Mary became close friends and there are several paintings by Degas featuring her as a named subject, including his 1880 painting *Mary Cassatt at the Louvre*. In these Mary's height, slenderness, natural grace and confident manner can be seen, as well as her flair for fashion.

Early paintings by Mary show Impressionist influence, in particular that of Degas in her *A Woman in Black at the Opera* and Manet in *Young Woman Sewing in the Garden* (1886). However, she never used the Impressionists' characteristic broken colour or complementary colours, and soon evolved her own style, which some argued was unmistakably American in its solidity and clarity of contour and detail. By the late 1880s she was concentrating on the theme of mother and child – for which she was to become most well known. Executing works in oil and pastel, she also became an acclaimed printmaker.

In 1890 Mary encountered a major influence on her work when she visited an exhibition of Japanese colour prints. Inspired by a series of woodblock prints, she produced a series of ten colour etchings, which showed a shift of emphasis from form to line and pattern, the use of rather acid colours, compression of space and amending perspective to emphasize certain details. They depicted scenes from a woman's day and included the now widely known pictures *The Letter*, *Woman Bathing* and *The Coiffure*. These were shown at her 1891 exhibition.

Mary enjoyed great success in France but was less recognized in America, although in 1893 she was invited to produce a mural for the Columbian Exposition in Chicago. The 89-foot work, *Modern Woman*, did not survive but the subject matter provided inspiration for future years. Although Mary felt more at home in France, where she felt women did not have to fight for recognition if they did serious work, at heart she retained her American sympathies. She contributed enormously to the promoting of Impressionism in America by advising her wealthy American friends, the Havemeyers, in forming their art collection.

In 1904 Mary was awarded France's prestigious Légion d'honneur. By 1912 she had developed cataracts that were operated on unsuccessfully and led to the end of her career as an artist. In her later years she became interested in the cause of women's suffrage, for which she held an exhibition in 1915. She died in her château at Beaufresne on 14 July 1926.

Mary never married. Her decision to become a professional artist was a brave one at a time when art was largely the preserve of men. Some regard her relationships with other artists as probably the most successful ones in her life because it was really only with them that she felt on an equal intellectual footing. Nonetheless, she produced incomparable depictions of that most essential human relationship, that of mother and child.

Emmeline Pankhurst

Emmeline Pankhurst was Britain's leading female suffragist. She encouraged the use of violence, public demonstrations and hunger strikes in the campaign for women's votes and was frequently imprisoned.

'The argument of the broken window pane is the most valuable argument in modern politics.'

BIOGRAPHY

Name:	Emmeline Goulden
Lived:	14 July 1858 – 14 June 1928
Place of birth:	Manchester, England
Place of death:	London
Nationality:	British
Famed as:	Social reformer; campaigner for women's suffrage

Emmeline Pankhurst was born to a middle-class family in Manchester. Her father was a businessman with radical political sympathies, who campaigned against slavery and the Corn Laws. Her mother was a feminist who campaigned for female suffrage. She took Emmeline to suffragist meetings when she was in her teens. After attending school in Manchester, Emmeline finished her education in Paris, like many well-off young women of her time.

In 1878 Emmeline returned to England and met Richard Marsden Pankhurst, a Manchester barrister who shared her belief that women should have the same rights as men. They married the following year. Richard Pankhurst drafted an amendment to the Municipal Franchise Act of 1869, which allowed unmarried women householders to vote in local elections, and he also wrote the Married Women's Property Acts in 1870 and 1882.

FACTFILE

- Suffragette Emily Davison died in 1913 when she was trampled by a horse as she staged a protest on the racetrack at the Derby. She was widely regarded as a martyr, but it is doubtful that she intended to commit suicide.

- Force feeding through the mouth was commonly used on suffragettes starting hunger strikes while imprisoned. Several died as a result of the process, which is now categorized as torture.

- During World War I, Emmeline was financially supported by the British government when she campaigned for women to take over men's jobs and free men for war service.

The Pankhursts had five children, including three daughters – Christabel, Sylvia and Adela – who would become active in the suffrage movement with their mother. Richard Pankhurst, who was 24 years older than Emmeline, died of a perforated ulcer in 1889, and in the same year Emmeline founded the Women's Franchise League. Four years later, she and Christabel formed the Women's Social and Political Union (WSPU).

In 1895 Emmeline became a Poor Law Guardian. Her work involved regular visits to the local workhouse where she was profoundly affected by the suffering of the inmates. She was particularly concerned by the treatment of women. She became convinced women's suffrage was the only way to tackle such difficult social problems. From this point she was driven by the fight for women to have the same political status as men, and to be entitled to vote.

The suffragettes, as they were called, rallied under the motto 'Deeds, not words'. At first, the movement was non-violent and consisted mainly of disrupting political meetings. Restrained though this may sound, this sort of activity by a group of well-to-do middle-class women was unheard of at the time. In October 1905 the suffrage movement started to attract much wider publicity when two of its members, Christabel Pankhurst and Annie Kenney, were jailed. They had been expelled from

TIMELINE

Date	Emmeline Pankhurst	Related events
1858	Born in Manchester	
1878	Marries Richard Pankhurst	
1889	Death of Richard Pankhurst Founds Women's Franchise League	
1893	Founds WSPU with Christabel	New Zealand becomes the first country in the world to grant women the vote
1906–20		Women granted vote in Finland, Norway, Denmark, Iceland, Sweden, Germany, Poland, Austria, Czechoslovakia, Luxembourg, Netherlands, Australia
1912	Imprisoned 12 times	
1913	Tours United States	
1918		Vote granted to married women, female householders and women over 30 with a university degree in Britain Canada grants vote to women
1920		US grants vote to women
1923		Ireland grants vote to women
1926	Returns to England Stands for Parliament	
1928	Dies in London	Vote for all British women over 21

an election rally after demanding a statement about votes for women, and were charged with assault – a policeman claimed they had spat at him – and fined. When they refused to pay the fines they were sent to prison. The case shocked the public and drew more attention to their cause.

Emmeline Pankhurst was a talented speaker who inspired many others to follow her. Fellow suffragette and novelist Rebecca West described her addressing a crowd: 'Trembling like a reed, she lifted up her hoarse, sweet voice on the platform, but the reed was of steel and it was tremendous.' She made hundreds of speeches during her life, all demonstrating her natural gift for rhetoric, including the following in 1908: 'I for one, friends, looking round on the muddles that men had made, looking round on the sweated and decrepit members of my sex, I say men have had the control of these things long enough, and no woman with any spark of womanliness in her will consent to let this state of things go on any longer. ...Perhaps it is difficult to rouse women; they are long-suffering and patient, but now that we are roused, we will never be quiet again'.

Between 1908 and 1909, Emmeline was imprisoned three times. On 18 November 1910, she and a group of WSPU members tried to gain admission to the House of Commons to interview Prime Minister Herbert Asquith and to protest against the dropping of the Conciliation Bill, which would have given women the vote. They were stopped and a riot developed as the women attempted to break through police lines. More than 100 women were arrested for disturbing the peace and assault. Many of the women accused the police of brutality and most of the charges against them were subsequently dropped. This event came to be known as Black Friday.

From 1912, Emmeline and her followers fought for the vote by increasingly violent means. Suffragettes smashed windows, chained themselves to railings and even attacked politicians. Christabel directed many of these activities from Paris, having fled there to avoid arrest for conspiracy. Emmeline herself was arrested on several occasions, and went on hunger strike. In 1912 alone she was imprisoned 12 times. Under the Prisoners Act of 1913, the so-called 'Cat and Mouse Act', hunger-striking prisoners could be freed for a time and then reimprisoned when considered strong enough to serve the rest of their sentences.

By 1913, the WSPU had become notorious for staging violent attacks on the property of people opposed to female suffrage, including very prominent places like Westminster Abbey. Yet the movement had still not succeeded in achieving its goal. It was in this year that Emmeline made perhaps her most famous speech, in America, in which she eloquently described the plight of women in Britain: 'I am not only here as a soldier temporarily absent from the field of battle; I am here... as a person who according to the laws of my country, it has been decided, is of no value to the community at all.'

With the outbreak of World War I, and the release of all suffragettes from prison, Emmeline and Christabel called off the suffrage campaign to support the war effort, and Emmeline turned her leadership skills towards urging women to work for their country. Perhaps reflecting this change of emphasis, in 1917 the WSPU changed its name to the Women's Party. During the war Emmeline made visits to the United States, Canada and Russia to encourage the mobilization of women. In June of 1918, the final year of the war, women over the age of 30 were given the right to vote in Britain.

After the war Emmeline lived in the US, Canada and Bermuda for several years, returning to Britain in 1926. In that year she stood for parliament as the Conservative candidate for a seat in East London, but became gravely ill and died before she could be elected. On 2 July 1928, just three weeks after her death, a law was passed allowing all women over the age of 21 to vote, finally establishing electoral equality with men. Of her three daughters, who campaigned so closely with her, Christabel emigrated to the US after World War I and became an evangelist preacher. Both Sylvia and Adela had broken with the WSPU in opposition to the use of violence. Sylvia became a committed political activist and Adela helped organize the Women's Peace Army in Australia during World War I.

Marie Curie

Marie Curie's discovery of radium helped revolutionize medicine. She was the first woman to win a Nobel Prize, the first person to win it twice and the only woman to have won it in two different categories.

'Nothing in life is to be feared. It is only to be understood.'

BIOGRAPHY

Name:	Marya Sklodowska
Lived:	7 November 1867 – 4 July 1934
Place of birth:	Warsaw, Poland
Place of death:	Sallanches, Haute Savoie, France
Nationality:	Polish
Famed as:	Nobel prize-winning discoverer of radium; innovator of X-ray technology

Marie Curie was born in Warsaw, Poland, the youngest of five children. At school she was a brilliant student, winning a gold medal in 1883 at the end of her secondary schooling. Her family valued education, but women could not attend university in Russian-dominated Poland at that time. Marie started to earn a living by giving private tuition and became involved with a group of young people who arranged their own studies in a loose organization known as the Floating University. In 1886 she became governess to a wealthy family, but she craved intellectual stimulation and research and became more and more determined to become a university student. In 1891 she went to Paris to live with her sister Bronya, who was studying medicine there. She adopted the French version of her name, Marie, and studied mathematics, chemistry and physics at the Sorbonne. She also became the first woman to teach there.

FACTFILE

- Marie's eldest daughter, Irène Joliot-Curie, became a physicist. In 1935 she and her husband won the Nobel Prize for chemistry for their work on the synthesizing of new chemical elements.

- In 1995, the bodies of Marie and Pierre Curie were reinterred in the Panthéon in Paris, the burial chamber reserved for heroes of the French Republic.

- Her picture appeared for many years on French banknotes and coins.

- Element 96 – Curium (Cm) – was named in honour of Marie and Pierre Curie.

In 1894 she needed a laboratory where she could work on her chosen field of research, the measurement of the magnetic properties of steel alloys. Colleagues suggested she approach Pierre Curie at the School of Physics and Chemistry. This proved a pivotal point in her life and career. She was impressed with Pierre from their very first meeting: 'He seemed very young to me although he was then aged 35. I was struck by the expression of his clear gaze and by a slight appearance of carelessness in his lofty stature. His rather slow, reflective words, his simplicity, and his smile, at once grave and young, inspired confidence. A conversation began between us and became friendly; its object was some questions of science upon which I was happy to ask his opinion.'

Marie and Pierre married in the summer of 1895. This was to be the start of a truly remarkable scientific partnership, and together they worked for many years on research projects, eventually concentrating their studies on the newly discovered phenomenon of radioactivity. They had two daughters, Irène and Eve, whom they brought up while maintaining a punishing schedule of research and publication, often in gruelling conditions, and at first under-supported by the French academic establishment.

Another French physicist, Antoine Henri Becquerel (1852–1908), had recently discovered natural radioactivity, given out by uranium. Marie was fascinated by this

TIMELINE

Date	Marie Curie	Related events
1867	Born in Warsaw	
1891	Moves to Paris to study medicine	
1895	Marries Pierre Curie	Wilhelm Conrad Rüntgen takes the first ever X-ray photograph (of his wife's hand)
1896		Becquerel discovers the radioactivity of uranium
1903	Nobel Prize for physics (shared with Pierre Curie and Antoine Becquerel)	
1906	Pierre Curie is killed	Charles Barkla discovers the X-rays of elements
1911	Second Nobel Prize (for chemistry)	
1914	Devises mobile X-ray ambulances Becomes first director of the Radium Institute in Paris	Ernest Rutherford suggests that the positively charged atomic nucleus contains protons
1921	Tours America	Albert Einstein wins Nobel Prize for physics
1934	Dies in Haute Savoie, France	The Radium Institute is renamed the Curie Institute
1935		Irène and Frédéric Joliot-Curie win the Nobel Prize for chemistry

finding and reached the conclusion that radiation was a property of uranium atoms and must therefore exist in some other elements as well. She began a systematic search for radioactivity and found it also in thorium. The Curies then investigated the substance known as pitchblende, the natural mineral from which uranium and thorium were extracted. They found, to their surprise, that this was more radioactive than could be explained by the amounts of uranium and thorium that it contained. Soon they had discovered two more highly radioactive elements, radium and polonium, the latter named after Marie's homeland.

A steady stream of scientific papers flowed from their discoveries, not only about the new elements but also about the effects of radiation on cells. One notable finding was that diseased, cancerous cells were destroyed more rapidly than healthy cells when exposed to radiation. This discovery was to have enormous implications in the development of treatments for many forms of cancer in the years to come, and radiotherapy is still one of the main weapons in the medical arsenal today.

International recognition soon followed this groundbreaking research, and in November 1903 the Royal Society of London awarded the Curies the Davy Medal. The following month they won the Nobel Prize for physics for their discoveries, sharing the award with Becquerel.

Fame abroad was matched by fame in France and Pierre Curie became Director of Research and Professor of Physics at the University of Paris, a post created especially for him. In 1905, a year after the birth of Eve, their second daughter, Pierre was elected to the prestigious Academy of Sciences and he delivered his and Marie's joint Nobel address in Stockholm, Sweden, on 6 June of that year.

In 1906 Pierre was killed when he was knocked down by a heavy horse-drawn wagon. Marie, alone and with two small daughters to bring up, was invited to take his place as professor of physics, the first woman to hold a post of this stature. In 1908 she started to give the first, and at that time the only, course on radioactivity in the world. She also worked hard at editing their collection of works, culminating in the *Traité de Radioactivité*, published in 1910.

Marie continued her work on radioactive elements and in 1911 won her second Nobel Prize, for chemistry. The award was made for her work isolating radium and studying its chemical properties, and was unshared. In 1914 she helped found the Radium Institute in Paris and was its first director. She realized that X-rays could help to locate foreign objects inside a body and facilitate surgery. During World War I she devised X-ray vans, which were sent out to treat wounded soldiers and which became known affectionately as 'little Curies'. Marie drove the vans to the front lines herself. The vans were equipped with radon, a radioactive gas given off by radium, that Marie personally collected and stored in glass tubes. To raise funds for the war effort, she sold her and Pierre's gold Nobel medals.

Marie was quiet, dignified and unassuming, and won the admiration of scientists everywhere. Her work is recorded in numerous papers in scientific journals and reflected in many awards. She was always wary of interviews and public speaking but in 1921 she toured the US and addressed many meetings, to huge acclaim. During her tour, President Harding, on behalf of the women of America, presented her with one gram of radium, 'more than a hundred thousand times dearer than gold', for her Institute.

She never lost her wonder at the natural world, nor the excitement of uncovering its secrets. In 1933 she defended advances in science against critics who were worried about the possible dehumanizing powers of such research: 'I am among those who think that science has great beauty. A scientist in his laboratory is not only a technician; he is also a child placed before natural phenomena which impress him like a fairy tale.'

On 4 July 1934, at the age of 67, Marie died of leukaemia, possibly the result of repeated exposure to the high levels of radiation involved in her research. After her death the Radium Institute in Paris was renamed the Curie Institute in her honour. Albert Einstein aptly said: 'Marie Curie is, of all celebrated beings, the only one whom fame has not corrupted.'

Emily Murphy
and the Famous Five

In 1927 five women united to bring to Canada's Supreme court the now notorious Persons Case, which examined whether women could be legally considered 'persons' and eligible for public office. The women – Emily Murphy (above, centre), Louise McKinney (bottom left), Nellie McClung (top left), Henrietta Edwards (top right) and Irene Parlby (bottom right) – were known as The Famous Five.

'Women, children, criminals and idiots are not legally "persons".'

Comment after the Canadian Supreme Court ruling in Edwards v. Canada, 1928

BIOGRAPHY

Name:	Emily Murphy
Lived:	14 March 1868 – 17 October 1933
Place of birth:	Cooksville, Ontario
Place of death:	Edmonton, Alberta
Nationality:	Canadian
Famed as:	Lawyer, writer and women's rights campaigner

Emily Murphy was the first woman magistrate in the British Empire. However, as she was about to pass sentence on her first case she was challenged by the defence lawyer, who questioned her authority, saying, 'You are not even a person.' He was referring to the wording of a British law of 1867 whereby women were not legal 'persons' and so did not have legal rights or privileges, although they could be subject to legal penalties.

Although Emily's position was later backed by the Supreme Court of Alberta, this was not the only time her authority as a judge was questioned. She was determined to confront this. In 1927 Emily joined forces with four other women and brought the Persons Case, to challenge the wording of section 24 of the British North America Act 1867 by which, so far, only men had been appointed to the Senate. Contemporary photographs of the Famous Five, as they quickly became known, suggest that they were stoical, determined, calm, questioning and without doubt persons to be reckoned with. Known to one another through their activism in women's rights, they held their first meeting over tea at Emily's house.

FACTFILE

- Since 1979, five awards have been made annually to Canadians who fought for sexual equality.

- Nearly 500,000 Canadians signed a petition asking that Emily Murphy be appointed to the Senate.

- Together with Thérèse Casgrain (feminist, reformer and politician) the Five have been commemorated on the new Canadian $50 note.

When the case was tried (Edwards v. Canada 1928) the Supreme Court of Canada ruled against the Five, stating that 'women, children, criminals and idiots are not legally "persons" '. The Court asserted that the word 'person' did not include women since those who framed the Act in 1867 would not have had women in mind as at that time women did not participate in politics.

The women were undaunted and went on to appeal to the Judicial Committee of the British Privy Council, the last resort for Canadian courts at that time. In 1930 it ruled that the word 'persons' covered both sexes and that Canadian women could therefore serve in the Senate. As this council was the final court of appeal for the whole British Empire the decision had far-reaching effects. Just four months later Canada had its first woman Senator, Cairine Wilson.

Emily Ferguson was born into one of Ontario's leading families and in 1887 married Arthur Murphy, a travelling missionary with whom she had two daughters. In 1904 they moved to Manitoba and then to Edmonton, Alberta and it was here that Emily became a social reformer. Her campaigning interests included fighting drunkenness and rural poverty, and promoting female suffrage and the legal rights of women.

She was particularly keen to see an established special court that would hear

TIMELINE

Date	Famous Five	Related events
1867	Henrietta Muir Edwards founds the Victorian Order of Nurses	
1906		Death of Susan B. Anthony, US suffrage campaigner
1913	Irene Parlby sets up the first women's group of the United Farmers of Alberta	
1916	Emily Murphy becomes the first woman magistrate in the British Empire	Manitoba becomes first province to allow women the vote and to hold provincial political office
1917	Louise McKinney becomes the first woman elected to a provincial legislature	Dower Act passed in Alberta providing a wife with a life interest in a homestead that cannot be disposed of without her consent
1918		Canadian women's suffrage finally won
1921	Nellie McClung elected as a Liberal member in the Alberta Legislature Irene Parlby becomes Alberta's first female cabinet minister	
1927	The Famous Five sign Emily Murphy's petition about the appointment of women to the Senate	
1928		Supreme Court rules that women are not 'persons' (Edwards v. Canada) Alberta government passes the Sexual Sterilization Act
1929		British Privy Council reverses the Supreme Court's decision in Edwards v. Canada

women's evidence in cases like divorce or sexual assault, and in 1916 the Women's Court was established in Edmonton. Emily became the first female police magistrate in the British Empire. It was while she was sitting in this court that she first encountered challenges to her authority that led to her bringing the Persons Case. Emily finally resigned her judicial post in 1931, although she carried on as supervisor of Alberta's prisons and asylums.

As well as her campaigning work, Emily wrote under the name Janey Canuck, using this pseudonym to describe slum conditions in Europe, life in Manitoba and Alberta and, more contentiously, to argue that immigration was weakening the social structure and morals of Canadian society. Although these opinions were widespread at the time, for some her achievements have been discredited by her racist views. For most, however, the contribution of the Famous Five to women's rights in Canada is inestimable. Their achievement is permanently commemorated in a lively sculpture on Parliament Hill in Ottawa, the only statues of non-elected individuals on the site.

The other members of The Famous Five

Henrietta Muir Edwards 18 December 1849 – 10 November 1931

An advocate for working women and founder of the Victorian Order of Nurses, Henrietta Muir was born in Montreal. Among the many causes she promoted were temperance, raising the age of consent, equal parental rights, mothers' allowances and the reform of the Canadian prison system. Her knowledge of the laws pertaining to women and children was unequalled in the country. In 1875 she set up the Working Girls' Association that provided vocational training for women. She also edited the journal *Women's Work* in Canada, and in 1893 co-founded the National Council of Women.

Nellie Mooney McClung 20 October 1873 – 1 September 1951

Initially a teacher and then a novelist, Nellie McClung was welcomed by the women's rights movement in Winnipeg as she was a lively and amusing public speaker. Through her work, Manitoba became the first province to enfranchise women. Nellie campaigned widely for legal and financial rights for married women, factory safety legislation and many other reforms. She also continued to write, and although her work was forgotten for a decade it was rediscovered by feminists in the 1960s. She was, however, a Eugenicist and an ardent campaigner for the sterilization of the 'feeble-minded' and 'immoral'.

Louise Crummy McKinney 22 September 1868 – 10 July 1931

After marrying and working as a teacher, in 1916 Louise McKinney became the leading member of the Non-Partisan League, an agrarian movement fighting for public ownership of grain stores and flour mills. In 1917 she was elected to the Alberta Legislature as candidate for the League, becoming one of two women first elected to the House of Commons of Canada and the first woman on any legislative body in the British Empire. She was also a senior member of the Canadian Temperance Movement and campaigned for female suffrage.

Irene Marryat Parlby 9 January 1868 – 12 July 1965

In 1913 Irene Parlby set up the first women's group of the United Farmers of Alberta, by 1921 had been elected to the Alberta Legislature and then went on to become the first woman cabinet minister in Alberta. Always concerned with the interests of rural women and children, as President of the United Farm Women of Alberta, Irene campaigned to improve public health care and set up hospitals and mobile medical and dental clinics. In recognition of her contribution to the province of Alberta, Irene received an Honorary Doctorate from the University of Alberta in 1935. She died at the age of 97.

Rosa Luxemburg

A contemporary of Lenin and co-founder of the German Communist Party, Rosa Luxemburg's incitement of social and industrial unrest in post-World War I Germany led to her arrest and murder by German soldiers.

'Freedom only for the members of the government, only for the members of the party – though they are quite numerous – is no freedom at all. Freedom is always the freedom of dissenters.'

Inscription on Rosa Luxemburg's tomb in Berlin

BIOGRAPHY

Name:	Rosa Luxemburg, Red Rosa
Lived:	5 March 1870 or 1871 – 15 or 16 January 1919
Place of birth:	Lublin, Poland
Place of death:	Berlin, Germany
Nationality:	Polish
Famed as:	Political economist and socialist revolutionary

Rosa Luxemburg was born in Poland in 1870, the fifth child of a middle-class Jewish merchant and his wife. When she was three, the family moved to Warsaw where Rosa's father was active in leading intellectual circles. Rosa suffered a serious illness when she was five, which left her with a limp and lifelong pain, but she had a superb mind and gained a place at the best girls' school in Warsaw, normally the preserve of Russians (the Tsarist empire ruling Poland was especially antagonistic towards Jews).

At school Rosa was influenced by the left-wing Polish group, the Proletarian, which she joined in 1887. When she organized a small, illegal discussion group her activities drew the attention of the Russian secret police and she was smuggled to nearby Switzerland for safety.

Rosa studied natural sciences and political economy at Zurich University before changing to law in 1892. She met representatives of the international socialist movement and Russian Social Democrat movement, as well as Leo Jogiches, head of the Polish Socialist Party, who was to become her lover and a long-term friend. Rosa went on to further study in Paris and in 1898 gained her doctorate with her dissertation 'The Industrial Development of Poland', which later served as a basis for the programme of the Social Democratic Party of Poland, which she co-founded with Jogiches in 1893. This marked the start of a huge output of writing from Rosa, who between 1892 and her death wrote a total of nearly 700 articles, books, speeches and pamphlets.

FACTFILE

- At university, Rosa studied history, economics, philosophy, politics and mathematics simultaneously. Her specialist subjects included the Middle Ages, the science of forms of state and stock exchange crises.

- Under Lichtenstein Bridge, in Berlin's Tiergarten, a large cast-iron plate marks the spot where the murdered revolutionary was thrown into the canal.

- A tortoise named Rosa Luxemburg was the regular winner of an annual tortoise race held between Balliol and Trinity Colleges at Oxford University. The official elected to organize her physical and ideological training programme was known as Comrade Tortoise. Sadly, Rosa the tortoise was stolen from Balliol in 2003 and never returned.

Throughout her life Rosa believed that the cause of international socialism was more important than nationalism, which she regarded as an unhelpful, middle-class preoccupation. She stubbornly underestimated the strength of nationalist feeling, a cause of major disagreement with the future Soviet leader Vladimir Lenin, who was committed to national self-determination.

In 1898 Rosa left Zurich for Berlin, where she joined the staff of a socialist paper and gained citizenship by marrying a German anarchist. She was soon at odds with a leading revisionist thinker in the German Social Democrat Party (GSDP), Eduard Bernstein. Bernstein believed Marxism was outdated and that parliamentary pressure was the only method to establish socialism in highly industrialized

TIMELINE

Date	Rosa Luxemburg	Related events
1870 or 1871	Born in Lublin, Poland	Birth of Lenin
1883		Death of Karl Marx
1887	Joins the left-wing Polish group, the Proletarian	Lenin arrested during a student protest and expelled from university
1892	Attends university in Switzerland	
1893	Co-founds the Social Democratic Party of Poland with Leo Jogiches	
1898	Joins the staff of a socialist paper in Berlin and marries	Russian Social Democratic Party and Labour Party formed; later splits into Bolsheviks and Mencheviks
1899/ 1900	Rosa Luxemburg's defence of Marxism, 'Reform or Revolution?', published	Lenin travels to Western Europe for the first time
1904– 1906	Imprisoned several times	Bloody Sunday in St Petersburg – start of the 1905 Russian Revolution
1914	Publication of Rosa Luxemburg's major theoretical work *The Accumulation of Capital*	Outbreak of World War I
1917		October Revolution, also known as the Bolshevik Revolution
1918	Released from prison; campaigns for a socialist revolution in Germany	End of World War I
1919	Murdered by the Freikorps in Berlin	Stalin elected as a member of the Politburo, the foremost policy-making body in the Soviet Union

nations. Together with Karl Kautsky, Rosa strongly opposed the revisionist line and in 1900 wrote an article 'Reform or Revolution?' in which she argued the continuing case for revolution, denouncing parliament as a bourgeois sham. As a result, revisionist views gradually lost popularity in German socialist circles and abroad.

From 1900 onwards Rosa attacked German militarism and imperialism in her newspaper articles, foreseeing war and trying to persuade the GSDP to move away from it. Her influence grew, due as much to her conspicuous physical courage as her theories. Between 1904 and 1906 she was imprisoned several times. Undeterred, she used a false passport to return to Poland, then part of Russia, to organize workers' revolts with Jogiches. She regarded the first Russian Revolution of 1905 as a defining moment in her life and world history. She wrote: 'For the first time the only power which historically is qualified and able to cast Tsarism into the dustbin and to raise the banner of civilization in Russia and everywhere has appeared on the scene of action'.

On her return from Poland in 1906, having broken with Jogiches, Rosa was imprisoned for urging a general strike in Germany. Between 1907 and 1914 she continued to agitate for mass action, which eventually led to a break with Kautsky. In 1907 she became an economics instructor at a school for party officials and in 1914 produced her most famous work, *The Accumulation of Capital*. In this she modified Marxist ideas by considering the new role of imperialism and argued that capitalism would survive until it dominated the world through imperialist expansion. Her theory stressed the potential revolutionary energy of the common people.

Rosa was appalled when the GSDP not only supported World War I in 1914 but also agreed to a truce with the government, promising not to strike for its duration. This was a personal crisis for Rosa, who left the party and briefly contemplated suicide, depressed that the revisionism that she had fought since 1899 had apparently triumphed.

Rosa spent most of the war in prison, from where she organized the illegal Spartacus League with Karl Liebknecht. The League was opposed to the socialists' nationalism. They wanted to bring an end to the war through revolution and establish a people's government. Rosa's ideas were disseminated through her pamphlet 'The crisis of social democracy' in 1919, written under her pseudonym Junius.

When Rosa was released in November 1918 she immediately began agitating for a socialist revolution in Germany, seeking political power for worker and soldier soviets (councils), but frustrated by the conservative establishment in Germany and the army. Together she and Liebknecht founded the German Communist Party, although Rosa tried to limit the influence of Russian Bolsheviks whom she considered dangerously dictatorial.

She and Liebknecht urged revolution against the German government, which had been in power since the armistice, and encouraged a wave of strikes, riots and violence that swept Germany. These culminated in the abortive Spartacus Uprising in Berlin in January 1919, which was brutally crushed by the national militia, the Freikorps. Rosa and Liebknecht were arrested. On their way to prison on 15 or 16 January they were murdered by the Freikorps. Rosa's body was thrown into a canal. The soldiers responsible were later acquitted of murder, a ruling that translated Rosa's death into martyrdom.

Standing barely five feet high, Rosa presented a frail physical appearance that belied the vast energy, dynamism and bravery she showed throughout her short life. In her lifetime, she was one of the most effective and respected leaders of the international socialist movement and after her death inspired countless radicals, including feminists. Although later criticized for her views by some Marxists, she is also revered by many other radicals who consider her the most outstanding personality in the international labour movement after Marx and Engels, as well as a martyr for the socialist cause, a woman of action and a major political theorist. The 1960s saw renewed interest in her life and a number of important publications about her appeared in the 1980s. An internationally acclaimed film about her life, directed by Margarethe von Trotta, was released in 1986.

Helena Rubinstein

Helena Rubinstein founded a global cosmetics empire that made her one of the richest women in the world. She used her enormous wealth to create a foundation that supports education, health, art and community service programmes for women and children in the United States.

'I believe in hard work. It keeps the wrinkles out of the mind and spirit.'

BIOGRAPHY

Name:	Helena Rubinstein, Princess Gurieli
Lived:	25 December 1870 – 1 April 1965
Place of birth:	Krakow, Poland
Place of death:	New York
Nationality:	Polish
Occupation:	Cosmetician, business executive and philanthropist

Glamorous, tempestuous and sophisticated, Helena Rubinstein was also a woman who could spot a business opportunity. While visiting relatives in Australia in her early thirties, she noticed the adverse effect of the hot climate on women's skin. Helena had with her a jar of facial cream mixed to a family formula. She realized she had found a simple business equation, one that would start her on the road to becoming a millionairess.

No beauty industry existed at the time, and women had to make their own beauty aids – the time was ripe for Helena's ideas and business flair. She went on to pioneer a wide range of products never before available to women, including tinted face powder and foundation. A mixture of business acumen, ambition, inventiveness, marketing skill, curiosity and foresight enabled her to open a string of beauty salons attracting wealthy clients, and later to turn to large-scale manufacturing and distribution of her cosmetics. She published several books passing on her ideas about beauty and health, and her genuine artistry is apparent in the comment made about her by Picasso: 'She is as much a genius as I.'

FACTFILE

- Helena Rubinstein and Elizabeth Arden were bitter rivals all their working lives, although they never met. Arden called Rubinstein 'that woman', while to Rubinstein Arden was 'the other one'.

- She encouraged women to pay attention to their physical health as well as their appearance, urging them to avoid smoking and drinking, to take exercise and to eat a healthy, balanced diet.

- When she died in 1965 her personal fortune was reported to be around $100 million.

After amassing a personal fortune of around $1,000,000, Helena was able to maintain homes in cities around the world and to become an important patron of the arts. She established a foundation to co-ordinate her philanthropic activities and made large donations to museums, colleges and institutions for the needy, especially women and children. She lived into her nineties, remaining active in the running of Helena Rubinstein Incorporated right up to her death. She is remembered now both for her generous support of many organizations and for bringing accessible glamour to the lives of women all over the world.

Helena was born on Christmas Day in 1870 in Krakow, the oldest of eight children of Horace and Augusta Rubinstein. Growing up in a Jewish merchant family with a tradition in medical work, Helena studied medicine for a short while in Zurich. However, in 1902 she left Switzerland for Melbourne, Australia, where she opened a beauty salon offering free advice to all women who purchased her skin-preserving face cream. She worked long hours, started to research dermatology and advertised her product widely. After a while she stopped importing the cream from Europe and set about manufacturing it herself. Within two years she had made £100,000. She

TIMELINE

Date	Helena Rubinstein	Related events
1870	Born in Krakow, Poland	Birth of Rosa Luxemburg, also born into a Jewish family in Poland
1878		Elizabeth Arden (Florence Nightingale Graham) born in Ontario, Canada
1902	Opens her first shop in Australia	
1908	Marries Edward Titus and opens her Maison de Beauté in London	
1910		Elizabeth Arden opens her first salon on 5th Avenue, New York
1912	Opening of her Paris salon	
1914	Opens a salon on West 49th Street, New York	Start of World War I (ends 1918)
1917	Begins the distribution of her products, one of her principal business activities	
1927		Max Factor introduces his first non-theatrical cosmetics
1937	Divorces Edward Titus and marries Artchil Gurieli-Tchkonia	
1953	Sets up the Helena Rubinstein Foundation	
1965	Dies in New York	

then left her sister in charge of the business in Melbourne and travelled to London to set up a new operation there.

Helena built on her early success by spending time studying dermatology with leading experts of the day before returning to her business. While in London she met Edward Titus, an American journalist whom she married in 1908. They had two sons, Roy and Horace. In the same year she opened her Maison de Beauté, which quickly attracted prestigious clients including Queen Alexandra. From the outset, her clientèle were rich and aristocratic women, who broke with social custom by visiting her salons. In 1912 Helena opened a salon in Paris that was patronized by, among others, the author Colette and actress Sarah Bernhardt.

After the outbreak of World War I, Helena and her husband went to New York, where she opened a salon on West 49th Street. She soon had salons in Chicago, Boston, Los Angeles and other cities all over the country through which she sold her products, with the stated aim of improving the 'terrible complexion' of American women. She sold her products through department stores and devised the idea of training travelling saleswomen to sell to smaller stores and households. She also created her own diet plan.

After World War I Helena returned to Paris, where she became recognized as Europe's leading cosmetician. She continued to show immense business flair and in 1929, shortly before the stock market crash, she sold her business to Lehman Brothers for $8 million. In 1930 she bought it back for $2 million. When asked how she had managed to make such a huge profit so easily she commented nonchalantly, 'All it took was a little chutzpah.'

Helena began to spend a great deal of time in her laboratories, developing products. She also employed chemists and researchers, who created and manufactured hundreds of new and improved beauty aids, including the first ever line of medicated skin care products. Eventually over 1000 products bore Helena's name. The wholesale distribution and manufacturing of her products then became the main thrust of her cosmetics empire. By the end of World War II manufacturing facilities had been set up in five continents.

In 1937 Helena divorced her first husband and married a Georgian prince 20 years her junior, Artchil Gurieli-Tchkonia. She became known as Princess Gurieli. She created a range of male cosmetics under her husband's name but these proved unsuccessful. Artchil, and Helena's son Horace, died in 1956.

As the beauty industry reached out to the middle classes, Helena's wealth grew and so did her interest in the arts. As well as accumulating many books on beauty and a famous collection of jewellery, she collected African sculpture, modern works, Oriental art and Egyptian antiquities. She had wide-ranging taste and enjoyed discovering and promoting the avant-garde, patronizing many artists who went on to become world famous. She became prominent in international society, although she was said to hate small talk. During her life, 27 portraits were painted of her by some of the greatest painters of her time, including Marie Laurençin, Raoul Dufy, Salvador Dali, Pablo Picasso and Graham Sutherland.

Although an extremely wealthy woman, Helena was very frugal and always brought a packed lunch to work. She did, however, dress in clothes from *haute couture* designers. She frequently gave executive positions in her organizations to relatives, valuing the family highly.

In 1953 she set up the Helena Rubinstein Foundation: 'My fortune comes from women and should benefit them and their children, to better their quality of life.' The foundation gave many donations and grants, and awarded scholarships to enable young women to take up higher education and follow non-traditional careers. Helena also made personal gifts to museums, particularly the one in Tel Aviv, to colleges and to medical research, as well as financing scholarships for Israeli citizens.

Helena continued to be involved with her organization even as her health failed. When she died in New York on 1 April 1965, she was one of the world's wealthiest women. Her foundation continues its philanthropic work and support for numerous charities, but by women around the world Helena Rubinstein will probably be best remembered for showing them how to feel and look more beautiful, and for providing the products that enabled them to do so.

Helen Keller

Helen Keller became deaf and blind at the age of 19 months but this eager, inquisitive child learned to communicate with finger signs, read with Braille and speak aloud. She overcame her disability to study for a degree from one of the leading universities in the United States and throughout her life she campaigned internationally to improve facilities for the deaf-blind.

'Her spirit will endure as long as man can read and stories can be told of the woman who showed the world there are no boundaries to courage and faith.'

Senator Lister Hill of Alabama

BIOGRAPHY

Name:	Helen Adams Keller
Lived:	27 June 1880 – 1 June 1968
Place of birth:	Tuscumbia, Alabama
Place of death:	Westport, Connecticut
Nationality:	American
Famed as:	International campaigner for the deaf-blind and disabled

Born in a small farm town in Alabama, Helen Adams Keller was the daughter of Arthur Keller, a captain in the Confederate Army, and his young second wife Kate Adams. She was an exceptionally intelligent and advanced child, imitating everything she saw and heard, and by six months was making her first attempts at speech. But her extraordinary development was cut short when she succumbed to a sudden illness at 19 months. Doctors described the condition, which left Helen unconscious, as 'acute congestion of the stomach and brain'. Helen was not ill for long and seemed to recover completely, but her parents' relief was cut short when they realized she had become deaf and blind.

FACTFILE

- Doctors today think Helen's childhood illness was probably scarlet fever, meningitis or rubella (German measles).

- Anne Sullivan had contracted trachoma as a child and went completely blind herself in 1935.

- Helen made two movies about her own life, the first in 1919 (*Deliverance*). She won an Oscar for the second, *Helen Keller in Her Story*, in 1955.

- Helen wrote enthusiastically about Communism after the Russian Revolution in 1917 and her communist sympathies were investigated by the FBI.

Helen soon forgot her memories of sights and sounds and grew used to silence and darkness. Her family developed ways to communicate with her, and Helen devised more than 50 signs of her own to transmit her needs and feelings, but her frustration was enormous and her behaviour deteriorated. At the age of seven, Helen was referred to the Perkins Institute for the Blind in Boston, Massachusetts, where it was confirmed that nothing could be done to improve her sight. However, specialists recognized Helen's exceptional intelligence and advised that she could be educated. A young teacher, Anne Mansfield Sullivan (shown on the right of the photograph opposite), was sent to work with Helen. It was the beginning of a relationship that ended only with Anne Sullivan's death.

Anne's first major difficulty was to impose some discipline on a spoiled, unruly and withdrawn child. She began to teach Helen the names of objects by spelling out letters on the palm of her hand but Helen could not relate these patterns to the things they described. A breakthrough came when Anne placed Helen's hand under running water. She spelled out the word 'water' and this seemed suddenly to unlock Helen's early memories of language.

Seeing Helen's confidence return, Anne opened up the concepts of abstracts and emotions. She also introduced Helen to Braille. In a process that took many years, she turned a child living in darkness and silence to one who could converse, express emotions and read. Helen's informal education in the surroundings of her home continued and she began to learn arithmetic, geography, zoology and botany.

TIMELINE

Date	Helen Keller	Related events
1880	Born in Tuscumbia, Alabama	
1882	Helen becomes deaf-blind	Alabama experiences an epidemic of rubella (German measles)
1887		Anne Sullivan begins to teach Helen
1900	Helen enters Radcliffe College and graduates *cum laude* in 1904	
1913		*Out of the Dark*, a book on Helen's socialist views, is published
1914–18	Foundation of Helen Keller International (1915)	Start of World War I (ends 1918)
1916	Joins the Industrial Workers of the World (IWW) and starts to write for them	
1919	Helen makes a film of her life, *Deliverance*	Foundation of the League of Nations Death of President Roosevelt
1920	Foundation of American Civil Liberties Union	Prohibition in the United States
1921		American Foundation for the Blind established
1932		Braille is accepted as the world's standard alphabet for the blind
1935		US Social Security Act provides unemployment insurance, retirement benefits and assistance for children and disabled
1936		Death of Anne Sullivan
1961	Makes her last public appearance, in Washington DC	
1964	Awarded Presidential Medal of Freedom	
1968	Dies in Westport, Connecticut	

In May 1888 they visited the Perkins Institute for the Blind and Helen was able to make friends and converse with other blind children. She wrote later, 'What joy to talk with other children in my own language! Until then I had been like a foreigner speaking through an interpreter.' The trip to Boston also offered new pleasures – trips to Bunker Hill and Plymouth and a holiday in Cape Cod. This visit marked the start of a pattern of summers spent at home and winters at the Institute.

In 1890, Helen learned to speak again. Helen understood the concept of speech, as Anne encouraged her to touch people's lips and sense the vibrations as they spoke, but with her deafness her own ability to speak had disappeared. Sarah Fuller, principal of the Horace Mann School for the Deaf, began to teach Helen in March 1890. She allowed Helen to put her fingers in her mouth and feel the movements of her tongue so that she could understand how spoken words were formed. Helen used this technique to teach herself to speak.

By 1893, Helen was reading English, French, German, Greek and Latin in Braille. The following year Anne went with her to the Wright-Humason School for the Deaf in New York where Helen stayed for two years.

In 1896, again accompanied by Anne, Helen enrolled at the Cambridge School for Young Ladies. She studied a variety of subjects including English history, English literature, German and Latin. Despite initial problems with the lack of Braille versions of textbooks, Helen took the preliminary examinations for Radcliffe College in 1897, eventually entering the college in the autumn of 1900. During her time at Radcliffe, Helen studied many subjects, including French, German, history and Latin, and graduated *cum laude* in 1904.

Although Helen's formal education ended with her degree, she continued to study. She had begun writing while at Radcliffe and had works published, including *The Story of My Life*, *Optimism* and *The World I Live In*. She also contributed to magazines and newspapers. She began campaigning on behalf of the deaf-blind and disabled.

Her fundraising efforts and public support for organizations that helped deaf-blind people in the United States were tireless. She travelled around the country giving lectures. She joined the staff of the American Foundation for the Blind and remained a member until her death. In 1924 she established the Helen Keller Endowment Fund.

Helen's work was not limited to the United States. In 1915 she was a founding member of the Permanent Blind War Relief, now known worldwide as Helen Keller International. Until Anne Sullivan's health made travelling impossible, she and Helen visited more than 40 countries. In time, Helen built up a wide circle of famous friends and contacts, including Alexander Graham Bell, who had first recommended the Perkins Institute to her parents, Mark Twain, Charlie Chaplin and Presidents Roosevelt, Eisenhower and John F. Kennedy. Helen was also a campaigner for social reform and an active member of the Socialist Party. She was one of the founders of the American Civil Liberties Union in 1920.

Anne, who had been ill for some time, lapsed into a coma and died in 1936, while Helen held her hand. After her death, which ended a friendship and association that had lasted nearly 50 years, Helen moved to Connecticut and others assisted her with her work.

In 1946, she began travelling again on behalf of the American Foundation for Overseas Blind, visiting 35 countries and five continents before 1957. Her international efforts brought her awards as diverse as Brazil's Order of the Southern Cross, Japan's Sacred Treasure and the Philippines' Golden Heart.

Helen's time after 1961 was spent at her home at Arcan Ridge in Connecticut with her family, friends, colleagues and books. She was awarded the Presidential Medal of Freedom by Lyndon B. Johnson in 1964 and in 1965 she was elected to the Women's Hall of Fame. She died on 1 June 1968 at Arcan Ridge, shortly before reaching her 88th birthday.

Virginia Woolf

Virginia Woolf was one of the most significant modernist novelists. A founding member of the Bloomsbury Group, her style and subject matter were controversial. The publishing house she owned with her husband, Leonard, published many books by unknown but now greatly respected authors such as Katherine Mansfield, T. S. Eliot, H. G. Wells and Gertrude Stein.

'A woman must have money and a room of her own if she is to write fiction.'

BIOGRAPHY

Name:	Adeline Virginia Stephen
Lived:	25 January 1882 – 28 March 1941
Place of birth:	London
Place of death:	Rodmell, Sussex
Nationality:	British
Famed as:	Author, feminist, publisher and a member of the Bloomsbury Group

Adeline Virginia Stephen was born in London in 1882 to Leslie Stephen – he was later knighted – a literary critic and creator of the Dictionary of National Biography, and his second wife Julia Jackson Duckworth, a member of the Duckworth publishing family. Virginia had three siblings, Thoby, Adrian and Vanessa, one step-sister, Laura, from her father's first marriage, and three half-brothers and sisters from her mother's first marriage, Gerald, George and Stella Duckworth. Virginia was educated at home by her father and given unlimited access to his library. Family life was punctuated with visits from distinguished literary figures of the time.

Despite this privileged lifestyle, Virginia's early life was seriously disturbed. She was sexually abused by her half-brother Gerald and the death of her mother in 1895, when Virginia was 13, prompted the first of many breakdowns. In July 1897, Virginia's half-sister Stella, who had taken the place of her mother in the household, died of peritonitis.

FACTFILE

- In 1909, Virginia and the writer Lytton Strachey decided to get married, only to change their minds three days later.

- In 1910, disguised and made up by Sarah Bernhardt's make-up artist, Virginia took part in the notorious Dreadnought Hoax, an anti-establishment prank in which she and others gained access to the top secret battleship by pretending to be visiting Abyssinian dignitaries.

- In 1927, Virginia received the award for Tallest Woman Writer from the *London Evening Standard* newspaper, beating the novelist Elizabeth Bowen.

- In 2002, Nicole Kidman was awarded an Oscar for Best Actress for her portrayal of Virginia Woolf in *The Hours*, a film based loosely on Virginia's life and her novel *Mrs Dalloway*.

In 1904, Virginia's father died of cancer and Virginia, Vanessa and Thoby moved to a house in Bloomsbury. Within a month her mental health had deteriorated and she was admitted to a nursing home. By the end of 1904, however, she had recovered and started teaching English and history at Morley College. In 1905, she began writing book reviews and articles for journals. Then the death of Thoby from typhoid fever in 1906 resulted in another prolonged breakdown.

Despite her mental fragility, Virginia was lively, generous and hardworking, but extremely shy. Although she suffered from mood swings and bouts of depression and elation during acute periods of illness, Virginia was, in fact, very sociable, and it was at the house in Bloomsbury that she, Thoby and Vanessa formed the centre of what became known as the Bloomsbury Group. Never a formal society, this was really a coming together of Cambridge graduates and their friends. The group became renowned for its rejection of Victorian values in religion, art and social and sexual conventions. Prominent members included Lytton Strachey, E. M. Forster, Dora Carrington, Duncan Grant, John Maynard Keynes and Roger Fry.

TIMELINE

Date	Virginia Woolf	Related events
1882	Born in London	
1912	Virginia marries Leonard Woolf	
1913		Roger Fry and Duncan Grant establish the Omega Workshops
1917	The Hogarth Press begins	
1918		Lytton Strachey, *Eminent Victorians* published
1924		E. M. Forster, *A Passage to India* published
1927	*To the Lighthouse* published	
1928	*Orlando* published	D. H. Lawrence, *Lady Chatterley's Lover* published
1929	*A Room of One's Own* published	
1932		Death of Lytton Strachey

Suicide of Dora Carrington |
1936		John Maynard Keynes, *General Theory of Employment, Interest and Money* published
1937	*The Years* published	
1941	Commits suicide	
1969		Death of Leonard Woolf

In 1911, Virginia moved into a house with members of the Bloomsbury Group, including Leonard Woolf – a civil servant and political theorist. They married in August 1912. Even in the early days of the marriage, Leonard was aware of symptoms of Virginia's illness. By 1913, Virginia had completed her first novel, *The Voyage Out*, but was left in a state of extreme physical, mental and nervous exhaustion. In September she attempted suicide.

In October 1915, following the publication of *The Voyage Out* and a further period of severe mental illness, Virginia and Leonard moved to Hogarth House in Richmond. In 1917 they set up a small hand press in their dining room, with the aim of publishing special editions of selected work by friends and acquaintances in the Bloomsbury circle. Begun as a hobby, with the intention of distracting Virginia from the emotional stress of her writing, the Hogarth Press grew into a substantial business in the inter-war years and production had to be undertaken by a commercial printer.

The first book by the Hogarth Press was a 32-page pamphlet entitled *Two Stories*, containing 'The mark on the wall' by Virginia and 'Three Jews' by Leonard. The catalogue of authors they went on to publish now reads like a roll-call of some of the greatest writers and artists of the twentieth century: Katherine Mansfield, T. S. Eliot, Clive Bell, Cecil Day Lewis, Robert Graves, E. M. Forster, Christopher Isherwood,

John Maynard Keynes, William Plomer, Vita Sackville-West, Roger Fry, Gertrude Stein, H. G. Wells, Vanessa Bell, Dora Carrington and Duncan Grant. The Hogarth Press also published the first English translations of Sigmund Freud and other psychoanalytical works. Virginia was involved with the business until 1938, after which Leonard ran it with John Lehmann until it was taken over by the publishers Chatto and Windus after World War II.

In 1919, Virginia and Leonard moved to Rodmell in Sussex. The Hogarth Press now became her publisher. In 1921 her novel *Monday and Tuesday* appeared. In this book, Virginia experimented with a new style of writing that allowed her to display her perception of the underlying psychological and emotional motives of her characters – stream of consciousness. *Jacob's Room* (1922) expanded on the technique. Virginia's illness seemed to be under control and in March 1924 the Woolfs returned to live in Tavistock Square, London.

Virginia's health remained stable and she entered a period of intense activity, in which she produced her best work. She published essays for periodicals, collections and critical writings in *The Common Reader* (1925). In the same year, the Hogarth Press published *Mrs Dalloway*, in which Virginia wove mental illness into a fictional story. *To the Lighthouse*, a strongly narrative novel, followed in 1927. *Orlando* (1928) traced the career of an androgynous protagonist from the court of Elizabeth I to the end of World War I: it was inspired by Virginia's same-sex relationship with writer Vita Sackville-West. *A Room of One's Own* (1929) examined the obstacles and prejudices confronting women at the time. In 1931 Virginia published *The Waves*, her most experimental novel, constructed from a series of monologues by the major characters.

In 1936, Virginia began once again to suffer bouts of mental illness. With the start of World War II, she and Leonard moved permanently to Rodmell. *Roger Fry* – a posthumous biography of the artist and critic – was published in July 1939, followed by *Between the Acts* in 1941. It was Virginia's last novel and was published posthumously. On 28 March that year she filled her pockets with stones and drowned herself in the river at Rodmell. She left Leonard a letter: 'I feel certain that I am going mad again: I feel we can't go through another of those terrible times. And I shan't recover this time.' Her body was not found for three weeks.

Her work quickly grew unpopular in the post-war period. Critics derided her characters as trivial and self-obsessed examples of an outmoded upper-middle-class intelligentsia – much like the members of the Bloomsbury Group themselves, who also fell out of favour. Virginia's reputation today rests mainly on the novels *To the Lighthouse* and *The Waves*. With their experimentation, rejection of traditional style and structure and exploration of psychological motive they established her as a leading modernist writer. In the 1970s, reassessment of these two novels by feminist thinkers and critics re-established Virginia Woolf as one of the twentieth century's greatest writers.

Coco Chanel

Coco Chanel revolutionized ideas of women's dress and elevated fashion design to an art form. The company she founded is an international presence in *haute couture*, designer clothing, scent and cosmetics.

'Fashion is not something that exists in dresses only. Fashion is in the sky, in the street, fashion has to do with ideas, the way we live, what is happening.'

BIOGRAPHY

Name:	Gabrielle Bonheur Chanel
Lived:	19 August 1883 – 10 January 1971
Place of birth:	Saumur, France
Place of death:	Paris, France
Nationality:	French
Famed as:	*Haute couture* designer and perfumier

Gabrielle Bonheur 'Coco' Chanel started life as an orphaned peasant but went on to become one of the most revolutionary fashion designers of all time. She changed the face of fashion to such an extent that she was the only couturier in *Time* magazine's 100 most influential people of the twentieth century and her ideas still permeate today in the work of modern designers. By redefining the way a woman should dress, taking masculine clothes and giving them a feminine twist, Coco also made a significant contribution to the women's rights movement.

Coco's style was universal and has proved timeless. The creations that made her famous in the 1920s, the 'little black dress' and jersey suits, are still widely produced today and continue to be based on her original designs. But her signature styles evolved partly out of necessity. Coco, known as 'Mademoiselle' by her inner circle, only learned how to be a seamstress because she could not afford expensive clothes created by designers. She instinctively created comfortable and loose-fitting clothes that immediately appealed to women, whose bodies had been squeezed and moulded by boned corsetry for many years. She would never have described herself as a feminist, but her revolution in women's dress design, and above all the freeing of women from the confines of corsets, coincided with the booming of the feminist movement. The way Coco integrated masculine and sporting elements of dress with women's clothing chimed with the ideals of the feminist movement.

FACTFILE

- Traditional Chanel accessories include gold chains, multiple strings of pearls, two-tone shoes and quilted handbags with gold chain shoulder straps.
- Chanel No. 5 was named after Coco's lucky number. All her new collections appeared on the fifth day of the month. Chanel No. 19, introduced in 1970, was named after her birth date.
- Her nickname 'Coco' means 'little pet'.
- Coco lived in private rooms in the Ritz Hotel in Paris for more than 30 years.

Coco had a secretive nature, aiming perhaps to deflect questioning about her poverty-stricken past. She would claim to have been born in 1893 in the Auvergne, when in fact she was born ten years earlier in the town of Saumur, to a workhouse mother who died soon after, leaving six children to a father who swiftly deserted the family. In 1905, at the age of 17, she left her job as a seamstress in order to make a living as a cabaret singer. She sang in Parisian cafés like La Rotonde in Montparnasse, and it was here that she first acquired the nickname Coco, from a popular song she sang. Her singing career was short-lived, but through it she became the mistress of rich men like Étienne Balsan and Arthur 'Boy' Capel, who would help her to set up her business and introduce her clothing to wealthy society women.

Coco's sense of style was too deep-rooted for her to be swept along by the currents of fashion and her creations were always original. In 1912, aided financially by Balsan,

TIMELINE

Date	Coco Chanel	Related events
1858		Charles Worth establishes the first *haute couture* fashion house in Paris
1883	Born in Saumur, France	
1912	Opens millinery shop in Paris	Jean Patou founds Maison Parry
1923	Chanel No. 5 launched Stage designs for *Antigone*	
1925	Signature cardigan jacket created	
1926	The little black dress created	
1927		Jeanne Lanvin launches her scent Arpège
1935		Elsa Schiaparelli opens a Paris salon
1937	Stage designs for *Oedipus Rex*	Cristóbal Balenciaga opens a salon in Paris
1946		Christian Dior opens a Paris salon and launches the New Look
1954	Reopens her showrooms for the first time since World War II The Chanel suit created	Elsa Schiaparelli declared bankrupt
1957		Death of Christian Dior. Yves Saint Laurent takes over the fashion house
1971	Dies in the Ritz Hotel, Paris	
1983		Karl Lagerfeld begins designing for the Chanel label

she opened her first millinery shop. Coco pioneered her own flapper style of hat instead of the *Belle Époque* type fashionable at the time, saying, 'How can a brain function under those things?' Her own well-functioning brain led to the rapid expansion of the Chanel company. In addition to her famed sense of style, she was also a strong businesswoman, talented at marketing. By the 1920s, Coco had attained legendary status. She was courted by Hollywood, in addition to the rich and famous, and the Chanel brand was booming. She also nearly married one of the richest men in Europe, the Duke of Westminster. When asked why she did not, she replied, 'There have been several Duchesses of Westminster. There is only one Chanel.'

It was during this decade that she launched her most timeless items. Her little black dress was created in 1926. There had been other little black dresses by other designers, but Coco's was the only one considered stylish enough for *haute couture*. Another lasting innovation was the scent Chanel No. 5, launched in 1923. With Chanel No. 5 she started the trend for fashion designers to produce signature scents. No perfume had ever been named after a clothes designer before. Chanel No. 5 has become the benchmark of designer perfumes and remains an important profit line for the modern Chanel organization. After No. 5 was launched, Pierre Wertheimer, head of the Bourjois company and probably her lover, became Coco's partner in the perfumery business. Chanel No. 5 has become synonymous with luxury and sensuality. Its abiding association with glamour and success was sealed in 1954 when Marilyn Monroe, asked in an interview what she wore to bed, replied 'Chanel No. 5'. Sales soared worldwide. Coco herself designed the classic stoppered bottle that the scent is still sold in. The perfume inside, she maintained, was more important than the packaging.

Coco's success made her part of the modern artistic movement, alongside Stravinsky, Picasso, Cocteau and Diaghilev. Indeed, Cocteau once said of her that 'she has, by a kind of miracle, worked in fashion according to rules that would seem to have value only for painters, musicians, poets.' Coco made the designs for Cocteau's stage plays *Antigone* (1923) and *Oedipus Rex* (1937). She also designed the costumes for many films. This association with highbrow culture set her apart from other contemporary fashion designers, and has meant that her designs have become regarded as works of art.

But Coco's reputation was not completely untarnished. During World War II, less palatable sympathies emerged as she allied herself with the Fascist movement. She displayed anti-semitic and homophobic tendencies, and in the course of the war she shut down her business and started a relationship with a Nazi officer, Hans Gunther von Dincklage. She was widely criticized for these actions and from 1939 until 1954 was effectively in retirement.

Then in 1954 Coco decided to reopen her business. She secured her comeback success with the creation of the Chanel suit, which is still worn and widely copied today. It had a knee-length skirt and fitted jacket of black woven wool, with gold buttons, and was typically worn with oversized costume jewellery. Karl Lagerfeld has said, 'By the 1950s she had the benefit of distance, and so could truly distil the Chanel look. Time and culture had caught up with her.' Once again, Coco's designs represented a fashion liberation. Her casual, relaxed shapes, in soft fabrics, were very different from the highly-structured post-war New Look of her rival Christian Dior.

The 1950s was the decade when Coco Chanel consolidated her influence. By the 1960s, she had become part of the same fashion establishment that she so rigorously rejected in the beginning and her name was almost synonymous with *haute couture*. In 1969 Katharine Hepburn played her on Broadway, and in a film of her life, *Chanel Solitaire* (1981), she was played by the French actress Marie-France Pisier. Coco was working right up to her death in 1971 and is buried in Lausanne, Switzerland. Despite her numerous love affairs, she never married. After her death the company was run by a number of her designers. Since 1983, the German designer Karl Lagerfeld has kept the Chanel name alive by successfully combining Coco's traditional style with more modern design.

Eleanor Roosevelt

Eleanor Roosevelt, wife of US President Franklin D. Roosevelt, was his indispensable political aide and an indefatigable human rights activist. As head of the United Nations Human Rights Commission she drafted the Declaration of Human Rights. President Harry S. Truman called her 'The First Lady of the World'.

'At all times, day by day, we have to continue fighting for freedom of religion, freedom of speech, and freedom from want – for these are things that must be gained in peace as well as in war.'

BIOGRAPHY

Name:	Anna Eleanor Roosevelt
Lived:	11 October 1884 – 7 November 1962
Place of birth:	New York
Place of death:	New York
Nationality:	American
Famed as:	First Lady and campaigner for human rights in the United States and worldwide

Anna Eleanor Roosevelt was born in October 1884 in New York. She was the eldest daughter of Elliott Roosevelt, the younger brother of Theodore Roosevelt, a Republican and the 26th President of the United States. Her childhood insecurity, due largely to what she described as her 'plain looks and lack of manners', made her shy and deferential, and caused her difficulties even in adulthood.

Eleanor's parents had marital problems and were separated for some time before her mother's death from diphtheria in 1892. During the same year, Elliott Roosevelt was confined to a mental institution where he died two years later of alcoholism. Eleanor and her younger brothers – Elliott and Hall – went to live with their maternal grandmother, a rather cold and distant figure.

In 1899, Eleanor's grandmother enrolled her at Allenswood School in England. This was a positive experience for Eleanor, as her tutor – Madame Marie Souvestre – was a progressive woman who helped her develop her self-confidence. After school, Eleanor became Madame Souvestre's travelling companion in Europe and she began to appreciate what life could be like for an independent woman.

FACTFILE

- Eleanor was a skilful archer and one of the first women to take part in the sport of bowhunting.

- Eleven Gallup polls named Eleanor as the most admired woman in the world. But her children were resentful of the time and attention she lavished on strangers, instead of on them, and all led troubled lives.

- She wrote her column 'My Day' six days a week, from 1935 until her death in 1962, taking only four days off when her husband died.

- Following Eleanor's death, her son Elliott wrote a series of best-selling detective stories in which his mother, as First Lady, acted as a detective and helped the police to solve crimes.

Nevertheless, a conventional and unexceptional upper-class life was what Eleanor was expected to aspire to. After three years in Europe, she returned to New York for her society debut in 1902. Three years later she married her distant and very eligible cousin, Franklin Delano Roosevelt. They had six children.

At first, Eleanor's life as a married woman in a certain class of society followed a predictable pattern. She became involved in the sort of acceptable voluntary organizations supported by women of her class: the National Consumer's League and the Junior League of New York, where she taught callisthenics and dancing to immigrants. Despite her background, she was rather naïve about politics. However, that was about to change. Franklin D. Roosevelt entered politics in 1910, when he ran as a Democrat for the New York State Senate. He became Assistant Secretary of the Navy in 1913 and Eleanor began to learn how political life in Washington worked.

TIMELINE

Date	Eleanor Roosevelt	Related events
1884	Born in New York	Statue of Liberty dedicated by President Grover Cleveland
1899	Attends school in England	
1905	Marries Franklin Delano Roosevelt	
1920	Accompanies Franklin during Vice-Presidency campaign	Congress passes 19th Amendment granting women the right to vote
1921	Franklin paralyzed by polio	
1925	Foundation of Val-Kil furniture factory	
1932	Franklin elected President of the United States	The Great Depression intensifies in America
1936	Franklin re-elected as President	
1939	Defies segregation laws	Hitler invades Poland and war breaks out in Europe
1945	Franklin dies suddenly	President Harry S. Truman authorizes use of atomic weapons against Japan
1946	Elected head of United Nations Human Rights Commission	
1948	Drafts Declaration of Human Rights	Declaration of Human Rights passed by United Nations
1952	Resigns from United Nations	
1961	Reappointed by John F. Kennedy to United Nations and the Commission on the Status of Women	John F. Kennedy becomes President
1962	Dies in New York aged 78	

In 1918, Eleanor discovered that her husband was conducting an affair with Lucy Mercer, Eleanor's social secretary. The couple did not divorce but the discovery strengthened Eleanor's independence and they began to lead separate lives. Eleanor had become genuinely drawn towards campaigns to tackle rising social problems and now became increasingly involved. She campaigned to abolish child labour, establish a minimum wage and pass legislation that would protect workers. In 1919, she visited World War I veterans at the St Elizabeth Hospital and volunteered at the International Congress of Working Women in Washington.

In 1920, Eleanor supported Franklin's campaign for the Vice-Presidency. When he was paralyzed by polio in 1921, her political activity increased, and she travelled around the United States on fact-finding missions on Franklin's behalf. She also became active in the Women's Division of the State Democratic Committee. In 1925, Eleanor set up the Val-Kil furniture factory, along with Marion Dickerman and Nancy Cook, on the Hyde Park estate in New York where the Roosevelts lived. In 1928, when Franklin was elected Governor of New York, Eleanor was elected Director of the Bureau of Women's Activities by the Democratic National Committee.

In 1932, Franklin ran successfully for the Presidency. As in his earlier bids for office, Eleanor worked closely with him and his aides throughout the campaign. By this time, her own social and political activity had begun to draw the attention of the press. Before the election there was a great deal of speculation about whether her independent work would have to be curtailed if she became First Lady. In the event, Eleanor made the role of First Lady her own. She undertook official entertaining, travelled around the country, gave lectures and radio broadcasts and had her own column in a daily newspaper.

Eleanor's anti-racist views were well known. When the black opera singer Marian Anderson was not allowed to sing in Constitution Hall in Washington in 1939, because of her colour, Eleanor arranged an alternative performance on the steps of the Lincoln Memorial. An audience of 70,000 watched the recital, which was broadcast nationwide on the radio. She lobbied her husband to sign a series of orders barring discrimination against blacks in his New Deal programmes in the South, and opposed internment laws against the Japanese in World War II. Eleanor's support for racial equality earned Franklin many African-American votes.

Eleanor also fought for equal rights for women and was the first president's wife to hold women-only press conferences – she knew the press would have to employ a woman reporter to have access to her. She discouraged women from marrying young and hastily, encouraged them to learn skills through employment and secured the first governmental funds for childcare centres.

After Franklin's death in 1945, Eleanor assumed that her public life was over, but by this time she had become a powerful public figure. In 1946, she was elected head of the United Nations Human Rights Commission. She began to draft the Declaration of Human Rights and started the pressure group Americans for Democratic Action, which focused on domestic and social reform and resistance to Russia and the Cold War. In 1948, the Declaration of Human Rights was passed by the United Nations.

Eleanor's social reform work continued, but in 1952 she resigned from the United Nations and backed Adlai Stevens' campaign for the Presidency. She visited the Soviet Union in 1957 as a representative for the *New York Post* and in 1958 spoke at a civil rights workshop in Tennessee, despite threats from the racist vigilante group, the Ku Klux Klan.

In 1961, President John F. Kennedy reappointed Eleanor to the United Nations and as Chair of the President's Commission on the Status of Women. During the last year of her life, she sat on the Commission of Inquiry into the Administration of Justice in the Freedom Struggle, which monitored and reported on the progress of the civil rights movement. She died of tuberculosis in 1962.

Eleanor Roosevelt grew up never expecting to be remembered other than as somebody's daughter, niece or wife. She became America's longest-serving First Lady and will be remembered in her own right for her commitment to international humanitarianism and her perseverance in translating ideas into actions.

Amelia Earhart

Amelia Earhart was the first woman to cross the Atlantic by plane and the first female pilot to make solo transatlantic and transpacific flights. A national heroine, she died in 1937 while attempting a round-the-world flight.

'Women must try to do things as men have tried. When they fail, their failure must be but a challenge to others.'

BIOGRAPHY

Name:	Amelia Mary Earhart
Lived:	24 July 1897 – 2 July 1937 (date conjectural)
Place of birth:	Atchison, Kansas
Place of death:	Near Howland Island, Pacific Ocean
Nationality:	American
Famed as:	Pioneering female aviator

Amelia Earhart's upbringing was overshadowed by her family's financial problems. Her father, Edwin Earhart, was an alcoholic and unable to hold down a job. She and her sister Muriel lived with their maternal grandparents for the first 12 years of Amelia's life. At school, she was a bright child who often clashed with authority and her tomboyish interests were atypical for her time. She was once quoted as saying 'Adventure is worthwhile in itself.' It might be said to be her ethos in life.

During World War I, Amelia went to Toronto with Muriel and worked as a nursing assistant, caring for wounded soldiers. After the war, she began training as a doctor in California but dropped out of the course. She had been seduced by aviation.

In December 1920, when she was 23, Amelia went up in a plane for the first time, as a passenger. She said later, 'By the time I had got two or three hundred feet off the ground I knew I had to fly.' She took lessons in California, insisting on having a female flying instructor. Neta Hook gave Amelia her first lesson in January 1921, and within the same year Amelia had saved enough money to buy her own plane, a Kinner Airstar two-seater. The plane was painted bright yellow and Amelia named it Canary.

FACTFILE

- Amelia Earhart was nicknamed 'Lady Lindy' because her posture, build and features resembled Charles Lindbergh.

- She never wore flying gear. Instead of a helmet, she preferred a close-fitting hat and flew either in a dress or a suit.

- She was a friend of Eleanor Roosevelt, who obtained her student pilot's licence so that Amelia could teach her to fly.

- When the British pilot Amy Johnson and her husband Jim Mollison were injured following a crash landing in Connecticut in 1933, Amelia invited them to stay and recover in her house.

- In 1937, the year of her death, Amelia met Orville Wright in Philadelphia.

In 1924 Amelia moved to Boston, where she began social work, but flying remained her passion. Aviation advances meant that flying was constantly in the news in the late 1920s. On 20 May 1927 Charles Lindbergh made the first solo crossing of the Atlantic, landing in Paris. A wealthy American, Amy Guest, offered to sponser a transatlantic flight by a woman and contacted publicist George P. Putnam, asking him to find a suitable candidate. Amelia was by now well known in amateur flying circles and George asked her to join Wilmer Stultz and Louis Gordon on a transatlantic flight. On 17 June 1928 the team set out in their Fokker F7 from Newfoundland towards the British Isles. They landed in Burry Port in Wales after 21 hours of flight. The trip gripped the public imagination and the team were greeted as heroes on their return. Amelia hit headlines worldwide. She had not piloted the plane but she was the first woman to fly the Atlantic. Newspapers loved her and

TIMELINE

Date	Amelia Earhart	Related events
1897	Born in Atchison, Kansas	
1903		Orville and Wilbur Wright accomplish the first sustained powered flight
1919	Begins medical studies	John Alcock and Arthur Whitten Brown make the first non-stop transatlantic flight
1921	Learns to fly	Bessie Coleman becomes the first African-American woman to receive Fédération Aéronautique Internationale pilot's licence
1927		Charles Lindbergh flies solo non-stop across the Atlantic
1928	First woman to fly the Atlantic	Bert Hinkler flies solo from England to Australia
1930		Amy Johnson is the first woman to fly solo from England to Australia
1931	Marries George Putnam	Reginald Mitchell's S6B Supermarine seaplane breaks the world speed record
1932	First solo crossing of the Atlantic by a woman	
1935	Flies the Pacific – twice	The world's first successful passenger airliner, the DC-3, takes off for the first time from Santa Monica, California
1937	Disappears over the Pacific	The explosion of the Hindenberg air balloon kills 36 people in New Jersey

from this point she became a public figure. Amelia and George, who had been brought together by the adventure, married in 1931.

On 20 May 1932, Amelia set out from Newfoundland on a solo crossing of the Atlantic, heading, like Lindbergh, for Paris. She made it across the ocean, but icy weather and mechanical problems forced her to land in Ireland. This exploit helped cement her fame. President Hoover presented her with the Gold Medal of the National Geographic Society, Congress awarded her the Distinguished Flying Cross and the French made her a member of the Légion d'honneur. Then, in 1935, Amelia was the first person to fly the Pacific solo and she did it twice, first from Honolulu to California and then from Mexico City to Newark.

Before Amelia Earhart's very public adventures, flying had been regarded as an exclusively male preserve. She was fully aware that the world viewed her as a pioneer of female as well as avionic achievement. She once said, 'Now and then women should do for themselves what men have already done – occasionally what men have not done – thereby establishing themselves as persons.'

Amelia had one major challenge left – to fly around the world. After some false starts, on 1 June 1937 she set off from Miami with her co-pilot and navigator Fred Noonan. The trip would cover 46,000 km. After many stops in South America, Africa, India and Asia, on 2 July they faced the final trans-pacific 11,000 km. Their journey was almost completed when there was confusion about their location, although weather conditions were not particularly bad. Eventually the coast guard lost contact with the plane, which was presumed to have come down in the sea.

The search and rescue operation that followed lasted 16 days, involved 4000 people from the US navy and coast guard and cost the US government $4 million. No trace of Amelia's plane was ever found. It seems clear that, disorientated, Amelia and Noonan ran out of fuel and perished somewhere in the Pacific. Like other prominent figures who have died in tragic circumstances, her death has been the subject of hysterical conjecture and enduring conspiracy theories. In 2005, the explorer David Jourdan planned a sonar search of the area where her plane is supposed to have gone down, hoping to solve the mystery – and the speculation continues.

Amy Johnson   1 July 1903 – 5 January 1941

A contemporary of Amelia Earhart, the British pilot Amy Johnson took up flying as a hobby while she was working as a solicitor's secretary in London. She was awarded her pilot's licence in 1929. The following year she became world famous when she flew solo from England to Australia, a distance of 17,600 km, in a de Havilland Gypsy Moth bi-plane, now exhibited at the Science Museum in London. She was trying to beat the record time of 15.5 days, set by Bert Hinkler, and was on track to do so until two crashes and lengthy repairs delayed her. An overnight celebrity, Amy was awarded the CBE.

In 1931 Amy flew from England to Japan co-piloted by Jack Humphreys, and in 1932 set a world-record time for a solo flight from England to South Africa. The record she beat had previously been set by Jim Mollison, a Scottish pilot whom she had met earlier that year. They decided to marry within hours of their meeting and afterwards flew together several times, including an abortive round-the-world trip in 1933. The marriage later foundered, partly because they continued to compete for supremacy as pilots, and they divorced in 1938. After Amelia Earhart's death, Amy abandoned record flights and took up gliding.

During World War II, Amy transported planes for the Royal Air Force. On 5 January 1941, she went off course in bad weather while flying from the north of England towards Oxford and, running short of fuel, baled out over the Thames estuary. She was seen in the water and an officer from a Royal Naval destroyer dived in to rescue her. As the ship manoeuvred to pick her up, Amy disappeared. Her body was never recovered.

Margaret Bourke-White

Margaret Bourke-White was the first western photographer allowed into the Soviet Union, the first female photojournalist for *Life* magazine, the first female war correspondent and the first photographer to be allowed to work in combat zones during World War II. She once said, 'Nothing attracts me like a closed door.'

'Work is something you can count on, a trusted, lifelong friend who never deserts you.'

BIOGRAPHY

Name:	Margaret White
Lived:	14 June 1904 – 27 August 1971
Place of birth:	New York
Place of death:	Stamford, Connecticut
Nationality:	American
Famed as:	Photographer and photojournalist

Margaret was the second of two children born to Joseph White, an inventor and engineer of Polish-Jewish background, and his Anglo-Irish wife Minnie Bourke. A strong believer in equality of opportunity for all his children, Margaret's father took her to see the printing machines in his workplace and she showed an early fascination with these. Her later achievements in what was then largely a man's world owed much to the influence of her father, whose motto was 'You can!'

Margaret had a strict upbringing in which frivolities like chewing gum, slang, cards and comics were banned. A strong-willed child, she often left home to explore, and her mother had to resort to sewing a sign on her jumper with her name and address, asking people to send her home. She inherited a strong work ethic from her father as well as a keen interest in wildlife. When she left school she went to Columbia University in New York to study reptiles. While there she developed an interest in photography – another thing she shared with her father – and signed up for classes with Clarence White, an advocate of 'pictorialism', when photographs are made to look like pictures through the use of soft focus. It was here that she developed her skills in photo composition.

FACTFILE

- During her career, Margaret was torpedoed, strafed by enemy fighters, shelled, stranded on an Arctic island and ditched in the Chesapeake River when the helicopter she was travelling in crashed.

- Her famous photograph of Gandhi at his spinning wheel was taken only hours before his assassination.

In 1925 Margaret married an engineering student she met at Columbia, Everett Chapman. However, the marriage only lasted a year, largely because of the influence of his highly possessive mother, and in 1926 Margaret returned to studying at Cornell University in New York, where she graduated in 1927. However, the unexpected death of her father left her without financial resources and she began to take photographic commissions to support herself.

Margaret specialized in photographing industrial subjects and architecture. In 1929 she set up her own studio in Cleveland and took the name Bourke-White, from her mother's and father's surnames. Her photographs of steel making attracted a great deal of attention and she was invited to work as the staff photographer for *Fortune* magazine, where she remained from 1929 to 1934. In 1930 she became the first foreigner admitted to the USSR when *Fortune* sent her there to document advances in industry since the 1917 Revolution. At this point in her career her method was to take many pictures in order to capture a single moment that conveyed the human drama of a situation. In 1934 she went to the American midwest to cover the drought conditions in the Dust Bowl and was deeply moved by the suffering of the farmers and their families. Individuals, as well as the drama, now began to be important to her.

TIMELINE

Date	Margaret Bourke-White	Related events
1904	Born in New York	
1908		Birth of Henri Cartier-Bresson
1930	Joins *Fortune* and photographs in USSR	First issue of *Fortune*
1936	Begins work for *Life*	Robert Capa photographs Spanish Civil War (until 1939)
		Alfred Eisenstaedt joins *Life* (until 1972)
1941–45	Works as war photographer with US forces	
1944		Capa photographs D-Day (6 June). The film is irreparably damaged during processing by lab assistant Larry Burrows
1945	Photographs liberated concentration camps, including Buchenwald	Alfred Eisenstaedt publishes iconic photograph of US soldier kissing woman in Time Square
1947	Travels to India	Capa founds Magnum Photos with Henri Cartier-Bresson and David Seymour
1954	Diagnosed with Parkinson's disease	Robert Capa killed by landmine while photographing Indochina War
1956		David Seymour killed by machine-gun fire in Suez
1971	Dies in Connecticut	Larry Burrows killed in helicopter crash covering the war in Vietnam

In 1936 Margaret began her lifelong connection with *Life* magazine, when her pictures of the construction of the Fort Peck Dam were on the cover of the first edition of what became one of America's most prominent picture magazines. Margaret's pictures of major national events like wars, floods and riots were soon a major feature in *Life*. She specialized in what were called photo-essays: a series of sequential photographs with captions that in a pre-television era gave people news stories and information in an innovative form. There was strong competition for good assignments and publication between photographers at *Life*. Margaret sometimes literally crawled between the legs of her male competitors to get photographs. Her success and aggressive drive made her unpopular, but one contemporary described her as the most hard-working woman he had ever met.

In 1937 Margaret met the man who was to become her second husband, the novelist Erskine Caldwell, when they worked together on the book, *You Have Seen Their Faces*, which recorded the experiences of rural black Southerners during the Depression. Although Margaret liked to pose her subjects, a technique she was criticized for, she produced images that were more revealing than the dispassionate pictures taken by official government photographers, and it was her images that helped to bring about legislation that improved the lot of sharecroppers.

In 1939 Margaret married Caldwell and they were together for three years. However, her continual absences through work during World War II meant that Caldwell eventually sought a divorce. Although Margaret subsequently had numerous romances, she never remarried.

During World War II Margaret covered the war for *Life*, and also worked for the US armed services as its first woman photographer. In 1941, she was on assignment in Russia once again. Foreign photographers were officially banned, but Margaret's earlier work earned her exemption. She was the only foreign photographer in Moscow when Germany invaded Russia that June. Her historic films were taken out of the country by a US diplomat. In 1942 she was crossing the Atlantic to North Africa in a transport ship that was torpedoed and sunk. She had to scramble to get into a lifeboat along with others, but later managed to take photographs of the relieved survivors waving to the British search plane. Later, she said: 'For me the indelible untaken photograph is the picture of our sinking ship viewed from our dangling lifeboat.' During the war Margaret was to take memorable photos of each of the Allied leaders: Churchill, Stalin and Roosevelt. Attracted to heights, she also shot photographs from a wide range of military and commercial aircraft and airships.

In 1943 Margaret became the first woman to fly on a combat mission. She then became the first Army Air Force woman photographer covering the allied infantry's first campaign in action in North Africa and Italy. At the end of the war she was attached to General Patton's Third Army when it crossed the Rhine, and was among the first to take pictures that shocked the world as they showed the truth about Nazi concentration camps. Her book *Dear Fatherland, Rest Quietly*, published in 1946, recorded her experiences as US troops liberated the camps.

After the war, Margaret travelled to India to record the migration of Hindus and Muslims as India and Pakistan were partitioned during Independence. She was the last person to photograph Gandhi before his assassination in 1948. From 1949 to 1953, she photographed life in South Africa under apartheid, as well as the Korean War.

On returning from Korea Margaret realized she was unwell, and her illness was diagnosed as Parkinson's disease. In order to help others suffering from the same condition, Margaret allowed *Life* to run a photo-essay in 1959 about her attempts to recover from an operation. But by 1969 she was forced to retire from the magazine. Her last two photo-essays were on Jesuits in America and America viewed from the air. As she became increasingly incapacitated, Margaret worked on her autobiography and in setting up an exhibition of her work in Boston. In 1971 she died in hospital.

Life published her best-known photographs in tribute and began their eulogy with the words 'Her pictures were her life'. Determined, aggressive and a perfectionist, she left a lasting memorial in her many iconic photographs of twentieth-century world events.

Katharine Hepburn

Confident, intelligent and witty, four-time Oscar winner Katharine Hepburn defied convention throughout her professional and personal life. The daughter of a suffragist, she specialized in portraying women who, like herself, steered their own course in life.

'If you obey all the rules, you miss all the fun.'

BIOGRAPHY

Name:	Katharine Houghton Hepburn, 'Kate'
Lived:	12 May 1907 – 29 June 2003
Place of birth:	Hartford, Connecticut
Place of death:	Old Saybrook, Connecticut
Nationality:	American
Famed as:	Award-winning stage, screen and television actress

Katharine was the second of six children in a wealthy New England family in Hartford, Connecticut. Her parents were noted liberals. Her father was a doctor, a urologist, and her mother was active in the cause of women's suffrage. Their well-publicized views on contentious issues of the time, such as birth control, the dangers of sexually-transmitted diseases and equal rights for women, meant that the family was sometimes ostracized, though Katharine later said, 'we grew quite to enjoy that'. Her background gave her both her distinctive, clipped New England accent and the capacity to ride out other people's disapproval, a useful life skill for a woman who always lived life on her own terms. Katharine was good at sports and achieved notable athletic success as a teenager in figure skating and golf. Later in her career she was able to harness her athletic ability to perform some of her own film stunts.

As a young girl, Katharine loved silent films and took odd jobs to earn the money to buy tickets for the latest releases. She made her first appearance as an actress in an amateur production when she was 12. Not particularly academic, she was sent to Bryn Mawr College to be educated, and although she managed to graduate in history and philosophy, she also spent a lot of time there acting in plays. The same year as her graduation, 1928, she made her debut on Broadway and married Ludlow Ogden Smith, a businessman and socialite. Their marriage was not a success, possibly because of Katharine's strong need for independence, and they soon separated amicably. They remained friends for life and only divorced in 1934 when Katharine had made her name in films.

FACTFILE

- The three-inch bronze sculpture of Spencer Tracy featured in the film *Guess Who's Coming for Dinner?* was created by Katharine Hepburn herself and was sold for $316, 000 in her estate auction in 2004.

- She based her interpretation of her character in *The African Queen* on Eleanor Roosevelt.

- Katharine received a record 12 Oscar nominations during her career. She held the record until 2003, the year of her death, when Meryl Streep overtook her.

Katharine continued to be given small parts on Broadway, in which she always made sufficient mark to ensure attention. In 1932, after receiving excellent reviews for a stage performance, the film studio RKO asked her to take a screen test for the film *A Bill of Divorcement*, which was to star John Barrymore, one of the top stars of his time. Although she was then earning only $80–$100 a week in the theatre, Katharine asked the studio for an incredible $1,500 per week. On the strength of her screen test they agreed, and she was contracted to make five films between 1932 and 1934. She won her first Oscar for her third film, *Morning Glory*, in 1933. Her fourth film, a 1933 version of *Little Women* in which she played the lead role of Jo March, was a massive box office success and the most successful picture of its day.

TIMELINE

Date	Katharine Hepburn	Related events
1907	Born in Connecticut	
1928	Broadway début Marriage to Ludlow Ogden Smith Wins Oscar for *Coquette*	Mary Pickford wins Best Actress
1933	Wins first Best Actress Oscar for *Morning Glory*	Charles Laughton wins Oscar for *The Private Lives of Henry VIII*
1939	Loses role of Scarlett O'Hara to Vivien Leigh	Vivien Leigh wins Oscar for *Gone with the Wind*, which also wins Best Picture
1940	Returns to screen success with *The Philadelphia Story*	James Stewart wins Best Actor Oscar for *The Philadelphia Story*
1941	Begins relationship with Spencer Tracy	
1951	Makes *The African Queen*; nominated for an Oscar	Humphrey Bogart wins Best Actor Oscar for *The African Queen*
1957		Humphrey Bogart dies aged 57
1967	Wins second Oscar for *Guess Who's Coming to Dinner?*	Spencer Tracy dies aged 67
1968	Wins third Oscar for *The Lion in Winter*, shared with Barbra Streisand (*Funny Girl*), the first ever tied vote	Academy Awards ceremony broadcast worldwide on television for the first time
1981	Wins fourth Oscar for *On Golden Pond*	Henry Fonda wins Best Actor Oscar for *On Golden Pond*
2003	Dies at her home in Connecticut	

However, although naturally delighted by the success of her films, RKO found Katharine's headstrong and independent style difficult to deal with. Her height, physique and bone structure made her a highly compelling screen presence, but off-screen she refused to conform in any way with the prevailing image of the Hollywood starlet. She usually dressed very casually in tennis shoes and overalls, wore no make-up and refused to pose for pictures or give interviews. The fact that she was a complete professional, letter perfect in her lines and totally researched in her roles counted for little in those days. Style was regarded as more important than substance.

The effect of this, and her reputation for being difficult, was that by 1938, when the critically acclaimed *Bringing Up Baby* demonstrated Katharine's strong flair for comedy, she had already lost box office appeal. When she failed to win the role of Scarlett O'Hara in the major adaptation of Margaret Mitchell's novel *Gone with the Wind*, she was labelled 'box office poison'. Undaunted, she returned to her stage roots on Broadway playing a wealthy socialite in *The Philadelphia Story*, a role specially written for her. Encouraged by her lover, multi-millionaire Howard Hughes, she bought the rights to the play and turned it into a hit movie in 1940, starring alongside Cary Grant and James Stewart. *The Philadelphia Story* resurrected her film career and has been voted one of the top 100 American films of all time by the American Film Institute. By now, she was in her early thirties and back at the top of her profession.

Katharine had numerous love affairs and almost married Howard Hughes, but called the engagement off at the last minute. Then in 1942 she worked with actor Spencer Tracy in the film *Woman of the Year*. This was the first of nine films they made together and the beginning of a 25-year love affair between the two. Tracy, a Roman Catholic, never married Katharine but their relationship lasted until his death in 1967. Their on-screen chemistry showed Katharine at her characteristic best – a feisty woman, with a mind of her own in a meeting of equals, a modern woman in a modern relationship. The pair brought out each other's strengths and became a legendary screen pairing.

As she grew older, Katharine survived as a screen star by choosing roles that suited her changing age. Perhaps the most memorable was *The African Queen* (1951), in which she starred with Humphrey Bogart and played a strait-laced missionary who falls in love with Bogart's alcoholic riverboat captain. The book she later wrote about the difficulties of making the film became a bestseller.

Acclaimed for her ability to master a range of roles, from the comedic to the dramatic and tragic, Katharine went on to play a series of middle-aged spinsters throughout the 1950s. During the 1960s she made fewer films, preferring to spend time with Tracy, who was now seriously ill. After a five-year absence they made their last film together in 1967, *Guess Who's Coming to Dinner?*, for which Katharine won her second Best Actress Oscar.

After Tracy's death, Katharine won her third Oscar for her performance as Eleanor of Aquitaine in *The Lion in Winter* (1968). In the 1970s she started making television films, which included memorable appearances in Tennessee Williams' *The Glass Menagerie* (1973) and Emlyn Williams' *The Corn is Green* (1969). Her fourth Oscar win was for her appearance in *On Golden Pond* (1981), which also featured Henry Fonda. Like Fonda, Katharine was also unwell, suffering from a neurological illness that caused uncontrollable shaking. It was the last film for Fonda, who died in 1982.

In 1991 Katharine published her autobiography, *Me: Stories of My Life*. She appeared in her last feature film in 1994. She then withdrew from public life as her health declined and died at her home in Connecticut in 2003, aged 96.

Although her family background gave her privileges to which many of her female fans could never aspire, Katharine Hepburn provided an image of an assertive woman whom they could watch and learn from. She showed that it was acceptable for a woman to speak her mind, be physically active, talk back in a relationship and refuse to bow down to the demands of even the most powerful Hollywood studios. Although this did not guarantee her popularity, and put her at odds with men – and women at times – she provided a role model for future generations and showed that women could take on a male and money-dominated system and triumph over it.

Simone de Beauvoir

Simone de Beauvoir was one of the greatest philosophers of the twentieth century. Her famous book, *The Second Sex*, in which she analyzed the systematic devaluation of women throughout history, scandalized post-war Europe.

'This has always been a man's world, and none of the reasons that have been offered in explanation have seemed adequate.'

BIOGRAPHY

Name:	Simone Lucie-Ernestine-Marie Bertrand de Beauvoir
Lived:	9 January 1908 – 14 April 1986
Place of birth:	Paris, France
Place of death:	Paris, France
Nationality:	French
Famed as:	Author, philosopher and feminist

Simone de Beauvoir was born into a middle-class French family, the eldest daughter of Georges Bertrand de Beauvoir, a lawyer, and Françoise Brasseur. Simone's mother was a devout Roman Catholic, and Simone and her younger sister Hélène were raised in a strict Catholic manner. The sisters were extremely close throughout their lives.

Although Georges' fortunes declined after World War I, the family was still wealthy enough to educate their daughters privately at a Catholic girls' school. Georges did not share his wife's religious conviction and encouraged his daughters to be free thinkers. Simone began to question Christian doctrine, and at the age of 14 she realized she no longer had a belief in God. She was a declared atheist from this time, resolved to live the life of the intellect, rather than the spirit.

An outstanding student, Simone was awarded honours in the *baccalauréat* in 1925. She and her sister knew that their father's precarious finances meant that they would have to work for a living, and Simone decided that she wanted to write and teach philosophy. In 1927 she began to study at the Sorbonne, in the University of Paris.

FACTFILE

- Sartre's nickname for Simone was 'Castor', the French for beaver, a pun on her name and a reference to her dedication to hard work. His letters to her almost invariably began 'My darling Beaver'.

- Simone and Sartre read and edited one another's novels from the beginning of their relationship. The full extent of her contributions to his work became known only after her death.

- Over 5000 people attended Simone's funeral in 1986.

In 1929 she attended classes at the École Normale Supérieure, an élite graduate school, to prepare for the *agrégation* in philosophy. This teaching qualification was competed for only by the most exceptional students. Her main competitors were three men: Jean-Paul Sartre, who was sitting the examination for the second time, Paul Nizan and Jean Hyppolite. All three were enrolled at the École Normale, while Simone attended classes informally. Sartre came first and Simone second. At 21, she was the youngest person ever to be awarded the qualification and became part of the rather forbidding, intellectually exclusive coterie that formed around Sartre. The two were to remain together for the rest of Sartre's life.

The *agrégation* virtually guaranteed Simone, Sartre, Nizan and other members of their circle jobs for life in the state education system. Simone taught in lycées all over the country for the next few years, and was working in Paris when the Germans invaded France in 1940. She left her post in 1943 and never taught again. Their philosophical coterie had largely ignored political events throughout the 1930s, but the occupation of France ended their detachment. Sartre, who had been conscripted, was briefly imprisoned by the Germans but released in 1941 and he and Simone remained in Paris throughout the war. Sartre became involved with the French

TIMELINE

Date	Simone de Beauvoir	Related events
1908	Born in Paris	
1929	Meets Jean-Paul Sartre	
1938		Jean-Paul Sartre publishes *Nausea*
1940		Paul Nizan killed at Dunkirk
1941		Sartre joins French Resistance with Albert Camus
		Camus publishes *The Stranger*
1943	*She Came to Stay* published	
1945	*The Blood of Others* published	Sartre publishes the first volume of his *Roads to Freedom trilogy*
1947	Meets Nelson Algren	Camus publishes *The Plague*
1948	*America Day by Day* published	Catholic church puts all of Sartre's works on its index of prohibited books
1949	*The Second Sex* published	
1955	*The Mandarins* wins the Prix Goncourt	
1957		Albert Camus wins Nobel Prize for Literature
1959	*Memoirs of a Dutiful Daughter* published	
1960		Death of Albert Camus
1980		Death of Jean-Paul Sartre
1986	Dies in Paris	

Resistance movement as did Simone to a lesser extent, and their increasing politicization drew them towards Communism.

Simone, having abandoned her career in teaching, began to write. In 1943 her first novel, *She Came to Stay*, was published, a lightly fictionalized account of her and Sartre's three-way relationship with one of Simone's students. During the war, Simone completed four further books: *Useless Mouths*, *Pyrrhus and Cineas*, *The Blood of Others* and *All Men are Mortal*. *The Blood of Others*, which explored the problems of political activism and dilemmas experienced by a French Resistance leader during the war, was published in 1945 and attracted a great deal of critical interest. After the war, there was a proliferation of literature and art based on existentialist philosophy, which emphasizes the essential importance of individual freedom and the responsibility of choice. Simone's and Sartre's novels on these themes were wildly successful and they moved in circles with intellectuals and artists like Albert Camus, Pablo Picasso and Georges Bataille. Together they edited the leftist journal *Les temps modernes* – a monthly review that put them at the focus of an active intellectual community.

In the public imagination, Simone and Jean-Paul Sartre modelled existentialism and made philosophy look chic against a backdrop of Paris cafés and jazz clubs. Their unorthodox relationship and the individuals they created in their novels – men and women striking out bravely against faith, authority and tradition – seemed to typify the turbulent atmosphere of the post-war years. Half a century later, it is difficult to appreciate how revolutionary their social and philosophical stance was.

Simone became increasingly critical of capitalism after World War II. A five-month visit to the United States in 1947 seemed only to confirm her beliefs, although while there she fell in love with the novelist Nelson Algren – it was the start of a 15-year on–off relationship. By agreement, her relationship with Sartre allowed contingent affairs and both had several. In 1948, Simone published *America Day by Day*, a work that described the social problems, class inequality and racism she witnessed during her American tour.

Then in 1949, Simone published what was to become her best known and defining work – *The Second Sex*. Her book deplored the oppression of women who, she argued, had been thwarted throughout history by the generally accepted view that men were the norm and women an aberration from it. She claimed that history, myth and literature reinforced the idea of women as an inferior sex and rejected the idea that the male ideal was the only one to which women could aspire. These were also ideas that she confronted and dramatized in her fiction, which largely focused on women who take control of their lives and accept responsibility for the consequences of their actions. *The Second Sex* was banned by the Catholic church, which did no harm to its appeal, and Simone was fêted and insulted by commentators in more or less equal measure.

In 1955 *The Mandarins*, considered by some to be her best book, was published. It was based loosely on her relationships with Algren and Sartre and won the Prix Goncourt – the highest literary honour in France. Again banned by the Catholic church, it was dedicated to Algren, despite his unhappiness with the contents. Between 1958 and 1972, Simone published four autobiographical works – *Memoirs of a Dutiful Daughter*, *The Prime of Life*, *Force of Circumstance* and *All Said and Done*. These all demonstrated that, as far as possible, she lived like her heroines: an independent woman shaping her life with decisions she made for herself.

In her later books, Simone turned her focus to the subject of decline and death, depicting the problems of ageing and society's indifference to older people in *A Very Easy Death* and *Old Age*. In 1981 she published *A Farewell to Sartre* – an account of the last years of Sartre's life.

Apart from her writing, Simone dedicated her later life to the feminist movement, speaking out against the institutionalization of poor and unmarried mothers and becoming involved with demonstrations to legalize abortion in the 1970s. After the death of Sartre in 1980, her mental and physical health rapidly deteriorated and she became dependent on alcohol and amphetamines. She died of pneumonia in Paris on 14 April 1986 and was buried beside Sartre in the Cimetière de Montparnasse. 'Our relationship,' she said, 'was the greatest achievement of my life.'

Mother Teresa

Mother Teresa of Calcutta spent her life among the destitute and dying. She founded the Missionaries of Charity, who work with the poorest people of the world. She was awarded the Nobel Peace Prize in 1979 and was beatified by Pope John Paul II after her death.

'Love begins at home, and it is not how much we do, but how much love we put in the action that we do.'

BIOGRAPHY

Name:	Agnes Gonxha Bojaxhiu, Blessed Teresa of Calcutta
Lived:	27 August 1910 – 5 September 1997
Place of birth:	Skopje, Yugoslavia
Place of death:	Calcutta, India
Nationality:	Albanian
Famed as:	Missionary to the destitute, sick and dying worldwide

Born on 27 August, 1910 into an Albanian family, Agnes Gonxha Bojaxhiu was the youngest of five children, only three of whom survived. Little is known about her early life, although she recalled that her religious interests were already beginning to form while she was at primary school. By the age of 12 she had developed a particular interest in overseas missions and felt that her vocation was helping the poor. Her inspiration to work in India came from reports sent home by Jesuit missionaries.

When 18 she left home to join the Sisters of Loreto, a community of nuns based in Dublin, Ireland, known for their missionary work in India. In Ireland she was plunged into a different culture. Unable to speak English, she was remembered as being 'very small, quiet and shy', and even described as 'ordinary'.

FACTFILE

- For someone to be beatified, there needs to be documentary evidence of a miracle. In 2002, an Indian woman claimed that her cancer had been cured when she placed a locket containing the image of Mother Teresa on her stomach. This was recognized as a miracle by the Vatican. Evidence of a further miracle will be required before Mother Teresa can be canonized (become a saint).

- Mother Teresa used to be a geography teacher.

- She was criticized for the practice of baptizing the dying, without regard to their own religion.

The year 1929 brought another change in her life, when she was sent to Darjeeling in India, to join the congregation of Sisters of Loreto there. It was here that she made her first vows and chose the name Sister Mary Teresa, in honour of the saints Teresa of Avila and Thérèse of Lisieux. From 1937 she was always known as Mother Teresa. Her service began with a posting to St Mary's High School for girls in a district of Calcutta, where she taught for almost 15 years.

On 10 September 1946, during a train journey to Darjeeling, she received what she took to be a call from God. She felt urged to leave her teaching post and devote herself to working with the poorest and neediest in India. In her own words, she 'heard the call to give up all and follow Christ into the slums to serve him among the poorest of the poor'.

Leaving the safety and sheltered life of the convent, however, was not a straightforward process: there were a number of obstacles to overcome. The Church was initially resistant to her forming a new community and she had to seek the intercession of the Archbishop of Calcutta. In 1948 the Vatican granted her permission to leave the Sisters of Loreto and to start her new work under the Archbishop's guidance. Exchanging her habit for the simple sari and sandals of an ordinary Indian woman, Mother Teresa left the safe confines of the convent and school for the open, dirty streets of the larger world. Photographs of Mother Teresa

TIMELINE

Date	Mother Teresa	Related events
1910	Born in Yugoslavia	Balkan War (1910–12)
1928	Joins Sisters of Loreto in Ireland	Mohandas Gandhi demands independence for India at the Calcutta Congress
1929	Moves to India with Sisters of Loreto	
1937	Takes vows and is known as Mother Teresa	Hindi becomes national language of India. Schoolchildren are required to salute the image of Mohandas Gandhi
1948	Founds Missionaries of Charity	Assassination of Mohandas Gandhi Nehru becomes India's first Prime Minister
1952	Missionaries of Charity open first house for the dying	
1979	Awarded Nobel Prize for Peace	
1985	Awarded the Medal of Freedom, highest US civilian award	
1986		First case of AIDS diagnosed in India
1996	Becomes only the fourth person to be made an honorary US citizen	
1997	Dies in Calcutta	
2003	Beatified by Pope John Paul II	

nearly always show her in her plain white sari with a blue border, a simple cross at the shoulder.

After undergoing medical training, she formed a group, the Missionaries of Charity, whose members took the usual vows of poverty, chastity and obedience, and also a fourth vow, to give free help to the poorest people. Their mission, in Mother Teresa's words, was to care for 'the hungry, the naked, the homeless, the crippled, the blind, the lepers, all those who feel unwanted, unloved, uncared for throughout society, people that have become a burden to the society and are shunned by everyone.' She began by teaching the children of the slums how to read and write and the principles of basic hygiene, but gradually extended this to visiting the sick and the old as well.

The Missionaries of Charity began their distinctive work of ministering to the dying in 1952, when they took over a Hindu temple to the god Kali in Calcutta. The temple became Kalighat Home for the Dying, a refuge where the poorest people could go to ease their departure. The main goal was to give dignity and love to the old and terminally ill, regarding every individual as uniquely precious in God's sight. Mother Teresa's aims were straightforward – to help the disadvantaged and reduce their suffering – and she believed fervently that by serving the poor in this way she was directly serving Christ. In her speech on receiving the Nobel Prize, she said: 'He died on the cross...for you and for me and for that leper and for that man dying of hunger and that naked person lying in the street not only of Calcutta, but of Africa, and New York, and London, and Oslo – and insisted that we love one another as he loves each one of us.'

In 1957, the Missionaries began to work with lepers, and slowly extended their educational work. They also opened a home for orphans and abandoned children. In 1959 they expanded further, spreading their work to other Indian cities. Their focus remained on the poorest of the poor: orphans, the dying and those ostracized from society by disease. They soon had centres in more than 22 Indian cities and Mother Teresa travelled to Australia, Africa and South America to begin foundations. Poverty in these countries owed much to population growth, but the Missionaries of Charity were firmly opposed to contraception and abortion, which Mother Teresa described as 'the worst evil, and the greatest enemy of peace'.

The Missionaries of Charity and affiliated lay groups widened their activities throughout the 1970s, and Mother Teresa received international recognition and financial support. By 1979, when she accepted the Nobel Prize for Peace, she and her affiliated groups had more than 200 different operations in over 25 countries around the world. Later she sent her Missionaries of Charity into Russia, China and Cuba. The hallmark of all of Mother Teresa's works – from shelters for those dying of AIDS, to orphanages and homes for the mentally ill – is service to the very poor and needy.

Tiny but energetic, in old age her wrinkled face and glowing eyes familiar through the media, Mother Teresa maintained an aura of sanctity, little changed by the worldwide attention she received. She was the recipient of some of the world's highest honours, including the Albert Schweitzer International Prize, the US Presidential Medal of Freedom and the Congressional Gold Medal. She declined the usual celebrity dinner when she accepted the Nobel Prize and requested that the money saved should go to funds for the poor in Calcutta. She came to be known as the 'saint of the gutters' and the 'angel of mercy'. Her practical nature was combined with a complete lack of cynicism and an absolute belief in the love of God for his poorest creatures. She was not without her detractors, however. Her wisdom in accepting aid from certain politicians and individuals was frequently questioned, as was the Vatican's refusal to disclose the amount of money belonging to the Missionaries of Charity.

At the time of her death, Mother Teresa was still working with the Missionaries of Charity and died of a heart attack on 5 September 1997, at the age of 87. The Indian government gave her a state funeral and her body was buried in the Mother House of the Missionaries of Charity. Long before her death, books and articles had started to revere her, and in October 2003 she was beatified by Pope John Paul II. Her own words best sum up her life and its guiding principles: 'By blood, I am Albanian. By citizenship, an Indian. By faith, I am a Catholic nun. As to my calling, I belong to the world. As to my heart, I belong entirely to the heart of Jesus.'

Dorothy Hodgkin

The research work of Dorothy Hodgkin, Britain's first female Nobel laureate, enabled the mass production of life-saving antibiotics, insulin and vitamin B12. In retirement she campaigned for disarmament and on behalf of underdeveloped countries.

'She will be remembered as a great chemist, a saintly, gentle and tolerant lover of people and a devoted protagonist of peace.'

Max Perutz

BIOGRAPHY

Name:	Dorothy Crowfoot Hodgkin
Lived:	12 May 1910 – 29 July 1994
Place of birth:	Cairo, Egypt
Place of death:	Shipston-on-Stour, England
Nationality:	British
Famed as:	Pioneer of crystallography and a campaigner for disarmament and international relations

In the small class held in the Rectory at Beccles, Dorothy and her fellow pupils grew crystals from solutions of alum and copper sulphate. They looked on in wonder as the solution slowly evaporated and crystals formed. Dorothy, then aged just ten, was later to write: 'I was captured for life, by chemistry and by crystals.'

And yet a career in science was hardly an obvious choice for a girl from her background. Dorothy was born in Cairo, Egypt, the eldest of four daughters. Her father, John, was an archaeologist and scholar working for the Ministry of Education while her mother, Molly, was an expert in Coptic textiles and a gifted botanic artist. She was also a confirmed pacifist and campaigner for disarmament, beliefs that she transmitted to Dorothy, whose work in the same field was to become an important part of her later life.

FACTFILE

- In 1934, Dorothy was diagnosed with rheumatoid arthritis. Despite the crippling effect this had on her hands as she grew older, she continued to be a 'bench scientist', working on practical research.

- In 2003 Tony Blair launched the Dorothy Hodgkin Postgraduate Award Scheme, a new UK initiative to bring outstanding students from the developing world to study for doctorates in leading UK research facilities.

For the first four years of Dorothy's life the family lived the comfortable life of English expatriates overseas, but with the onset of World War I in 1914 Dorothy's mother feared for her daughters' safety outside the UK and took them home, placing them with John's parents. That task completed, she took a flight back to Egypt to be with her husband, and for the remainder of their childhood Dorothy and her sisters never lived with both parents for more than a month or two – an experience to which Dorothy credited her independent spirit and self-determination.

In the mid-1920s, Dorothy's parents were living in Sudan and Dorothy and her sisters were at school in England. Dorothy's passion for chemistry had been encouraged by her mother with the gift of Sir William Bragg's two published lectures, entitled *On the Nature of Things* and *Old Trades and New Knowledge*, which explained how scientists used X-rays to 'see' atoms and molecules. For Dorothy, the books were a revelation. At school, where the teaching was divided along traditional lines, only Dorothy and one other girl were allowed to join the chemistry class. Dorothy sat her School Leaving Certificate in 1927 and was awarded distinction in six subjects and an award of £30. The following year she was accepted to study chemistry at Somerville College, Oxford.

At that time, chemistry was chiefly an experimental discipline with rigid boundaries between its different branches. Students were called on to memorize vast amounts of information and carry out a set series of tests in practical classes. No one tried to explain why a particular element might be more reactive than another, or how the structure of a molecule might relate to its function. This was

TIMELINE

Date	Dorothy Hodgkin	Related events
1910	Birth of Dorothy Crowfoot	
1928		Alexander Fleming identifies penicillin
1932	Graduates from Oxford	Vitamin C isolated
1937	Awarded a PhD from Cambridge University Marries Thomas Hodgkin	
1945	Identifies the structure of penicillin	Alexander Fleming awarded Nobel Prize for Medicine
1947	Awarded Fellowship of Royal Society	
1953		Crick and Watson discover the structure of DNA
1956	Takes first photographs of vitamin B12	
1958		Fred Sanger awarded Nobel Prize for chemistry for identifying structure of the insulin molecule
1964	Nobel Prize for chemistry	
1967	Elucidates structure of insulin	
1994	Dies from a stroke	Death of Nobel Prize winning chemist Linus Pauling

not what Dorothy had come to Oxford for and she set about trying to learn more about the study of crystals – the subject that had first ignited her interest in chemistry. She was encouraged by her tutor to attend a special course in crystallography – a method used to determine the structure of molecules. Once molecular structure could be identified, ways of making synthetic versions of materials could be found, enabling the mass production of chemicals and drugs. Dorothy was fascinated by this process and began working on the structure of highly toxic thallium. She graduated in 1932 with a first-class degree.

That year, Dorothy moved to the University of Cambridge to begin research for her PhD, working on the structure of proteins and steroids, which she studied using X-ray crystallography. In 1933, Somerville College awarded her an unusual research fellowship, financing one year at Cambridge followed by another at Oxford.

Her first task on returning to Oxford was to do what she had been prevented from doing while she was at Cambridge – studying some crystals through to a complete analysis of their structures. Her colleague Robert Robinson, who helped Dorothy to obtain the funds she needed to equip her laboratory, saw that research in his own field of organic chemistry stood to benefit from the work of crystallographers. Dorothy was only too pleased to help him out. For his part he returned the favour; knowing of her previous work on the digestive enzyme pepsin, he gave her a small sample of protein to photograph. That protein was insulin.

The breakthrough in Dorothy's research came when she was still only 24. She specialized in tackling problematic subjects, and the structures of the three molecules on which she concentrated – insulin, penicillin and vitamin B12 – are particularly complicated. In 1934, she was able to crystallize and photograph the insulin molecule, a vital step in her research, she was to continue for nearly 40 years.

In 1937, Dorothy was awarded her PhD from Cambridge and married Thomas Hodgkin, an expert on African affairs, who came from a family of high academic achievers. There was no thought in Dorothy's mind that marriage would prevent her from working, even though, at that time, all women were still required to resign their college Fellowships on marriage. However, by this time, any women who wished to be reinstated almost always were, and Dorothy was no exception. She and Thomas went on to have three children. Friends recall their family home as an open house for students and visitors, bustling with activity.

From 1942 Dorothy worked on penicillin and, three years later, she identified the structure of the penicillin molecule. This work led to other scientists being able to modify the structure of penicillin and create many varieties of antibiotic, adapted to fight specific infections. In 1947 Dorothy was awarded the Fellowship of the Royal Society, Britain's élite scientific association.

As well as her research work, Dorothy was a fellow and chemistry tutor at Somerville College, where she taught Margaret Thatcher, the future British Prime Minister. She also visited universities around the world, although she was denied a visa to attend a scientific conference in the US in 1953 because she had been a member of Science for Peace – a group that had Communist connections.

In 1956 Dorothy took the first photographs of vitamin B12, but it was another five years before she was able to determine the vitamin's structure, working with Kenneth Trueblood, a young American crystallographer. Among crystallographers, the success with vitamin B12 was instantly recognized as setting a new standard. In 1964 Dorothy was awarded the Nobel Prize for chemistry, 'for her determinations by X-ray techniques of the structures of important biochemical substances'.

In 1967, Dorothy finally elucidated the complicated structure of insulin, which was to lead to an understanding of how insulin reduces the symptoms of diabetes. Three years later she was elected Chancellor of Bristol University, where she remained until her retirement in 1977.

Dorothy's retirement was not to be restful. From 1977 to 1989 she was president of Pugwash, an international organization of scientists who, during the Cold War, tried to further communication between scientists on both sides of the Iron Curtain. A lifelong supporter of campaigns for world peace and disarmament, she advocated aid for countries in the developing world. Dorothy continued to campaign for the use of science as a way of promoting international understanding until prevented by poor health. She died at her home from a stroke in 1994.

Rosa Parks

Rosa Parks changed the course of American history when she refused to give up her bus seat to a white man on a routine journey in 1955. She became a figurehead for generations of black Americans, to whom she was 'the mother of the civil rights movement'.

'Our mistreatment was just not right, and I was tired of it.'

BIOGRAPHY

Name:	Rosa Louise McCauley
Lived:	4 February 1913 – 25 October 2005
Place of birth:	Tuskegee, Alabama
Nationality:	American
Famed as:	Iconic figure of US civil rights movement

The actions of this extraordinary woman marked the beginning of the modern civil rights movement in the United States. On 1 December 1955, Rosa, a seamstress in Montgomery, Alabama, refused to give up her bus seat to a white male passenger. Rosa was weary after a long, hard day's work, but this was by no means her sole reason for refusing to leave her seat. She was also tired of the treatment she and other African-Americans were made to endure every day of their lives under the racist laws of the time, which endorsed social segregation. Rosa was arrested and fined for disorderly behaviour. Her solitary act of rebellion not only inspired freedom-lovers everywhere but also led ultimately to the end of legal segregation in America.

FACTFILE

- Rosa tried to register to vote – her legal right – three times between 1943 and 1945. She was successful on her third attempt.

- In 1965, she joined Coretta Scott King, wife of Martin Luther King, to speak before the national meeting of the Women's Public Affairs Committee, a multiracial group dedicated to racial harmony.

- In 2000, the Rosa Parks Museum was dedicated at Troy State University, Montgomery, in her presence.

- Rosa was the first woman whose body was displayed for public viewing in the Rotunda of the Capitol, an honour normally reserved for presidents and war heroes.

Rosa's father, James McCauley, was a carpenter and her mother, Leona McCauley, a teacher. Her grandparents had been slaves. She grew up in extremely difficult times for black citizens, as racism was rife and segregation was strict, involving the brutal exclusion of black citizens from many public places. In an interview, she recalled the fear she used to feel as a child: 'Back then we didn't have any civil rights. It was just a matter of survival, of existing from one day to the next. I remember going to sleep as a girl hearing the Klan ride at night and hearing a lynching and being afraid the house would burn down.'At the age of 11 Rosa enrolled in the Montgomery Industrial School for Girls, a private, all-black, liberal school that had a philosophy of self-value that no doubt influenced Rosa in later life. Her schooling shaped her personality and sense of morality: she always had a strong desire to right society's wrongs. In her autobiography, published in 1993, Rosa said that school taught her 'that I was a person with dignity and self-respect, and I should not set my sights lower than anybody else just because I was black.'

Rosa attended Alabama State Teachers College, but had to leave before qualifying to nurse her sick grandmother. She met and married Raymond Parks, a member of the National Association for the Advancement of Colored People (NAACP), and they settled in Montgomery where Rosa had a job as a seamstress. The couple worked for many years to improve the lives of African-Americans. They also campaigned for

TIMELINE

Date	Rosa Parks	Related events
1913	Born in Tuskegee, Alabama	
1942		Congress of Racial Equality formed
1943	Becomes secretary of the Montgomery NAACP	
1948		President Truman orders the desegregation of all US troops
1955	Arrested for not giving up her seat on a Montgomery bus	Montgomery bus boycott begins Martin Luther King leads the Montgomery Improvement Association
1960		Civil Rights Act signed into law
1962		President John F. Kennedy sends the National Guard to support black student James Meredith when he registers at the University of Mississippi
1963	Attends the March on Washington	Martin Luther King delivers 'I have a dream' speech Assassination of President John F. Kennedy
1968		Assassination of Martin Luther King
1987	Founds Rosa and Raymond Parks Institute for Self-Development	
1996	Awarded Presidential Medal of Freedom	
1999	Awarded Congressional Gold Medal	
2005	Dies in Detroit, Michigan	

the defence of the Scottsboro boys, nine black youths who were accused of the rape of two white women in 1931. Despite overwhelming evidence of their innocence – including an admission from one of the women that she had lied in accusing them – they were sentenced to death. It took 20 years of appeals and retrials before they were acquitted.

By the time of the Montgomery bus incident in 1955, Rosa was a seasoned civil rights campaigner. In an interview in 1995, she was asked if she had felt anger at being asked to give up her seat on that particular day. She replied: 'I don't remember feeling that anger, but I did feel determined to take this as an opportunity to let it be known that I did not want to be treated in that manner and that people have endured it far too long. However, I did not have at the moment of my arrest any idea of how the people would react.'

But reaction was immediate and highly effective. The very next day, the Montgomery Improvement Association was formed, led by the young pastor of the Dexter Avenue Baptist Church, Dr Martin Luther King Jr. They called for a boycott of the city-owned bus company by all its black customers. The boycott lasted 382 days and buses stood idle for months. A Supreme Court decision ended the boycott, and Rosa was fined, but racial segregation on public transport was outlawed.

In 1957 Rosa and Raymond moved to Detroit and continued to work in civil rights. They struggled financially until Rosa was hired as an administrative assistant by congressional representative John F. Conyers Jr, from 1965 until 1987. After the death of her husband in 1977, Rosa established the Rosa and Raymond Parks Institute for Self-Development. The institute is dedicated to spreading the knowledge of civil rights history among young people. It sponsors an annual summer programme for 11–18 year olds called Pathways to Freedom, which allows young people to tour the country in buses, visiting the scenes of critical events in the civil rights movement and learning about the history of their country.

The phase of the civil rights movement that began with Rosa's bus protest and climaxed with the assassination of Martin Luther King in 1968 was scarred by a series of violent demonstrations and murders. Yet the movement was supported by legislation and grounded in the principle of non-violent protest. Rosa never endorsed violence, which contradicted her deep Christian faith. Her belief in God, she claimed, had given her strength throughout her life. In August 1994, when she was over 80, she was attacked in her home by a young man who wanted money. Rather than condemning the man, she sympathized with him and prayed for him, blaming instead 'the conditions in our country that have made him this way'.

Rosa received numerous awards, including honorary degrees from several universities, the Martin Luther King Jr Award in 1980 and the Eleanor Roosevelt Women of Courage Award. In 1996, President Bill Clinton awarded her the Presidential Medal, the highest award that can be given to a US citizen, and in 1999 she was awarded the prestigious Congressional Gold Medal, which had previously been awarded to Mother Teresa in 1997 and to Nelson Mandela in 1998.

Rosa was a vocal opponent of apartheid in South Africa and travelled the world meeting community and political leaders. In the last years of her life, she still made around 30 personal appearances a year. Known throughout the United States as 'the mother of the civil rights movement', she was always modest about her achievements: 'Four decades later I am still uncomfortable with the credit given to me for starting the bus boycott. I would like them to know I was not the only person involved. I was just one of many who fought for freedom.'

Rosa could not have foreseen or planned it, but her spontaneous decision to remain seated on the bus on 1 December 1955 changed the lives of hundreds of thousands of black Americans. She became a symbol of hope for those who suffered the daily indignities of life in a racist society. In 1995, she said, 'We still have a long way to go, we still have many obstacles and many challenges to face. It's far from perfect, and it may never be, but I think as long as we do the best we can to improve conditions, then people will be benefited.' Rosa died peacefully at her home in Detroit on 25 October 2005, aged 92.

Jiang Qing

Jiang Qing's marriage to Chairman Mao transformed her from a minor actress into one of the most infamous political figures of the twentieth century. As a member of the Chinese Politburo, and the notorious Gang of Four, she was responsible for the imprisonment and murder of countless numbers of artists and intellectuals, deemed enemies of the Cultural Revolution.

'I was Chairman Mao's dog. What he told me to bite, I bit.'

BIOGRAPHY

Name:	Luan Shu-meng, Jiang Qing, Madame Mao
Lived:	March 1914 (date uncertain) – 14 May 1991
Place of birth:	Shandong Province, China
Place of death:	Beijing, China
Nationality:	Chinese
Occupation:	Actress, member of Chinese Politburo, one of the Gang of Four

Jiang Qing, or Chiang Ch'ing, was born Luan Shu-meng in Shandong Province in China in 1914. The daughter of a carpenter, she was brought up by her grandfather, and had some drama training during her teens. She went on to study literature at Qingdao University and while there came into contact with left-wing ideas.

A beauty in her youth, Jiang Qing wanted to be an actress and in 1929 she became a member of a theatrical troupe. Going by the stage name Lan P'ing in Shanghai during the 1930s, she gained various roles in films and on the stage, including that of Nora in Ibsen's *A Doll's House*. In 1937, when the Japanese attacked Shanghai, she fled to the Chinese Nationalist wartime capital and worked for the government-controlled Central Movie Studio. She then crossed national lines to join Communist forces in Yan'an.

FACTFILE

- During the Cultural Revolution, traditional opera was banned in China. To replace it, Jiang Qing devised *Yang Ban Xi* – operas with an uplifting Communist message. Among the titles were *On the Docks, Red Detachment of Women, Taking Tiger Mountain by Strategy* and *The White Haired Girl*.

- So desperate was Jiang Qing to read Erich Segal's novel *Love Story* that she summoned a translator, who had been demoted to pig farmer during the Cultural Revolution, to appear before her and translate the novel.

- Jiang Qing loved luxury, at least in her later years. During the Cultural Revolution, she watched films that the rest of the population were forbidden to see in her private screening room and had access to private estates.

At Yan'an she began to study Marxist-Leninist theory formally and received some military training. She also worked as a drama instructor at the Lu Hsun Art Academy and it was here she met Mao when he visited the school. He was so irresistibly drawn by her beauty, sophistication and poise that in spite of Party disapproval he divorced his then ailing second wife to marry her. He did, however, agree to one proviso from the Party – that this new wife should not become involved in politics. For 30 years Jiang Qing did, indeed, stay outside the political arena, simply acting as an appropriate consort for the Chairman by hosting events for foreign visitors and sitting on a few cultural committees. This was not, however, because she had no political views of her own, nor because she lacked ambitions for power. The extent of these was to become apparent during the 1960s as she gradually gained ascendancy during the Cultural Revolution.

By 1959 it was clear that confidence in Mao had declined following the failure of his plan to industrialize China, his Great Leap Forward, which resulted in a terrible famine during which millions died. From the guarded compound where he and his wife lived, though in separate quarters, he began to plan the launch of the last government campaign of his life: his Cultural Revolution, encouraged by his wife and left-wing supporters. Now that Mao was in disagreement with the Party

TIMELINE

Date	Jiang Qing	Related events
1914	Born in Shandong Province, China	
1929	Joins a theatrical troupe	
1933	Joins Communist Party of China	
1934		Start of Mao's Long March
1937		Start of Second Sino Japanese War (ends 1945)
1938	Marries Mao Zedong	
1949	People's Republic of China established	Chinese custom of foot binding banned by Communists, but carries on in some areas until 1957
1958–60		China's Great Leap Forward – ends in failure
1966–76		Cultural Revolution in China
1966	Appointed deputy director of Cultural Revolution	
1969	Elected to the Politburo	
1972		President Richard Nixon visits China
1976	Mao Zedong dies. Gang of Four, including Jiang Qing, arrested	Major earthquake in northern China; government refuses outside aid
1981	Trial of the Gang of Four. Jiang Qing condemned to death, commuted to life imprisonment	
1991	Released on medical grounds Commits suicide	

establishment, Jiang Qing no longer felt restrained by their requirement for her to remain outside politics. Through the 1960s she built a role for herself as an individual, rather than Madame Mao, and this was reflected in her appointment to the Politburo, the chief governing body in China at the time.

The goals of the Cultural Revolution were 'to smash those Capitalists in power, to criticize the reactionary bourgeois "authorities" in science, to transform education, to transform literature and art'. Jiang Qing ardently attacked feudal and bourgeois influences in the arts and literature. She and other radicals wanted to rid the arts of what they viewed as its obsession with subjects like monarchy, romance and beauty. She encouraged the creation of new works with proletarian and revolutionary themes. However, this programme of change was not limited to modifying art forms and became a vehicle for the persecution, torture and murder of thousands of artists and intellectuals.

As one of the few people Mao still trusted, Jiang Qing was appointed First Deputy Head of the Cultural Revolution. This gave her far-reaching powers that she exploited mercilessly to suppress a wide range of political and non-political cultural activities and to spread terror throughout China. She also pursued personal vendettas against her political enemies, whom she had hunted down, publicly humiliated and killed. Deng Xiaoping, who was to be China's senior leader after Mao's death, was one of many Party Members who was physically abused and disgraced. In addition, Jiang Qing whipped up the Red Guard with strong speeches, stirring up much of the senseless violence that swept the country during this time. The Red Guards carried out random executions of 'counter-revolutionaries', and destroyed religious buildings, ancient artefacts, paintings, sculptures and libraries. Anyone who could be labelled an intellectual, on any pretext, was in danger. It is not entirely clear whether Jiang Qing had Mao's active support or just his passive acceptance. As his health began to decline her power increased, although she was obstructed by the more moderate prime minister, Zhou Enlai.

Jiang Qing's powers declined in the late 1960s but, although now widely hated, she was safe while Mao lived. As he grew older, Mao had named Hua Guofeng as his chosen successor. Hua was not the choice of Jiang Qing or other members of the Gang of Four, the name given to the group of Jiang Qing's sympathizers by Chinese moderates. In the weeks before Mao's death in September 1976 it seemed that the Gang were planning some sort of coup. However, they were thwarted by the quick thinking of their political opponents. Posters began to appear denouncing the Gang, and in October they were arrested. Vilified by monstrous cartoons in the press, Jiang Qing became the main object of propaganda against the Gang of Four, probably intensified by ambivalent feelings in China towards women, especially their involvement in politics.

Jiang Qing was, by now, widely hated for the terror she had helped inflict on the country. The Gang of Four were accused of subverting the government and 'framing and persecuting to death' many thousands of innocent people. The trial was televised. It was dramatic and compelling viewing. Jiang Qing claimed angrily that she had acted only to carry out Mao's wishes. She challenged the court to execute her and on several occasions had to be removed from the defendant's stand. The death sentence initially passed on her was commuted to life imprisonment. Her worst punishment was probably having to watch while Deng Xiaoping, her old enemy, began to transform the country she had for a while ruled.

Jiang Qing hanged herself while on release from prison in 1991 for treatment for throat cancer. The death of the woman who had known fame in many different forms was barely mentioned in the Chinese press. In 1984 a biography of her had been published, entitled *The White-Boned Demon*. It identified her as rage-filled, demonic, vindictive, cruel and emotionally needy. This seems to be how history is content to recall her. Inspired originally by genuine political enthusiasm for socialism, Jiang Qing still has her admirers in hard-line Communist circles, but for most she exemplifies the saying that all power corrupts and absolute power corrupts absolutely.

Billie Holiday

Billie Holiday was an international jazz star who gave definitive interpretations of some of the greatest songs of the twentieth century. Despite her talent, beauty and success, she struggled all her life with the legacy of her broken childhood, the lure of destructive relationships and a fatal addiction to drugs.

'You can be up to your boobies in white satin, with gardenias in your hair and no sugar cane for miles, but you can still be working on a plantation.'

BIOGRAPHY

Name:	Eleanora Fagan
Lived:	7 April 1915 – 17 July 1959
Place of birth:	Philadelphia, Pennsylvania
Place of death:	New York
Nationality:	American
Famed as:	Jazz singer

Never taught, Billie Holiday had an innate musical sense that was to earn her the title First Lady of the Blues. Her combination of skilful phrasing, emotional depth and a laconic poignancy was a unique talent, and many consider hers to have been the most expressive jazz voice of the twentieth century.

It seems highly likely that the emotional truth Billie brought to her performances was fuelled by her tempestuous personal experiences. Both an alcoholic and a drug addict, attracted to abusive men and full of behavioural contradictions, Billie was someone whose professional and financial success was not mirrored in her private life. Unable to conquer her drug addiction, she squandered and was cheated of her money, and her career was punctuated by periods in hospital and prison. When she died, aged 44, her voice was ravaged by her lifestyle, although her technical mastery remained. Her talent lives on in the recordings that are still widely sold today.

FACTFILE

- While Billie broke the colour barrier by becoming one of the first black jazz singers of that era to perform with white musicians, nevertheless she was still made to use the back entrance of some clubs and forced to wait in a dark room away from the audience before appearing on stage.

- UK music and entertainment magazine *Q* has identified *Strange Fruit* as one of ten songs that actually changed the world.

- Billie's autobiography (1956) was ghost-written by William Dufty. It was called *Lady Sings the Blues*, but Billie had wanted to call it *Bitter Crop*.

- 'Jazz royalty' is a term that reflects the great jazz musicians who have some sort of royal title in their name or nickname. Billie Holiday was known as Lady Day, Ella Fitzgerald was the First Lady of Song. There was also the King (Jo Oliver), the Duke (Duke Ellington), the Count (Count Basie) and the Earl (Earl Hines).

Billie was born Eleanora Fagan in Philadelphia, the daughter of a black domestic aged 13 and a professional jazz guitarist aged 15 – a couple who lived together only briefly. She was brought up in Baltimore and New York City. The precise facts of her early life are unknown. She never read her ghost-written autobiography and was a skilful fabricator. It seems she dropped out of school when very young and first came across jazz while carrying out errands for a brothel owner, who allowed her to listen to recordings of Louis Armstrong and Bessie Smith. These were to be her role models as she practised singing.

Billie and her mother worked as prostitutes before they moved to New York in the early 1930s, where they struggled to make a living. Settling in Harlem in 1931, Billie found work as a singer in various bars and was an instant success. It was in one of these nightclubs that she was discovered by the producer John Hammond. He gave her an introduction to Benny Goodman in 1933 and she made her first recording with Goodman's band. The professional name she chose for herself came from the

TIMELINE

Date	Billie Holiday	Related events
1915	Born in Philadelphia	Trumpeter King Oliver forms a band with clarinetist Sidney Bechet
1920		Birth of the Jazz Age Start of Prohibition
1930	Moves to New York City to join her mother	Duke Ellington records *Mood Indigo*
1933	Makes first recording, with Benny Goodman	Bessie Smith makes her final recording
1934	Appears with Duke Ellington in the film *Symphony in Black*	Clarinetist Jimmy Dorsey and trombonist Tommy Dorsey form the Dorsey Brothers Orchestra
1935–42	Makes many classic recordings with pianist Teddy Wilson, including *What a Little Moonlight Can Do*	Ella Fitzgerald makes her first recordings
1937	Debut with Count Basie's Band	Bessie Smith dies in a car accident
1939	Records *Strange Fruit*	Glenn Miller records *In The Mood*
1946	First solo concert in New York's Town Hall	Charlie Parker and Dizzy Gillespie perform at 'Jazz at the Philharmonic' in Los Angeles
1954	Tours Europe and plays the Royal Albert Hall, London	The Dave Brubeck Quartet records *Jazz Goes To College*
1959	Arrested for possession of drugs and dies in New York	Miles Davis records *Kind of Blue* Clarinetist Sidney Bechet dies

first name of the film star Billie Dove and the surname of her father, Clarence Holiday.

From 1935 to 1942 Billie gained public recognition through more than 100 recordings she made with small jazz groups, most of which featured the pianist Teddy Wilson. These recordings, made rapidly and at minimum cost, were to become jazz classics. Their success at the time led to Hammond arranging for her to appear with the best musicians of the day, the Count Basie Orchestra in 1937 and Artie Shaw's Band in 1938. However, Billie was not happy for long with life in a big band and from January 1939 appeared solo for nine months at the new Greenwich Village club, Café Society. Here she introduced the extraordinary song with which she is most associated, *Strange Fruit* – a protest song about lynching written by Abel Meeropol (Lewis Allan). The stark simplicity of the lyrics and Billie's delivery instantly marked *Strange Fruit* as a part of American, and musical, history. At this time she also made many recordings with the saxophonist Lester Young, with whom she had a relationship. It was Young who gave her the sobriquet Lady Day.

By the end of the 1930s Billie was a well-established star, and was to remain one for 20 years in spite of a highly tempestuous personal life. Her first public solo concert took place in 1946 at New York's Town Hall and she also appeared in several films, including *New Orleans* in 1947 with Louis Armstrong.

Billie's relationships with men were often brief and disastrous. She was married for a short time in 1941 to Jimmy Monroe, and later to trumpeter Joe Guy, with whom she toured in 1945 – together running a band that lost large amounts of money. These personal and business failures, together with a heroin addiction that began in the 1940s and heavy drinking, combined to produce a decline in Billie's health and circumstances. She spent increasing lengths of time in prison and hospital. In March 1948, immediately after release from a prison term, she gave a triumphant concert in Carnegie Hall and for another ten years she continued to work, although her criminal record meant that she was banned from many New York clubs and her dependence on drugs meant that stage performances were sometimes poor.

In 1954 Billie made her first trip to Europe, touring in eight countries with a group of American jazz musicians. She was rapturously received and then went on to perform solo in Britain, where she met with huge success at London's Albert Hall. However, some feel this success was due in part to pity from audiences seeing a decline in her talent that seemed to mirror her private sorrows. A further marriage in the mid-1950s to Louis McKay, who had associations with organized crime, quickly went wrong.

Her final appearance was in June 1959 at a benefit concert in New York. A few days later, as she lay dying from cirrhosis of the liver in the Metropolitan Hospital, she was arrested for the possession of illegal drugs. When she died she was virtually penniless, apart from a cash advance from a magazine for some articles about her life that was found strapped to her leg.

Remembered variously as self-destructive, independent but at times pathetically reliant, Billie was reckless in love and highly promiscuous before her drug-addiction set in. However, she was also said by those who knew her well to have been charismatic and to have a deep gift for friendship. The most famous photograph of her is a sophisticated image of her in evening dress with white gardenias in her hair. Other more candid photographs reveal her pensiveness and vulnerability.

Billie Holiday's singing style was distinguished by her ability to bring deeply personal interpretations to her songs. Although she had no technical training and a limited vocal range, by singing slightly behind the beat and subtly altering a melody or the phrasing of a lyric she achieved a vocal effect that resembled a jazz instrument. Her voice could be at once quiet and powerful. Songs such as *Gloomy Sunday* and *God Bless the Child* expressed both her great talent and her incredible pain. Once asked about her skill, she said simply that she did not know any other way to sing: 'I've lived songs like that.' Some critics have argued that her forte was not so much jazz as her ability to bring jazz qualities to other types of popular music. Her voice can be heard at its best in the vintage recordings made between 1936 and 1945, during her professional liaison with Lester Young.

Eva Perón

Both hated and adored in her lifetime, Eva Perón, second wife of President Juan Perón of Argentina, was the champion of the poor in her country. Her beauty and dedication drew her admiration from around the world and her tragic early death confirmed her as one of the female icons of the twentieth century.

'I have one thing that counts and that is my heart. It burns in my soul, it aches in my flesh and it ignites my nerves: that is my love for the people and Perón.'

BIOGRAPHY

Name:	Maria Eva Duarte, also known as Evita
Lived:	7 May 1919 – 26 July 1952
Place of birth:	Los Toldos, Argentina
Place of death:	Buenos Aires, Argentina
Nationality:	Argentinian
Famed as:	Actress, politician, heroine of the Argentinian people

Eva Perón was one of five illegitimate children of an unmarried cook, Juana Ibarguren, and her married lover, Juan Duarte. Her mother and sisters earned money by working for wealthy families. At an early age Eva was aware of the gulf in Argentinian society.

Eva went to school but was not a promising pupil. However, her early love of acting and drama was apparent even then. Her teachers recalled her entertaining the lower grade children with songs and poems and stories. She became known locally for her skills in poetry recitation and, after a part in a school play, became determined to be an actress.

FACTFILE

- Eva died of uterine cancer, the illness that killed Perón's first wife.

- Juan Perón married his third wife, nightclub singer Isabel Martínez de Perón, in 1961.

- In 1987 Juan Perón's tomb was violated and the hands of his corpse stolen. This was seen, in retrospect, as some justification for moving Eva Perón's body so often.

- *Evita*, a musical by Andrew Lloyd Webber based on the life of Eva Perón, was a huge stage hit in London and New York and made into a film starring Madonna.

Eva encouraged a degree of obscurity about her past and a number of stories are told. One is that when Eva was 15, a tango singer called Agustín Magaldi persuaded her mother to let her go to Buenos Aires with him. Eva went, but for four years life there was difficult. She was extremely beautiful, but very thin and in poor health. This made it hard for her to secure many acting roles. However, after landing some modelling jobs and a few acting roles in the theatre and on screen, in 1939, aged 20, she was given an important role in a radio soap opera. She became a popular radio actress, starring in many plays and in particular a series starting in 1943 on Radio Belgrano on the lives of important women, in which she played Elizabeth I of England and Catherine the Great, among others.

In 1943 the political atmosphere in Argentina was tense. On 4 June a military coup installed General Pedro Ramirez as President. As his Secretary of Labour he chose the then little-known General Juan Perón. Perón used this position to build the foundations for his future popularity and support from the working classes. The following year an earthquake in the Andes killed 7000 people and Perón organized a national campaign of relief, inviting most of the popular stars of the day to attend. It was at a benefit festival on 22 January that he and Eva met and fell in love. They were apparently well suited: Perón was dashing, handsome and recently widowed, Eva young and glamorous, and both were equally ambitious. Eva was his mistress for two years and during that time Perón gradually rose to power.

Perón's popularity with the working people was vital when he was imprisoned in 1945 by Ramirez, who was angered by Pérón's increasing power base. Eva rallied

TIMELINE

Date	Eva Perón	Related events
1919	Born in Los Toldos	Mussolini founds the Fascist movement in Milan, Italy
1939	Appears in first radio show	Start of World War II
1945	Marries Juan Perón	End of World War II
1946	Visits Europe and meets heads of state, including Spain's General Franco	First meeting of the United Nations
1951	Withdraws her candidacy as Vice-President	Juan Perón re-elected as President of Argentina
1952	Dies in Buenos Aires Her body is embalmed and displayed until 1955	National revolution in neighbouring Bolivia
1955	Eva's body is flown to Spain	Overthrow of Juan Perón, who takes refuge in Paraguay
1971	Eva's body returned for burial in Buenos Aires	
1973		Perón returns to Argentina as President. His wife Isabel serves as Vice-President, continuing as President after his death in 1974
1976		Military junta takes control in Argentina
1978		*Evita* opens in London's West End

support in the trade unions and managed to get him released, confirming his status as most powerful man in Argentina. Perón and Eva married quietly in 1945, partly because of her lowly status as an actress and because, having been his mistress, she was disliked by Perón's army friends and women in higher social circles. Eva seemed to adore Perón as much as he did her: 'I was not, nor am I, anything more than a humble woman, a sparrow in an immense flock of sparrows. But Perón was, and is, a gigantic condor that flies high and sure among the summits and near to God. If it had not been for him who came down to my level and taught me to fly in another fashion, I would never have known what a condor is like, nor ever have been able to contemplate the marvellous and magnificent immenseness of my people. That is why neither my life nor my heart belongs to me, and nothing of all that I am or have is mine. All that I am, all that I have, all that I think and all that I feel, belongs to Perón.' However, in later years tensions became apparent in their relationship. Although Eva was always careful to concede precedence to her husband, the personality cult that began to surround her seemed to diminish him and after her death, his popularity fell.

Soon after their wedding Perón became President. During his presidential campaign Eva had won adulation from the masses, whom she addressed as *Los descamisados*, 'the shirtless'. As his wife Eva was now able to enjoy public attention and a degree of power. She was given her own office in the capital, where she worked extremely long hours organizing work and aid for the poor and needy. She established her own foundation, the Eva Perón Foundation, which was funded by the 'voluntary' annual donation of a day's salary from all citizens of Argentina. This money was used to set up thousands of hospitals, schools, orphanages and homes for the elderly.

In 1946 Eva went on a tour of Europe to gain support for the Perón regime, now widely viewed as fascist in the post-war world. In Spain she was warmly greeted by Franco who wanted to improve trade relations with Argentina. While there she visited the tombs of Spain's first absolutist monarchs, Isabella and Ferdinand. She briefly met the Pope but was coolly received in France and when she discovered that she would not be invited to Buckingham Palace, she cancelled her trip to England. Despite her mixed reception, Eva's tour established her as a player on the world's political stage. When she returned to her own country she was treated with adulation and near worship.

Eva achieved important progress for women in Argentina by pressing through a bill granting female suffrage. She became hugely popular, and at the rally nominating Perón for a second term more than a million people voiced aloud a cry for Eva to stand as Vice-President. She did so but soon withdrew. The army, with whom she continued to be unpopular, was determinedly opposed to her appointment. However, by this time Eva's health was failing. She was in fact extremely ill and dying of cancer.

Eva was by Perón's side at his second inauguration but this was her last public appearance. On 26 July 1952 she fell into a coma and died surrounded by her family. The country went into a state of mourning. The rush to see her body was so great that eight people died and hundreds were injured. After her death, her legend – and her mortal remains – fuelled a propaganda war between pro- and anti-Perónists. Her body was embalmed and moved several times over the next two decades. It was feared that Eva's body would become a shrine, the focus of pro-Perónist feeling, if it remained for too long in one place. It was finally interred in the Duarte family crypt in a cemetery in Buenos Aires.

A complex and ambitious woman, Eva Perón was tireless in fighting for the poor and refused to slow down when ill, arguing 'I don't have time; I have too much to do.' An inspiring and persuasive orator, she was also intolerant of opposition and could be extremely ruthless – together with Perón she suppressed all criticism of the presidential regime by banning hundreds of independent newspapers. She believed herself wrongly accused of seeking personal power and always tried to stress her husband's achievements. Despite her success in gaining the vote for Argentinian women, and her rise to the top of Argentinian society, she was never entirely accepted by the upper classes in her country. She remained the people's heroine. The poor of Argentina came to regard her as a near saint, calling her 'Evita', the affectionate diminutive of her name that she consciously encouraged.

Betty Friedan

Betty Friedan's best-selling book *The Feminine Mystique* shook the world with its revelation of the deep dissatisfaction of an entire generation of American women. Widely regarded as one of the most influential American books of the twentieth century, it changed the lives of countless women and directed the course of feminist thinking.

'We're only beginning to know what we're capable of.'

BIOGRAPHY

Name:	Elizabeth Naomi Goldstein
Lived:	4 February 1921 – 4 February 2006
Place of birth:	Peoria, Illinois
Nationality:	American
Famed as:	Feminist and social reformer

Betty Friedan was born in Peoria, Illinois, to a Russian Jewish immigrant family. Her father, Harry Goldstein, had an upmarket jewellery business and her mother, Miriam Horowitz, had been the women's page editor of the Peoria newspaper. She gave up her career when she married. From early on, Betty sensed that her mother was dissatisfied as a homemaker. In an interview in 2003 she said, 'I was so aware of the crime, the shame that there was no use of my mother's ability and energy. And I think her frustration … She was a beautiful woman and she was a very able woman. But she dominated her husband and made her children's life slightly miserable.' Betty was a self-confident, intelligent young woman who planned to have an academic career.

Like her mother, Betty was also drawn to journalism. She started writing for the school newspaper when she was in elementary school and later, at high school, she set up a campus magazine with two classmates. Betty also encountered anti-Semitism at high school: 'Being Jewish, you didn't get into a sorority. I really didn't want to spend an Emily Dickinson adolescence reading poetry on gravestones, which I did. I would have much rather been in the jalopy with the kids, going to Hunt's for hamburgers.'

FACTFILE

- Betty and Carl Friedan's marriage ended bitterly after 19 years with each accusing the other of violence.

- By 2002 *The Feminine Mystique* had sold over nine million copies worldwide.

- In 2005, a panel of academics voted *The Feminine Mystique* one of the ten 'most harmful books' of the last two centuries. Other titles included Hitler's *Mein Kampf, Das Kapital* by Karl Marx and *The Kinsey Report*.

Betty's consolation was work. She graduated from high school at 17 and was accepted by all the leading women's colleges – Smith, Vassar, Wellesley and Radcliffe. She decided to go to Smith College, Massachusetts, the biggest and best women's college and the one that her mother had wanted to attend. She majored in psychology and edited a college newspaper, turning it from a once-weekly to a twice-weekly edition and employing a manager to sell the advertising to finance it. She graduated *summa cum laude* in 1942.

While still preparing for an academic career in 1944, Betty was offered a major fellowship to study for a PhD at the University of California, Berkeley. Faced with the realization of her early ambitions, Betty decided that she did not want to be an academic after all: 'While I had been, I guess, quite brilliant, academically, in my college years, I also had been editor of the paper, and I loved that. And that was a much more active thing. And I missed it when I was doing graduate work.'

Betty moved to New York and worked as a freelance journalist. In 1947, she met and married Carl Friedan, an actor. Shortly after, she gave birth to their first child and

TIMELINE

Date	Betty Friedan	Related events
1921	Born in Peoria, Illinois	Margaret Sanger founds the American Birth Control League
1937	Enrolls in Smith College, Massachusetts	
1952		Gloria Steinem attends Smith College
1963	*The Feminine Mystique* published	
1966	President of National Organization for Women	Death of Margaret Sanger
1968		Shirley Chisholm elected to Congress
1970		Germaine Greer publishes *The Female Eunuch*
1971	Founds National Women's Political Caucus with Gloria Steinem, Shirley Chisholm and Bella Abzug	Bella Abzug elected to Congress
1972		Gloria Steinem founds *Ms* magazine Shirley Chisholm runs for the US Presidency
1975	Named Humanist of the Year	
1981		Sandra Day O'Connor first female member of US Supreme Court
2005		Death of Shirley Chisholm
2006	Dies in Washington, DC	

took two years' maternity leave. She returned to work for the workers' magazine *UE News* until she became pregnant again. When her employers realized that she would qualify for further maternity leave, she was fired. Like her own mother, Betty became a full-time housewife and the family moved to Rockland County, where their third child was born.

For the next ten years Betty was chiefly a wife and mother. But she 'had to do something' and began working as a freelance magazine writer. In 1957 she was asked to devise a questionnaire about education, experience and satisfaction with life for the 15th alumni reunion at Smith College. The responses suggested that many of Betty's contemporaries were dissatisfied with their lives and felt incomplete and depressed if they had not had a career. At the same time, the received opinion that women should be completely fulfilled supporting their families left many of these 'over-educated housewives' with a burden of guilt.

The survey formed the basis of an article that Betty submitted to several women's magazines. Unprecedentedly – she had never had an article turned down before – they all rejected her work. 'I realized that what I was saying was threatening, somehow, to the editors of these women's magazines. That it threatened the very world they were trying to paint, what I then called the "feminine mystique". And I would have to write it as a book, because I wasn't going to get it in a magazine. And the rest is history.'

It was another five years before her book was published. Betty expanded her research, interviewing women throughout America. Her findings substantiated her main theme, that women endured pervasive discrimination, typified by patronizing advertising campaigns that pigeon-holed women as homemakers. She extolled the importance of women combining a career with family life to retain their sense of self-respect and self-worth.

The Feminine Mystique was published in 1963 and became a bestseller, with three million copies sold by 1966. Betty received many letters from women whose lives had been dramatically affected by her book. She realized that there was a significant, unexpressed movement for social change and started touring the United States to give lectures. Her constructive ideas included professional training, shared jobs and split-hour working for women, childcare facilities near workplaces and both maternity and paternity leave, so that fathers could also be involved in their children's early upbringing. And she demanded a legal end to sexual discrimination.

In 1966, Betty was a founding member of the National Organization for Women (NOW) – the largest body of feminist activists in the United States today. She was the first president and used her position to focus on Title VII of the Civil Rights Act of 1964, which outlawed discrimination on the basis of race and sex but was not strictly enforced. The following year, after leading 20,000 women through Washington to campaign for legalization of abortion and birth control, Betty resigned as president of NOW, concerned at the dominance of the organization by women who claimed female superiority. She wanted to focus on political reform, teaching and writing.

During the 1970s, Betty wrote a monthly column in *McCall's* magazine that was regularly read by eight million people. She was a founding member of the National Women's Political Caucus in 1971, which brought together a number of leading feminists and female politicians, and director of the First Women's Bank and Trust Company in 1973. Two years later the American Humanist Association named her Humanist of the Year, an award made 'to recognize a person of national or international reputation who, through the application of humanist values, has made a significant contribution to the improvement of the human condition'.

More recently, Betty taught in universities, campaigned for the Equal Rights Amendment and wrote. In 1993, she published *The Fountain of Age*, in which she claimed that old people in modern society are as invisible as women were 30 years previously. She told an interviewer: 'We are talking about the fastest-growing group of the population, people over 60. You're not affirming their existence, and you should.' Betty continued to write, teach and lecture: 'For my generation and those that followed us, of educated women, you could be plenty busy as a housewife, mother, when your kids were little, but it's not enough. When [the] life span of American women is approaching 80 years, as ours was, having kids is not going to take it up.'

Margaret Thatcher

Margaret Thatcher's years of power as Britain's first woman Prime Minister reshaped the social and economic landscape of the country. The Iron Lady was famed for her firmness and determination. 'You turn if you want to,' she once said: 'the lady's not for turning.'

'In politics if you want anything said, ask a man; if you want anything done, ask a woman.'

BIOGRAPHY

Name:	Margaret Hilda Roberts, Baroness Thatcher
Lived:	13 October 1925 –
Place of birth:	Grantham, England
Nationality:	British
Famed as:	First female British Prime Minister

Margaret Thatcher was born into the family of a self-made and prosperous grocer in Lincolnshire. Her father, Alfred Roberts, was active in local politics. A bright child, Margaret was educated at Grantham Girls' School, before going on to Oxford University to study chemistry. While at university she became President of the University Conservative Association, only the third woman to hold the position.

From 1947 Margaret was employed as a research chemist. She also continued her political activities and in 1950 and 1951 stood unsuccessfully as the Conservative candidate for Dartford in Kent, although she increased the local Tory vote by 50 per cent. Early pictures show her hallmark blonde coiffure, feminine features and winning smile. An authoritative speaker, her unforgettable delivery was once described as a 'honey-sweet voice of solicitous purity'.

FACTFILE

- In 1984, the IRA blew up the Grand Hotel in Brighton, where many members of the Conservative cabinet were staying for the Conservative Party conference. Five people were killed and many injured. Margaret insisted that the conference should continue and gave her speech as planned the following day.

- Her favourite television programme was the political comedy *Yes, Minister* (later *Yes, Prime Minister*) and she appeared in the show's Christmas special in 1984.

Through her involvement in the Conservative Party, Margaret met Denis Thatcher, a wealthy businessman whom she married in 1951. Denis supported Margaret while she studied to become a barrister, which she did while pregnant with twins. In 1953 Margaret qualified, specializing in taxation, and stood for a number of constituencies before winning the seat for Finchley in North London in April 1958.

After serving as a junior minister in Harold Macmillan's government, Margaret became a member of Edward Heath's cabinet in 1970. During the Conservative government of 1970–74 she was Secretary of State for Education and Science. Between 1974 and 1979 Margaret was shadow spokesman on the environment and financial affairs and it was during this time that she criticized Edward Heath for being insufficiently Conservative. When she challenged him for the party leadership in 1974 neither he nor she expected her to win the first ballot but, having done so, she was soon made party leader. For the rest of her period in opposition she united her party in opposing government spending, and argued the case for curbing trade union power and for reducing immigration.

The 1979 election followed the 'winter of discontent' during which the Labour government had struggled with the unions. The Conservatives won the election with a large majority and Margaret became Prime Minister. Her philosophy from the start was that Britain was over-governed and over-taxed. She aimed to make industry and public services more efficient by cutting subsidies, to privatize government-owned industries, to reduce trade union power, to fight inflation and to encourage home ownership.

TIMELINE

Date	Margaret Thatcher	Related events
1925	Born in Grantham, Lincolnshire	
1959	Becomes MP for Finchley	Conservatives win the General Election
1967	Joins shadow cabinet	
1970	Secretary of State for Education and Science	Tories win the General Election 18 year olds vote for the first time
1972		British troops kill 13 in Ulster (Bloody Sunday)
1975	Leader of the Conservative Party	
1979	Becomes Prime Minister	New Ulster Secretary Airey Neave murdered by the IRA
1981		Riots in London and Liverpool IRA hunger striker Bobby Sands dies
1982	Son Mark Thatcher goes missing for nine days on the Paris-Dakar car rally	The Falklands War
1983	Second term in office	
1984	Secures a £2 billion annual rebate from the European Union Survives assassination attempt	Miners' strike (ends 1985)
1987	Third term in office	
1990	Resigns Awarded the Order of Merit	John Major becomes Prime Minister
1992	Created Baroness Thatcher	
2003	Death of Denis Thatcher	

She achieved her goal of reducing inflation but at a heavy cost: unemployment nearly tripled in her first two terms in power. In 1981 there was the worst recession in Britain since the 1930s and rioting in deprived inner-city areas. Opinion polls showed her to be the most unpopular Prime Minister since 1945. However, the surprise invasion of the British-owned Falkland Islands by the Argentinians in 1982 gave Margaret an opportunity to tackle an external challenge decisively and turn public opinion in her favour. Media acclaim for her leadership of the Falklands War helped her to another term in office.

Margaret's second term as Prime Minister was crowned by her triumphant negotiation of a £2 billion annual rebate from the European Union in 1984. The rebate made up the shortfall between what Britain paid into the EU and what it received from it in subsidies. The UK has continued to benefit from the agreement ever since. However, there were corresponding low points, including a long, bitter and highly divisive strike by miners during 1984–85, which the government eventually broke through the preventative measures it had taken against coal shortages. The arts and education in Britain saw cuts in funding and in protest Oxford University twice refused to award Margaret the customary honorary degree given to Prime Ministers. This slight from her former university prompted Margaret to donate her personal papers to Churchill College, Cambridge, where they are stored with Sir Winston Churchill's.

Having survived an assassination attempt by the IRA in 1984, Margaret went on to win a third consecutive term of office and to become the longest-serving post-war Prime Minister. The large majority gained in the election was attributed by some commentators to the increased number of property owners that she had created through her policy of allowing tenants in municipal housing to buy their houses. Thatcherism was now an accepted political phenomenon, with its stress on policies that embodied Margaret's widely quoted belief that 'there is no such thing as society. There are only individual men and women and there are families'.

Margaret was an outspoken critic of Communism and a loyal supporter of American foreign policy under the Reagan administration. However, she respected the Soviet leader Mikhail Gorbachev, saying he was a man she 'could do business with'. With President Ronald Reagan she had a genuine personal friendship. He admired her intelligence and resilience and she was charmed by his humour and easy manners. She asserted a strong commitment to NATO by the UK and upheld the importance of Britain's independent nuclear deterrent. The ironic label by which she was known in the Soviet press – the Iron Lady – delighted her and became permanently coupled with her name.

In 1989, several events were set in train that led to her eventual downfall. They included the introduction of the deeply unpopular poll tax to fund local government, quarrels with senior colleagues and a downturn in the economy. In 1990 Margaret's leadership of the Conservative Party was formally challenged while she was out of the country. Her failure to win an outright victory in the first ballot of the leadership election took her by surprise. She quickly recognized that defeat was likely and resigned.

In her retirement Margaret has remained active, establishing the Thatcher Foundation to promote free enterprise and democracy throughout the world. In 1992 she was made a life peer and chose the title Baroness Thatcher of Kesteven. Since a series of minor strokes in 2002, her health has been frail. Her tribute at the funeral of Ronald Reagan in June 2004, a year after the death of her husband, was one of the most moving parts of the service. Although ill health meant that she had to record her address, she insisted on attending in person.

Many consider that Margaret Thatcher transformed Britain greatly for the better and re-established it as an economic force; others believe she damaged Britain's manufacturing base and created a divided society. She showed by example that it was possible for a woman to rise to the highest office in British politics and to stay there – a feat she accomplished with a level of assertiveness rarely equalled by her male predecessors.

Marilyn Monroe

Marilyn Monroe's extraordinary screen presence and stunning looks made her an enduring sex symbol. From a childhood of poverty and abandonment, she rose to become the greatest film star in the world and a legend in her own lifetime.

'Hollywood's a place where they'll pay you a thousand dollars for a kiss, and fifty cents for your soul.'

BIOGRAPHY

Name:	Norma Jean Baker
Lived:	1 June 1926 – 5 August 1962
Place of birth:	Los Angeles, California
Place of death:	Brentwood, California
Nationality:	American
Famed as:	Iconic film star

Marilyn Monroe, whose real name was Norma Jean Baker, was the illegitimate daughter of Gladys Baker, a film editor at RKO studios. Her mother's mental health deteriorated after Norma Jean's birth and she was eventually sent to a mental institution in Santa Monica. Norma Jean spent much of her childhood in foster homes and orphanages.

In 1941 her legal guardian, Grace McKee Goddard, who had been a friend of her mother, took Norma Jean in to live with her and her husband. Grace's passion for the cinema, and particularly the blonde film star Jean Harlow, had a huge influence on Norma Jean, who began fantasizing about becoming a star herself. In 1942 Grace's husband was transferred to the East Coast and the couple could not afford to take Norma Jean with them. She was now 16 and did not want to be put back into care. Grace McKee encouraged Norma Jean's relationship with her 21-year-old neighbour, James Dougherty, seeing marriage as the better option for her.

FACTFILE

- When asked about posing for the notorious *Playboy* photographs, Marilyn said, 'It's not true I had nothing on. I had the radio on.'

- The dress Marilyn wore to sing *Happy Birthday* to President John F. Kennedy was sold at auction by Christie's in 1999 for a world-record $1.3 million.

- Joe DiMaggio arranged Marilyn's funeral, to which no Hollywood figure was invited. For 20 years afterwards he delivered flowers to her grave three times a week.

- Marilyn's last film, *The Misfits*, was also the last film made by actors Montgomery Clift and Clark Gable before their deaths.

On 19 June 1942, Norma Jean and James married after dating for six months. Two years later James was sent to the South Pacific when he joined the Merchant Marines. During this time, Norma Jean worked in a factory in Burbank, California, where she was spotted by photographer David Conover, who was doing a photo-story on women contributing to the war effort for *Yank* magazine. Conover recognized how naturally photogenic Norma Jean was and his work brought her several modelling jobs.

Norma Jean caught the attention of Ben Lyon, a talent scout for 20th Century Fox film studios. She was given a six-month contract during which she did little but learn about hair, make-up and costumes. However, her contract was renewed and Norma Jean Baker metamorphosed into Marilyn Monroe, the name she and the studio jointly decided upon. Her hair was dyed platinum blonde, like Jean Harlow's, and she began to get bit-parts in films. James Dougherty returned home to a different woman in 1946 and the couple divorced.

Marilyn was a natural in front of the camera lens. Photographer Richard Avedon said, 'She gave more to the still camera than any actress, any woman, I've ever photographed, infinitely more patient, more demanding of herself and more comfortable in front of the camera than away from it.' Her ease in front of the

TIMELINE

Date	Marilyn Monroe	Related events
1926	Born in Los Angeles, California	
1946	Contract with 20th Century Fox	Arthur Miller writes *All My Sons*
1949		Arthur Miller's *Death of a Salesman* wins Pulitzer Prize
1952	Meets Joe DiMaggio on a blind date	
1953	Marries and divorces Joe DiMaggio *Gentlemen Prefer Blondes* and *How to Marry a Millionaire* released	Frank Sinatra wins Oscar for Best Supporting Actor (*From Here to Eternity*) Arthur Miller's *The Crucible* opens on Broadway
1954	Studies at the Actors' Studio, New York	
1955	Forms her company, Marilyn Monroe Productions	Sinatra releases *In the Wee Small Hours of the Morning*
1956	Converts to Judaism in order to marry Arthur Miller	Arthur Miller appears before the House Un-American Activities Committee
1959	*Some Like It Hot* released	
1961	Meets President John F. Kennedy *The Misfits* released	
1962	Dies at her home in California	
1999		Death of Joe DiMaggio
2005		Death of Arthur Miller

camera reflected perhaps a sadder truth about uneasiness in the real world. For Marilyn, Hollywood glamour offered escapism from the realities of a world that seemed to have let her down. Her superstar existence provided the attention and love that had been absent for so much of her childhood and adolescence. Her disjointed upbringing influenced her view of herself and her relationships. She once said, 'I knew I belonged to the public and to the world, not because I was talented or even beautiful, but because I had never belonged to anything or anyone else.'

Marilyn's first serious acting job was a small role in the John Huston thriller *The Asphalt Jungle* in 1950. Her first leading role came in *Don't Bother To Knock* (1952), and was followed by several more films, but it was her performance in *Niagara* (1953) that established her as a star. That same year, two films were released that established her as America's leading film actress, *Gentlemen Prefer Blondes* and *How to Marry a Millionaire*. In December, nude photographs of Marilyn appeared in the first edition of *Playboy*. The photographs, by Tom Kelley, had been taken while Marilyn was struggling to make her way into films but by the time they were published she was a superstar. *Playboy* appeared only a month before her wedding to her lover of two years, baseball star Joe DiMaggio, himself a national hero. Joe wanted a wife and family, not to share his marriage with the media, and he was wounded by Kelley's candid shots of his wife and some scenes in her films. Only nine months after their wedding they divorced.

In 1954, after making *The Seven-Year Itch*, Marilyn broke her contract with Fox and went to study acting at the Actors' Studio in New York. She wanted to escape the dumb blonde roles that the studio forced her to play. Fox were inflexible and began grooming blonde clones to fill her place, but the runaway success of *The Seven-Year Itch* forced them to change their minds. Marilyn returned to Hollywood with a new contract from Fox and formed her own company, Marilyn Monroe Productions, with photographer Milton H. Greene. The company produced *The Prince and the Showgirl*, co-starring Laurence Olivier, and her most famous film, the comedy classic *Some Like It Hot*, for which she won a Golden Globe.

On 29 June 1956, Marilyn married for the third time. Her husband, Arthur Miller, was an acclaimed playwright and a leading member of the arts intelligentsia. During their marriage Marilyn miscarried twice and became increasingly dependent on drugs and alcohol. She and Miller divorced in 1961, the year in which her last film *The Misfits*, scripted by Miller as a Valentine's gift to her, was released.

For her fans, Marilyn embodied the idealized victim-turned-star whom everyone loved to pity and adore. But the reality was that she was unhappy and unhealthy. By the early 1960s, her increasing substance abuse began to take its toll. She was difficult to work with, notoriously late on set and frequently unsure of her lines. Rumours began to circulate about her relationships with singer Frank Sinatra and both President John F. Kennedy and his brother Robert, the Attorney General. In May 1962, she sang a famously breathy and seductive version of *Happy Birthday* at a televised party for the President. She arrived, as usual, late and Kennedy later thanked her, with irony, for singing to him in 'such a sweet and wholesome way'. For the gossips her performance was a very public demonstration of their supposed affair.

It was also one of her last public appearances. Her mental and emotional health worsened and she spent months moving from one treatment centre to another. At this point, Joe DiMaggio re-entered her life. He supervised her medical care and left his job in order to be able to live closer to her. Inevitably, rumours of their remarriage spread. But shortly after Marilyn was named World Film Favourite at the Golden Globes in 1962, she was found dead at her home in California. It is likely she died from an accidental drug overdose – for which she had had to be hospitalized several times before – rather than committing suicide.

Death transformed Marilyn Monroe from a film star into an icon. Her ageless image, immortalized by countless photographs and Andy Warhol's screen prints, is as familiar to people born after her death as it was to her contemporaries. The circumstances of her death, together with her highly publicized relationships with celebrities and political figures, gave rise to conspiracy theories that persist today. Yet her own motivation was touchingly simple: 'I am not interested in money,' she once said, 'I just want to be wonderful.'

Anne Frank

Anne Frank's heartbreaking story is known to us through the diary she kept for two years while in hiding from the Nazis from 1942 to 1944. Although she was only 13 when she started the diary, the maturity of her observations on what she endured is remarkable. Anne's diary is one of the most poignant records of life during the Holocaust to have survived.

'Despite everything, I believe that people are really good at heart.'

BIOGRAPHY

Name:	Annelies Marie Frank
Lived:	12 June 1929 – March 1945 (date uncertain)
Place of birth:	Frankfurt, Germany
Place of death:	Bergen-Belsen, Germany
Nationality:	German
Famed as:	Diarist

Annelies Frank, always known as Anne, was born into an upper-class Jewish family in Frankfurt, Germany, and for the first four years of her life led an ordinary, happy childhood. In 1933 Adolf Hitler became Chancellor of Germany and the anti-Semitism encouraged by Nazi policies began to impinge on Jewish families. Otto Frank decided to leave Germany to escape persecution and moved to Amsterdam, where he started a business, the Dutch Opekta Company.

In 1934, Anne, her older sister Margot and their mother joined Otto Frank in the Netherlands. Anne and Margot attended a local school, where Anne showed a talent for writing and was described as an outspoken, intelligent and extrovert child.

In 1940, Germany invaded the Netherlands and Anne was forced to leave her school and attend the Jewish Lyceum. The following year saw Nazi horrors increase, including the rounding up of the Jews for transportation to concentration camps. Realizing that it would be very difficult to flee the Netherlands, now that it was occupied by the Nazis, Anne's father, together with trusted members of his staff, prepared a hiding place above his business premises. It would be a safe place to go if his family was threatened.

FACTFILE

- Anne Frank's diary has sold over 25 million copies worldwide.

- With the profits from the sale of the diaries, Otto Frank set up a charitable foundation to help pay for the medical expenses of Christians who had helped Jews during the war.

- Nearly a million people visited the Anne Frank House in Amsterdam in 2004.

On her thirteenth birthday, Anne was given a small book that she had pointed out to her father in a shop window. It had a checked cloth cover and a lock on the front. It was meant to be an autograph book but Anne decided to use it as a diary. Now segregated from her school friends, she addressed her diary as 'Kitty' and wrote as if she was writing letters to a friend. The early entries are mostly about her school days, and the boys and places she liked, but there are also references to life under the occupation, to the yellow star that she was forced to wear as a Jew and other daily persecutions she and her family had to deal with:

> *Our many Jewish friends and acquaintances are being taken away in droves. The Gestapo is treating them very roughly and transporting them in cattle cars to Westerbork, the big camp in Drenthe to which they're sending all the Jews. … If it's that bad in Holland, what must it be like in those faraway and uncivilized places where the Germans are sending them? We assume that most of them are being murdered. The English radio says they're being gassed.*

Three weeks after Anne's birthday, the family had to go into hiding.

Anne and her family spent the next 25 months in a cramped and damp series of rooms at 263 Prinsengracht in Amsterdam. Anne called it the secret annexe. They

TIMELINE

Date	Anne Frank	Related events
1929	Annelies Marie (known as Anne) born in Frankfurt am Main	
1933	Otto Frank moves to the Netherlands	Adolf Hitler becomes German Chancellor The first concentration camp is built Jews banned from public office
1938		Germany invades Austria Jewish synagogues and businesses destroyed during Kristallnacht
1940	Otto Frank's business moves into 263 Prinsengracht in Amsterdam	Germany invades the Netherlands
1941		Reinhard Heidrich authorized to find the 'final solution to the Jewish problem'
1942	Anne receives a diary for her 13th birthday The Frank family goes into hiding	Death camps established
1944	The families in the annexe are betrayed and sent to Auschwitz	D-Day
1945	Anne and Margot die in Bergen-Belsen Otto Frank returns to Amsterdam	The camp is liberated by allied troops a month after Anne's death Adolf Hitler commits suicide Germany surrenders
1947	Otto publishes Anne's diary	
1960	Anne Frank House opens at 263 Prinsengracht	
1980	Death of Otto Frank	

also sheltered the family of Hermann Van Pels, Otto's business partner, and, later, Fritz Pfeffer, an elderly dentist.

Life for everyone in the annexe was monotonous and confining. They had to stay silent during the day as even the smallest noise would give away their presence to the people working below. Supplies and news from the outside world were brought to them by four trusted friends, who risked their lives to help the Frank family. The penalty for anyone found sheltering Jews was death.

Anne spent her time in the annexe writing and trying to continue her education. She wrote short stories, fairy tales and essays and even began a novel. She dreamed of becoming a writer or journalist after the war. But principally she kept her diary and in it she wrote about daily life in the annexe, the tensions between members of her family and the others who shared the rooms with them, the boredom, and her deepest thoughts about life, the war and her longing for peace. The experience she had to endure matured her beyond her years:

> *It's utterly impossible for me to build my life on a foundation of chaos, suffering and death. I see the world being slowly transformed into a wilderness, I hear the approaching thunder that, one day, will destroy us too, I feel the suffering of millions. And yet, when I look up at the sky, I somehow feel that everything will change for the better, that this cruelty too shall end, that peace and tranquillity will return once more.*

In March 1944, the people in the annexe heard on the radio that diaries and other important documents would be collected after the war as a record of what had happened to Dutch people. Anne immediately set about editing and revising her diary, making simple corrections to the text and deleting whole sections if she considered them to be too personal.

Then without any warning, on 4 August 1944, the annexe was raided by the Nazis – the Franks and their friends had been betrayed. Anne, her family, and the others living with them were arrested and deported to Auschwitz. The four friends who had helped them were arrested but released. Two of them, Miep Gies and Bep Voskuijl, returned to the annexe and found Anne's papers scattered on the floor. They collected them and kept them safe.

On arrival at Auschwitz, Anne, Margot and their mother were separated from Otto. They believed that he had died but he survived the war. Anne and Margot were moved to Bergen-Belsen concentration camp in March 1945 and there, nine months after their arrest, they died of typhoid fever. Anne was just 15 years old. Their mother died in Auschwitz.

When Otto Frank returned to Amsterdam after the war, he advertised widely for news of his family and learned from Dutch survivors of Belsen-Bergen and Auschwitz that his wife and daughters were dead. When Miep Gies learned the news she gave Otto the diary she had rescued. Otto barely recognized his daughter from what he read and the experience was so painful that initially he hesitated to publish the diary, although it was clear from what Anne had written that she had intended to do so. The first edition of the diary, called *The Secret Annexe*, was published in the Netherlands in 1947. It was translated into English and adapted as a play, which triggered the enormous and abiding interest in Anne's story when it was staged in New York. Otto Frank himself could never bear to watch the dramatization of his family's experiences.

Today, 263 Prinzengracht has been renamed the Anne Frank House. It is a museum and international research centre providing educational resources and documentation about the holocaust. The *Diary of Anne Frank* has been translated into 67 languages and is one of the most widely read books in the world.

Dian Fossey

Dian Fossey followed her childhood dream of working with animals and spent her life with the mountain gorillas in central Africa. Her work saved the species, one of the most threatened in the world, but led ultimately to her own death.

'No one loved gorillas more.'

Inscription on Dian Fossey's original grave marker

BIOGRAPHY

Name:	Dian Fossey
Lived:	16 January 1932 – 27 December 1985
Place of birth:	San Francisco, California
Place of death:	Virunga, Rwanda
Nationality:	American
Famed as:	Zoologist and conservationist; champion of the mountain gorilla

Dian Fossey's early life was fractured by her parents' divorce when she was six. Her unhappy and difficult childhood was complicated by her relationship with her mother's second husband, whose coldness and rejection made her position in the family uncomfortable. Always an animal lover, she was forbidden by her stepfather to have any pets and grew up insular and introverted.

Her stepfather's reluctance to finance her education meant that she was supported by an aunt and uncle, who paid for her to train as an occupational therapist. She worked at various hospitals in California before moving to Kosair Children's Hospital in Louisville, Kentucky, where she became director of the occupational therapy department.

FACTFILE

- Louis Leakey facetiously suggested that Dian should have her appendix removed as a precaution before living in a remote area. He later wrote to say that he was not being serious but it was too late – Dian had already undergone the surgery.

- Dian's health did suffer from her extended periods of field research. She developed respiratory and cardiac problems and had to work with untreated fractures to her ribs and feet.

- Sigourney Weaver received an Oscar nomination as Best Actress for her portrayal of Dian in the film *Gorillas in the Mist*.

For years, Dian had been fascinated by the mountain gorillas of Rwanda, having read studies by George B. Schaller, who worked with them in the late 1950s. In 1963, she financed a study trip to Africa, an experience that marked a turning point in her life. In Rwanda she met Dr Louis Leakey, a British palaeontologist who was studying primate fossils to discover what they could reveal about human evolution. Leakey was initially wary of Dian but was won over by her single-mindedness: 'Some day I plan to come here to live and work,' she told him. Dian was overwhelmed by her first sighting of the gorillas: 'Their bright eyes darted nervously from under heavy brows as though trying to identify us as familiar friends or possible foes. Immediately I was struck by the physical magnificence of the huge jet-black bodies blended against the green palette wash of the thick forest foliage.'

Three years after her trip, Dian met Leakey again at a conference in the United States. He was looking for someone to undertake a long-term research project on mountain gorillas and offered Dian the job. In 1966, Leakey sent Dian to study the gorillas in the Democratic Republic of the Congo, then called Zaire, but the political situation in the country was highly volatile and she had to abandon her studies and take refuge in Rwanda. Here, with funding from the National Geographic Society and others, she established the Karisoke Research Centre in the Virunga national park.

The centre became the focus for intensive research over a period of 22 years and brought Dian to international attention. Her research method was to become

TIMELINE

Date	Dian Fossey	Related events
1932	Born in San Francisco	
1963	Makes trip to Africa to study mountain gorillas and meets Louis Leakey	
1966	Moves to Africa and starts work as a researcher for Louis Leakey	
1967	Establishes the Karisoke Research Foundation	
1973	Receives PhD from Cambridge University	Census records 275 Virunga gorillas
1978	Digit murdered	
1979		Mountain Gorilla Fund set up
1980	Moves to Cornell University	
1981		Census records 250 Virunga gorillas
1983	Publishes *Gorillas in the Mist*	
	Returns to Rwanda	
1985	Found murdered in her cabin in Virunga	
1988		The film of *Gorillas in the Mist* released
2004		Census records 380 Virunga gorillas

physically close to the gorillas, living alone with them for long periods and gaining their trust. She also began to feel intense emotional attachment to the animals. 'I feel more comfortable with gorillas than people,' she said. 'I can anticipate what a gorilla's going to do, and they're purely motivated.' Using skills learned in child therapy, she was a meticulous and patient observer, recording the behaviour of the gorillas in a virtually undisturbed state. This involved learning to recognize, and often naming, each individual. Dian discovered that they all had their own personalities, and that their lives were complex and highly social. One of the animals closest to her was a young gorilla she named Digit and she watched his progress as he grew from a small baby.

Dian's findings changed the general image of wild gorillas from dangerous and unfriendly animals to a true understanding of their intelligence, gentleness and social skills. The gorillas in Virunga trusted Dian to the extent that they would elicit contact with people who visited her to observe her work. This behaviour worried Dian as much as it delighted her: trust of this nature would make the gorillas easy game for the poachers and hunters who worked in the region. Gorillas were frequently killed for bush meat and there was a ready market for their heads, hands and feet. Many young gorillas were left orphaned through poaching.

In 1970 Dian reluctantly left Africa for England to work on a PhD at Cambridge University. Her work would not progress without further funding and to obtain that she needed academic credentials. She returned to Rwanda in 1973 and found she was spending less time in the field. Funding now supported a team of research students, and the administrative work of the project had grown correspondingly. As head of the project, Dian was obliged to spend more time at her headquarters. The late 1970s were a difficult period for her and she suffered spells of loneliness and depression, exacerbated by heavy drinking. Then in 1978 the body of Digit was discovered. He and other members of the troop had been killed and their bodies mutilated by poachers. The horror of this discovery was another turning point for Dian. It spurred her to launch an international campaign against poaching. By now, her reputation gave her influence with the authorities and rangers began to patrol the Virunga reserve. She also took matters into her own hands, arming her students with guns, naming suspected poachers and offering a bounty for their capture. Among the poachers, her activities made her enemies.

When Dian's article about the death of Digit appeared in *National Geographic* magazine, donations began to reach her from around the world. This money formed the basis of the Dian Fossey Gorilla Fund (DFGF), which is dedicated to the protection and preservation of mountain gorillas, and which now manages 20 projects in Rwanda, Congo and Uganda. These include educational programmes for schools, help with sustainable agriculture for local farmers, tree planting, research into gorilla DNA, and funding ranger patrols. In 1979, the independent Mountain Gorilla Project was set up. This has exploited worldwide interest in gorillas by encouraging gorilla tourism. The income from this has in turn motivated the government to crack down on poaching, which is far less prevalent today.

By 1981, Dian's activism and erratic behaviour had created such an atmosphere of tension around her research centre that she was advised to take extended leave from the project and Rwanda. She returned to the US and worked as an Associate Professor at Cornell University, in New York State. In 1983 she published her famous book, *Gorillas in the Mist*, a best-selling account of the observations she made over many years of fieldwork. The money Dian made from sales of her book enabled her to return to Rwanda later that year.

On 27 December 1985 Dian was found murdered in her cabin at the research centre. Her killers have never been identified. Members of her research team first fell under suspicion but it was generally accepted that she had been killed by poachers, who resented her campaign against their lucrative trade. Evidence has recently emerged implicating Rwandan politicians, who were later involved in the genocide of 1994. However, the mystery of her death will probably never be solved.

A census of Virunga mountain gorillas in 1996 put the total at 325, despite wars and general unrest in the area. The most recent census, in 2004, puts the figure at 380, with a world population of 700. Rwanda has now adopted the mountain gorilla as its national symbol. It appears on passports, tourist visas and currency. It is highly likely that, without the pioneering research and dedicated fieldwork of Dian Fossey, this gentle primate would now be extinct.

Mary Quant

Mary Quant brought fun and fantasy to fashion in the 1960s. The creator of the mini skirt and hot pants, she showed a generation how to dress to please themselves. Her instant success made traditionally cautious designers change their attitudes and make their designs appeal to the newly important youth market.

'Good taste is death. Vulgarity is life.'

BIOGRAPHY

Name:	Mary Quant
Lived:	11 February 1934 –
Place of birth:	London, England
Nationality:	British
Famed as:	Fashion designer

In an interview with the BBC in 1999, Mary Quant said: 'I grew up wanting to design clothes. The whole thing hit me at a very early age. In fact, I'm still in disgrace for cutting up a bedspread when I was ill with measles, aged something like six or seven.' Mary was born in Blackheath, London, the daughter of two Welsh teachers. Like many children growing up in London during World War II, she was evacuated to the countryside to escape bombing strikes on the capital.

As a young woman Mary returned to London to study art and illustration at Goldsmiths' College. She was interested in colours and patterns and the ways in which they contrasted, merged and balanced one another. After completing her studies she took a job with a couture milliner. This involved spending up to three days stitching a single hat for one customer. Mary became disillusioned with the state of the fashion industry and felt passionately that style and design should be available to everyone, not just the select few who could afford to pay high prices for hand-made, customized clothes.

FACTFILE

- When asked what had inspired her to design the mini skirt, Mary stated simply, 'Legs. I had good legs.'

- Mary's shift dress was seen as the perfect dress in which to do the twist, the dance that became all the rage in 1963 with Chubby Checker's hit *Let's Twist Again*.

- The introduction of the mini skirt forced a change in the UK tax system. Tax on women's clothes had previously been determined by skirt length and the mini skirt was tax exempt because it qualified as a child's size. In the mid-1960s women's clothes started to be classified by bust size, for tax purposes.

In 1955, Mary, her partner Alexander Plunkett-Greene and accountant Archie McNair opened Bazaar, one of London's first fashion boutiques on the Kings Road in Chelsea. Mary had a gift for marketing and an instinctive understanding of the needs and desires of her customers. In an interview with *American Vogue*, she described her shop as 'a sophisticated candy store for grown ups. I want women to come in here and play with colour and have fun.' Mary believed that fashion was the preserve of the young and should promote a sense of freedom, especially for women. In her autobiography she wrote: 'I had always wanted young people to have a fashion of their own, absolutely twentieth century.'

Within the first week of Bazaar's opening, the shop had taken five times as much money as Mary had anticipated. She soon realized that its success depended on stocking a large number of different designs, and this inspired her to design her own clothes to sell. One of the first lines she tried was a pair of 'mad house pyjamas': they became a must-have item for customers and Mary sold the design to an American manufacturer who produced their own version. Mary's single sewing machine in her London studio flat soon expanded into three full-time machinists whom she employed to sew her designs for Bazaar.

TIMELINE

Date	Mary Quant	Related events
1934	Born in London	
1955	Opens Bazaar in Chelsea, London	
1957	Marries Alexander Plunkett-Greene	Givenchy launches the sack line, later adapted by Mary for her mini shift dress
1958		Paris fashion houses show above-the-knee skirts
1960	Introduces the mini skirt	
1961	Opens second Bazaar in Knightsbridge	
1963	Forms the Ginger Group	Vidal Sassoon pioneers the five-point hair cut, adopted by Mary Barbara Hulanicki opens Biba
1964	Introduces the micro mini skirt	Tights hit the market: mini skirts make stockings unwearable
1965		Beatles awarded the MBE
1966	Receives the OBE *Quant on Quant* published	Model Twiggy named 'The face of 1966' by the *Daily Express*
1967		Laura Ashley opens her first shop in Kensington, London
1969	Launches hot pants	Zandra Rhodes opens her first shop in Fulham, London
1970		The Beatles disband
1975		Biba closes down
1981		Vivienne Westwood and Malcolm McLaren's first catwalk show
1990	Hall of Fame Award of the British Fashion Council	
2000	Resigns as director of Mary Quant Ltd	

Mary was not afraid of novelty and experimentation. Some of her most popular designs were sweater dresses with plastic collars, balloon-style dresses, and knickerbockers and stretch stockings in all colours and patterns. Other typical designs included knee-length white plastic lace-up boots, tight sweaters in bold striped or check patterns and plastic raincoats. These clothes became part of the 'London Look' and Mary Quant became synonymous with trendiness.

Ernestine Carter, one of the most authoritative and influential fashion writers of the twentieth century, wrote: 'It is given to a fortunate few to be born at the right time, in the right place, with the right talents. In recent fashion there are three: Chanel, Dior and Mary Quant.' The 1960s were the right time for Mary. The decade was characterized by the rise of youth culture in Britain. Young people of all classes had independence, employment and disposable incomes. Style and image were everything, visible on television, purchasable in shops, available to all. Glamour was no longer an elusive quality epitomized by heroes and heroines on the cinema screen: 1960s' role models were pop singers, models, sporting figures, television stars. If the 1960s was the right time, 'Swinging London' was the right place. Pop culture influenced what people wore as well as what they listened to.

The trio who had established Bazaar were quick to spot these new trends. 'Fashion reflects what is really in the air,' said Mary in an interview. 'It reflects what people are reading and thinking and listening to, and architecture, painting, attitudes to success and to society.' In 1961 they opened a second store in Knightsbridge, which enjoyed the same levels of success and profit as the original shop on the Kings Road. As Mary's designs took off, mass-production seemed the inevitable step forward, and in 1963 she began exporting her designs to the US. This was the start of a period of worldwide demand for her clothes. She set up the Ginger Group, which marketed her designs, and 'Mary Quant' became an international brand. Many of her designs were bought by the American chain store J. C. Penney, through which they were mass-produced and sold cheaply to a wide range of consumers. By 1966 Mary had also brought out a range of affordable cosmetics bearing her trademark daisy logo. She encouraged users to use make-up brushes for applying eyeliner and blusher to achieve the doe-eyed, hollow-cheeked look of top model Twiggy.

Of all Mary's designs, the mini skirt is by far the most widely recognized and the one for which she is still famed. Although André Courrèges had modelled above-the-knee couture designs in the early 1960s, Mary's designs were revolutionary: it was suddenly acceptable and even – such was the power of affordable fashion – mandatory to show a lot of leg. Some commentators saw the innovation in terms of female liberation – women could now move easily instead of being hampered by long skirts and underskirts. But Mary herself saw things in more basic terms: 'The fundamentals of fashion remain the same. Women wear clothes to feel good and to feel sexy. Women turn themselves on. Men like to look at women to be turned on – to feel sexy is to know you're alive.' For the first time clothes were being designed to uncover the body rather than dress it and the public consequences were far-reaching.

With the introduction of hot pants in 1969, Mary took the skirt hem as high as it could go and took shorts out of the school gym, but by the end of the decade her designs had lost their popularity. Throughout the 1970s and 1980s, she concentrated on the household goods and cosmetics side of Mary Quant, eventually selling the company to a Japanese consortium in 2000. Although she is no longer associated with the brand name, its success rests on her enduring reputation as a fashion innovator. In 1966 Mary was awarded the OBE for her outstanding contribution to the fashion industry. She accepted the award in her inimitable style, arriving at Buckingham Palace in a micro-mini skirt and black cut-out gloves. In 1990 she won the Hall of Fame Award of the British Fashion Council. 'Fashion, as we knew it, is over,' she once said. 'People wear now exactly what they feel like wearing.'

Germaine Greer

Outrageous and outspoken, Germaine Greer has always described herself as an anarchist. Her book *The Female Eunuch* was a manifesto for the sexual and feminist revolution of the late twentieth century.

'If a woman never lets herself go, how will she ever know how far she might have got? If she never takes off her high-heeled shoes, how will she ever know how far she could walk or how fast she could run?'

BIOGRAPHY

Name:	Germaine Greer
Lived:	29 January 1939 –
Place of birth:	Melbourne, Australia
Nationality:	Australian
Famed as:	Writer, broadcaster and academic

Born in Melbourne, Australia into a middle-class family, Germaine Greer was educated at a local convent. Her father was a distant figure to her, whose past she was later to research and write about in her autobiographical book *Daddy, We Hardly Knew You*, and her mother a conventional woman with whom Germaine found it hard to identify.

Germaine took her first degree at Melbourne University, then went on to Sydney University where she was awarded an MA in 1963. Here she encountered the left-wing and anarchistic Push group, who promoted sexual freedom. She said of this time: 'I was already an anarchist... I just didn't know why I was an anarchist.' Her experiences had a lasting influence on her thinking and activities – initially fuelling her promotion of sexual liberation while she was in England and later causing her to reflect bitterly on its false promises.

FACTFILE

- Germaine had a brief three-week marriage to Paul Du Feu, an Australian journalist, in 1968. He later married the US author Maya Angelou.

- She was arrested and fined £15 for public swearing during a speech in Auckland, New Zealand, in 1972.

- In 2000, she was attacked in her own home by a disturbed young woman who had become obsessed with her. She dismissed the incident, in which she was injured, saying, 'Ever since I published *The Female Eunuch* there's been an off-chance that some nutter is going to pick me off.'

Germaine went to England on a Commonwealth Scholarship in 1964 to study for a doctorate at Newnham College at the University of Cambridge. She was a startling presence to her contemporaries. The journalist and academic Lisa Jardine remembers Germaine failing to hear a request for silence at a formal dinner and continuing to talk into a suddenly hushed room: 'We were too astonished at the very idea that a woman could speak so loudly and out of turn, and that words such as "bra" and "breasts" (or maybe she said "tits") could be uttered amid the pseudo-masculine solemnity of a college dinner.'

During her time at Cambridge, Germaine joined the Cambridge Footlights, which put her in contact with the radical arts and media world of the 1960s. She began to write for several reviews, including a gardening column under the *nom de plume* Rose Blight for the satirical magazine *Private Eye* and articles for *Oz*, an underground magazine run by fellow Australian Richard Neville. Having gained her PhD in 1967 with a thesis on Shakespeare's early comedies, Germaine became a lecturer at Warwick University where she was to work until 1973. Here she wrote the work that was to make her an overnight success and bring international recognition, *The Female Eunuch*.

TIMELINE

Date	Germaine Greer	Related events
1939	Born in Melbourne	
1949		Simone de Beauvoir publishes *The Second Sex*
1961		First edition of *Private Eye*
1964	Attends Newnham College, Cambridge Joins Footlights	Fellow Footlights members include Graeme Garden, John Cleese, Eric Idle, Bill Oddie, Clive James, Tim Brooke-Taylor and Graham Chapman
1967	Awarded PhD Goes to Warwick University	*Oz* magazine is first published in London
1970	*The Female Eunuch* published	Kate Millett publishes *Sexual Politics*
1971		The editors of *Oz* magazine are acquitted of obscenity charges
1989	Returns to Newnham College *Daddy, We Hardly Knew You* published	
1990		Naomi Wolf publishes *The Beauty Myth*
1996	Resigns from Newnham College	
1998	*The Whole Woman* published	
2000	Attacked and imprisoned in her home	
2004		Death of Susan Sontag
2005	Appears on *Celebrity Big Brother*	Fellow contestants included Brigitte Nielsen, Caprice, Bez and John McCririck

With its striking cover of a woman's torso hung up on a coat hanger, the book's title came from its central theme that marriage was a form of legalized slavery and that women had been castrated of their essential selves. As a result, Germaine argued, women do not realize how much men hate them and how much they hate themselves. Published in October 1970, the book was hugely successful and caused wide debate. By March 1971 *The Female Eunuch* had sold out its first printing and been translated into eight languages. After a worldwide tour to promote the book, Germaine left Warwick. She became involved in a variety of new activities, including presenting a TV comedy show and writing a column for *The Sunday Times*. She also became a contributor to magazines as diverse as the radically feminist *Spare Rib* and the men's magazine *Esquire*. In 1971 she was one of a panel of feminists who challenged the novelist Norman Mailer in a widely publicized debate on women's liberation. The organizers hoped for drama but unfortunately produced farce, although the invited audience contained many distinguished women's rights leaders, including Betty Friedan and Susan Sontag.

In 1979 Germaine produced her second book, *The Obstacle Race*, in which she considered the difficulties facing women in the world of art. The following year she became Director of the Tulsa Centre for the Study of Women's Literature in Oklahoma. In 1981 she spent three months in India researching her next book, *Sex and Destiny: The Politics of Human Fertility*. Published in 1984, the book was later described as 'revisionist feminism' as she apparently reversed many of her earlier ideas, arguing for sexual restraint and an enhanced status for motherhood. She criticized the developed world's attempts to implement population control in developing countries and opposed sexual promiscuity, which together with modern forms of contraception she felt had harmed women.

It has been argued that Germaine's books have always reflected the major themes she has struggled with in her own life, including her desire to have children, in which she was unsuccessful. However, no book was more revealing, or arguably more readable, than her search for the hidden life of her father. *Daddy, We Hardly Knew You* was published in 1989 and chronicles her travels in search of her ancestors. In the same year, Germaine returned to Newnham College but resigned in 1996. She objected to the college's appointment of a transsexual to the teaching staff, which she believed contravened the statutes of the all-female college.

As she grew older Germaine began to see the process of ageing as a form of liberation. Sexually promiscuous as a young woman – the media always mentioned her physical beauty, long legs and sexual bravado – she now grew more introspective. She described her views in her book *The Change: Women, Ageing and the Menopause* (1991) in which she tried to dispel myths about the menopause and ill-health.

Germaine also produced a number of academic works and collections of essays and promoted neglected writers, sometimes publishing their work under her own imprint. However, her fame and popularity as a writer rests inevitably on her first famous book. She was reported to have been paid £500,000 in 1998 to write a sequel – *The Whole Woman*, a work in which she attacks trends in contemporary feminism.

She continues to attract, even to court, controversy. In 2003 she published her illustrated book *The Beautiful Boy* – while some saw this as a valid art historical project, others dismissed it as prurient. In early 2005 she was once again front page news when she participated in the television programme *Celebrity Big Brother*. She had previously derided the producers and viewers of the show, saying 'Reality TV is not the end of civilization as we know it, it is civilization as we know it.' However, she was tempted by the prize money, which contestants could donate to a charity of their choice, and Germaine's was 125 acres of rainforest in Queensland, Australia. In the event she walked out of the show, to even more publicity, when she saw her fellow housemates subjected to what she considered bullying. With typical robustness, she told an interviewer, 'Persecution is what happens, holocausts are what happen when good people do nothing.'

Mairead Corrigan and Betty Williams

The tragic deaths of three children on a Belfast street started Mairead Corrigan's (above left) and Betty Williams's (above right) quest for an end to violence in Northern Ireland. Their story shows how ordinary women can accomplish extraordinary things.

'The voice of women has a special role and a special soul force in the struggle for a non-violent world.'

Betty Williams' Nobel address

BIOGRAPHY

Name:	Mairead Corrigan and Betty Williams
Lived:	27 January 1944 – and 22 May 1943 –
Place of birth:	Belfast, Northern Ireland
Nationality:	British
Famed as:	Peace campaigners

Mairead Corrigan and Betty Williams unlocked an enormous desire for peace within the hearts of the Northern Irish people. They founded the Community of Peace People with journalist Ciaran McKeown in 1976. Together they shared the Nobel Peace Prize and the Norwegian People's Peace Prize in 1979, were given honorary Doctorates of Law from Yale University and were awarded the Carl Von Ossietsky Medal for Courage.

Their commitment to peace was sparked by a tragic episode in 1976. Throughout that year there had been an escalation of violence in Northern Ireland involving civilians on both sides of the sectarian divide, members of Catholic and Protestant paramilitary organizations and British forces stationed in the province. In August alone there were 20 deaths associated with the troubles. On 10 August, a car driven by an IRA gunman who had been shot fleeing from British soldiers smashed into a family group in a residential street. Two children were killed outright, a third was mortally injured and their mother was critically wounded. The horror of this event produced a wave of revulsion against the sectarian violence then sweeping Northern Ireland.

FACTFILE

- Since the Nobel Peace Prize was established in 1901, only 12 women have won it.

- Betty Williams has been awarded the Schweitzer Medallion for Courage, The Martin Luther King, Jr Award, the Eleanor Roosevelt Award and the Frank Foundation Child Assistance International Oliver Award.

- In 2003 Mairead Corrigan was among a group of about 50 protestors arrested at a non-violent prayer protest against the war in Iraq outside the White House in Washington.

- In 1976 the Nobel Foundation had not awarded a Peace Prize. Mairead and Betty received the 1976 award post-dated in 1977, the year in which Amnesty International was honoured.

Mairead was the aunt of the dead children and Betty went to the scene when she heard the shooting that killed the car driver. This appalling incident was the starting point and inspiration for the founding of the Community of Peace People.

The Peace People promote the peaceful interaction of Protestants and Catholics in Northern Ireland. Among other projects, they organize summer camps in various European countries to provide a setting in which young Catholics and Protestants from Northern Ireland can meet and get to know one another. The Peace People also manage liaison projects for prisoners and their families on both sides of the sectarian divide.

Mairead was born in Belfast towards the end of World War II. Her father was a window cleaner and her mother a housewife. The Corrigans had five other daughters and two sons. Mairead went to school in the city and left at 16 to train as a secretary. She worked for a succession of Belfast companies. She also undertook

TIMELINE

Date	Mairead Corrigan and Betty Williams	Related events
1943	Betty Williams born	
1944	Mairead Corrigan born	
1948		Irish Free State (Eire) granted full independence from Britain. The six northern counties remain part of the United Kingdom
1961	Betty marries Ralph Williams	
1969		British troops sent to Northern Ireland to intervene in sectarian violence between Protestants and Roman Catholics
1972		Bloody Sunday Northern Ireland government suspended
1976	Founded the Community of Peace People	
1979	Awarded the Nobel Peace Prize	
1981	Mairead marries Jackie Maguire Betty moves to the US	
1985		Anglo-Irish Accord
1987	Mairead honoured by UN Program for Women of Achievement	
1993	Travel to Myanmar in support of Aung San Suu Kyi	Downing Street Declaration – people of Northern Ireland free to decide their own future
1997		IRA agrees to ceasefire
1998		Good Friday Agreement signed
2005		IRA offers to put weapons 'beyond use'

voluntary work, helping to establish clubs for physically handicapped children, teenagers and pre-school playgroups.

Through the Peace People, Mairead has travelled to more than 25 countries to endorse the establishment of justice and peace by non-violent means. She visited Latin America as the guest of Nobel laureate Adolfo Perez Esquivel, whom she had nominated for the prize. Throughout the course of her work, Mairead has met world leaders like Pope John Paul II, Queen Elizabeth II and former US President Jimmy Carter. Over the last 20 years she has been honoured by numerous organizations, including the United Nations, and has been invited to speak at conferences for the world's leading peace initiatives.

In January 1980, the Corrigan family suffered another bereavement when Mairead's sister Anne committed suicide. She had never recovered from the death of her three children. The following year, Mairead married Anne's widower, her brother-in-law

Jackie Maguire. She is the stepmother of three children and she and Jackie have two sons of their own.

Betty was also born and grew up in Belfast. Her father was a butcher and her mother a housewife. Betty married young and had two children but she and her husband later divorced. She was working as an office receptionist when she witnessed the death of the Maguire children. Betty's response was to contact the Irish media and petition them to highlight the horror of the incident. Her efforts brought her together with Mairead and Ciaran McKeown, Northern Ireland correspondent for the Irish Press Group.

In 1982, Betty married her second husband, James Perkins. They moved to the US, where Betty lectures extensively, and from where she continues to campaign on behalf of peace groups. She has been a visiting professor in Political Science and History at Sam Houston State University in Huntsville, Texas and is currently President of World Centres of Compassion for Children. In 1993, she and Mairead were part of the Nobel laureate group that travelled to Thailand, in a vain effort to enter Myanmar (Burma) to protest against the detention of laureate Aung San Suu Kyi.

Mairead and Betty made enormous advances towards peace in Northern Ireland. Within the first six months of the Peace People being set up, there was a 70 per cent drop in the rate of violence in the province. Violence never returned to the level experienced in 1976 when it seemed the community might erupt into full-scale civil war. In 1979, Betty incorporated the Peace People's Declaration in her Nobel acceptance address:

> We have a simple message for the world from this movement for peace. We want to live and love and build a just and peaceful society. We want for our children, as we want for ourselves, our lives at home, at work and at play, to be lives of joy and peace. We recognize that to build such a life demands of all of us dedication, hard work and courage. We recognize that there are many problems in our society, which are a source of conflict and violence. We recognize the use of the bomb and the bullet and all the techniques of violence. We dedicate ourselves to working with our neighbours, near and far, day in and day out, to building that peaceful society in which the tragedies we have known are a bad memory and a continuing warning.

Mairead and Betty are still active in peace efforts worldwide and advocate creating peace by uniting people of different backgrounds. This method is founded on the belief that people cannot harm others that they have grown to know and befriend. Betty has talked of the need to break down the physical, emotional and ideological barriers that divide people. The only force that can break these barriers, she concludes, is the 'force of love'. Their efforts, born out of their personal witness of the tragedy of violence, have shown what exceptional women, from ordinary backgrounds, can accomplish. 'We are for life and creation', Betty stated in her Nobel lecture, 'and we are against war and destruction.'

Billie Jean King

One of the world's greatest athletes, Billie Jean King was a trailblazer for women's tennis. She fought for its parity with the men's game and dominated the world's major championships for two decades.

'Ever since that day when I was 11 years old, and I wasn't allowed in a photo because I wasn't wearing a skirt, I knew I wanted to change the sport.'

BIOGRAPHY

Name:	Billie Jean Moffitt
Lived:	22 November 1943 –
Place of birth:	Long Beach, California
Nationality:	American
Famed as:	Record-breaking tennis player

Billie Jean King is one of the most celebrated tennis players of all time. She won a record number of grand slam titles, was ranked number one in the world five times between 1966 and 1972, and spent a total of 17 years in the top ten of women's tennis.

Everyone in Billie Jean's family was involved with sport. Her father, Bill Moffitt, after whom she was named, was a Long Beach fireman and an athlete, and her brother Randy Moffitt became a pitcher for the San Francisco Giants baseball team. Billie Jean fell in love with the sport as soon as she started playing at the age of 11, winning her first championship when she was 14. She recalls the 'burning, tingling, literally white-hot feeling' she had when she first held a racket and maintains that even today, whenever she makes a good shot, 'My heart pounds, my eyes get damp, and my ears feel like they're wiggling.' At that time tennis was principally a men's sport and the women's game was regarded as an entertaining and attractive sideshow. Billie Jean transformed and dominated the game for nearly 20 years and destroyed that opinion for ever.

FACTFILE

- Billie Jean bought her first tennis racket with money she saved doing odd jobs. It cost $8.

- In 1973, *Sports Illustrated* magazine broke with tradition and, instead of naming its annual 'Sportsman of the Year', featured Billie Jean on the cover as 'Sportswoman of the Year'.

By the age of just 16 she was ranked nineteenth in the country, and former American champion Alice Marble began coaching her. 'She was so crazy about tennis,' Alice later said, 'I'd have to lock her in her room to do her homework.' Under Alice's influence Billie Jean rose to fourth in the national rankings in under a year. In 1961, when she was 17, she won the women's doubles at Wimbledon with 18-year-old Karen Hantze. They were the youngest team ever to win the tournament, and their victory brought Billie Jean international recognition. This was the first of her 20 Wimbledon titles, the record number of titles an individual has ever won.

While studying history at Los Angeles State College, she met law student Larry King, whom she married in 1965. From then on a generation of tennis fans became used to seeing 'Mrs L. W. King' on Wimbledon score boards – a naming convention that has now been dropped.

Billie Jean was named Outstanding Female Athlete of the World in 1967 and in 1968 she became the first woman to sign a professional contract to tour in a tournament group with Rosie Casals, Françoise Durr and Ann Haydon Jones, forming the women's section of the National Tennis League. This included six men: Rod Laver, Ken Rosewall, Pancho Gonzalez, Andres Gimino, Fred Stolle and Roy Emerson, the greatest players of their day.

TIMELINE

Date	Billie Jean King	Related events
1943	Born in California	
1951		Maureen Connolly becomes youngest woman to win the US singles championship in tennis
1958	Wins first singles tournament	
1961	Wins first Wimbledon title	
1965	Marries Larry King	
1966	Wins Wimbledon singles for first time	Losing finalist Maria Bueno, three times champion
1967	Wins the singles, doubles, and mixed doubles at Wimbledon and US Open singles and doubles	John Newcombe wins men's singles at Wimbledon and US Open
1971	First female athlete to earn over $100,000	Evonne Goolagong wins Wimbledon
1973	Beats Bobby Riggs in the 'battle of the sexes'	US Open equalizes men's and women's prize money
1975	Wins her last Wimbledon singles title	Losing finalist Evonne Goolagong, twice champion
1983	Retires from the professional game	Martina Navratilova wins Wimbledon and US Open
1996	US Olympic tennis coach	

The year 1971 was to prove a defining one. Billie Jean became the first woman to earn more than $100,000 in prize money in a single year, an achievement that brought her a personal telephone call from President Richard M. Nixon. Out of the 31 singles tournaments in which she participated she won 17, out of 26 doubles she won 21. Although her total earnings came to $117,000, this was a fraction of the sum a male player would have won for the same performance. Billie Jean began to campaign for equal prize money for the men's and women's championships and convinced her fellow players to form a union, the Women's Tennis Association. In 1972, when she won the US Open and was paid $15,000 less than Ilie Nastase, who won the men's singles, she refused to return to defend her title the following year unless the prize money was increased. In 1973 the US Open became the first major international tournament to offer equal prize money for men and women and Billie Jean became the first president of the WTA.

The same year brought a match that, despite all her record-breaking achievements, is the event that many people will best remember her for. Billie Jean agreed to take part in a $100,000, winner-takes-all match against Bobby Riggs, a previous Wimbledon champion who, at 55, was the same age as her father. Her decision prompted considerable criticism from people who queried whether a win or loss against a man so much older than her would accomplish anything, either for women's tennis or feminism in general. But Billie Jean, a women's rights campaigner who had the future of women's tennis at heart, saw things differently: 'I didn't feel it was a very big accomplishment athletically. But psychologically and emotionally, it was a big deal. I knew it might provide a springboard for girls and women in athletics.' The publicity surrounding the event was considerable, with a record crowd of nearly 31,000 in the Astrodome in Houston, Texas and a television audience of 50 million. Billie Jean won easily in three straight sets – the match was to be played as a men's single, with up to five sets.

In 1974 Billie Jean became the first woman to coach a professional male and female team when she served as a player-coach for World Team Tennis, which she and her husband Larry had helped establish. In 1975 she was part of the team that created both the World Team Tennis League and the Women's Professional Softball League, and also helped launch *Women's Sports Magazine.*

The list of Billie Jean's titles is impressive: Wimbledon singles 1966, 1967, 1968, 1972, 1973 and 1975 – she was also the finalist in 1963, 1969 and 1970; the US Open singles in 1967, 1971, 1972 and 1974; the French Open singles in 1972; and the Australian Open singles in 1968 and 1971. She was only the fifth woman to win all four major singles titles. In her whole career, including both the amateur and open eras, she won 67 professional titles and 37 amateur titles, and reached 38 other professional finals, while amassing impressive total prize money of $1,966,487.

In 1981, Billie Jean's personal life became news when she was sued by a woman who had been her companion for some years. She was the first American athlete to acknowledge a same-sex relationship and her openness won her general respect. Billie Jean and Larry King divorced in the mid-1980s.

Billie Jean's final act as a player came in 1983 at the grand age – for a sports person – of 39 at her most successful event, Wimbledon. She lost in her fourteenth semi-final appearance to 18-year-old Andrea Jaeger 6-1, 6-1. However, seven years after that she made a cameo appearance in the Boca Raton tournament in Florida, winning a doubles match with 13-year-old Jennifer Capriati.

Even after her official retirement from the game, achievements and awards continued to accumulate. In 1990, *Life* named her one of the 100 most important Americans of the twentieth century, and in 1994 she was ranked number five in *Sports Illustrated*'s top 40 athletes of all time, for her role in significantly altering and elevating the sport over four decades. In 1996 she coached the US team to the Davis Cup, beating Spain, and as US Olympic coach she guided Lindsay Davenport, Gigi Fernández and Mary Joe Fernández to gold medals.

Billie Jean now lives in Chicago, Illinois. She serves on the board of directors for the Women's Tennis Association, the Elton John AIDS Foundation and the National AIDS Fund, and is a member of the International Tennis Hall of Fame and the National Women's Hall of Fame. Her commitment to women's tennis remains undimmed, and she has inspired many of today's greatest female players.

Benazir Bhutto

The first woman to lead a Muslim country in modern times, Benazir Bhutto strove to improve conditions for women and the underprivileged in Pakistan. A woman of courage and conviction, she has lived in exile since 1999 after her government was deposed for corruption charges.

'When I was growing up I thought a woman could have it all and now I find that, yes, a woman can have it all – but she has to be prepared to pay the price.'

BIOGRAPHY

Name:	Mohtarma Benazir Bhutto
Lived:	21 June 1953 –
Place of birth:	Karachi, Pakistan
Nationality:	Pakistani
Famed as:	First woman to lead a Muslim country in modern times

Benazir Bhutto is the eldest daughter of Zulfikar Ali Bhutto, who was prime minister of Pakistan during the early 1970s. For three generations her family has been among the most powerful and wealthy of the ruling class in Pakistan. After primary and secondary education in Pakistan, Benazir went to Radcliffe College in Harvard, where she graduated with a degree in political science in 1973.

Life in America was a revelation to Benazir. She wrote later: 'I was a very shy girl who led an insulated life, it was only when I came to Harvard that suddenly I saw the power of people. I didn't know such a power existed, I saw people criticizing their own president, you couldn't do that in Pakistan, you'd be thrown in prison. I saw the press take on the government. I was determined to go back home and to give to my people the freedoms and the choices – the individual dignity – which I saw my college mates and everyone else in the West have.'

FACTFILE

- Benazir's huband, Asif Ali Zardari, was the investment minister in her government and gained the nickname Mr Ten Per Cent for the size of the cut he allegedly demanded on every deal.

- When the Taliban took power in Afghanistan in 1996, Benazir's government was one of only three nations to recognize it.

- Benazir has condemned the 11 September terrorist attacks on the United States, commenting that they do not serve Islam.

In 1973, Benazir went to Lady Margaret Hall at the University of Oxford, where she read for a degree in politics, philosophy and economics and became president of the Oxford Union debating society. Her life as an undergraduate was dogged by media attention, as her father's administration was challenged at home and abroad. Zulfikar Ali Bhutto had overseen the implementation of a new constitution, under which he became prime minister, a position of considerable power. He had pushed through socialist reforms and Islam had become the national religion of Pakistan. He took Pakistan out of the Commonwealth and formed alliances with other Islamic states. However, democracy within the country was fragile and political opposition was repressed.

Benazir returned to Pakistan for the election in June 1977. She wanted to work as a diplomat or a journalist but her father had other plans. He had groomed her, his oldest child, for political office. In the aftermath of the election, which led to widespread social unrest, martial law was imposed by General Zia-ul-Haq. Zulfikar Ali Bhutto was arrested and Benazir was placed under house arrest. The restrictions on her movements were to continue for more than six years.

Zulfikar Ali Bhutto's trial began in October 1977. Its blatant prejudice was condemned by commentators around the world, but appeals for clemency from numerous heads of state were ignored by the Pakistani regime. Zulfikar Ali Bhutto was hanged on

TIMELINE

Date	Benazir Bhutto	Related events
1953	Born in Karachi	
1956		Pakistan becomes an Islamic republic
1969	Admitted to Harvard University's Radcliffe College	
1971		Civil war in Pakistan: East Pakistan (Bangladesh) declares independence
1973	Graduates from Harvard Enrols at Oxford University	Zulfikar Ali Bhutto becomes Prime Minister of Pakistan
1976	Graduates from Oxford	
1977	Placed under house arrest Benazir's father arrested	Martial law imposed in Pakistan
1979		Zulfikar Ali Bhutto hanged
1984	Moves to England	
1986	Returns to Pakistan	
1987	Marries Asif Ali Zardari	
1988	Sworn in as Prime Minister	Zia killed in plane crash
1993	Re-elected as Prime Minister	
1996	Removed from office on charges of corruption	
1999	Goes into exile Sentenced to prison *in absentia*	Military coup in Pakistan
2004	Makes her home in Dubai	

4 April 1979. After her father's death, Benazir found herself *de facto* leader of the Pakistan People's Party. Her house arrest continued until January 1984, when she was eventually allowed to travel abroad on medical grounds.

For two years, Benazir remained in England, leading a political party in exile that had no power in its own country. Then in 1986 martial law was lifted in Pakistan and she judged the time was right to return to her country. She was met by hundreds of thousands of people on her arrival at Lahore airport on 10 April and hailed as the symbol of the anti-Zia movement. Vast rallies in support of the PPP were held across the country. On 18 December 1987, she married politician Asif Ali Zardari.

In 1988 Zia-ul-Haq announced the first elections that had been held in Pakistan for 11 years. Benazir was expecting her first child and Zia might have hoped that her pregnancy would limit her political activities. He was facing a delicate situation. Her return to the country had rekindled support for the PPP and opposition within and beyond Pakistan's borders was growing. After an appeal from Benazir, the Supreme Court ruled that the elections should be open to all political parties. Despite her pregnancy, Benazir campaigned for 15 hours a day and even after her child was born prematurely, she returned to the election campaign. General Zia-ul-Haq was killed in an air crash in dubious circumstances on 17 August 1988 and Ghulam Ishaq Khan became acting president. The PPP won 94 of 207 seats in the National Assembly and with the support of other smaller parties achieved a clear majority. On 2 December, Benazir was named Prime Minister – Pakistan's youngest and the first woman to lead a Muslim nation in modern times.

During Benazir's time in office, she focused on social issues, health and sex discrimination, and initiated projects to set up women's police stations, courts and development banks. She started the People's Programme for economic improvement and lifted a ban on student and trade unions. Despite some well-intentioned policies, Benazir's government was marked by intrigue and achieved little. In August 1990, President Ghulam Ishaq Khan accused her and her husband of corruption and dismissed her government. The PPP then lost the elections in late 1990. Benazir's husband was held in custody between 1990 and 1993 on various charges, although he was eventually acquitted.

For the next three years, Benazir campaigned as the opposition leader to Nawaz Sharif, attempting to improve programmes for health, social welfare and education for the underprivileged. In October 1993, she ran for election again. She was now a more experienced politician and had formed alliances to help her address Pakistan's deep-seated problems. When the PPP coalition won the election, Benazir returned as Prime Minister and stayed in office for the next three years.

In 1996, the upheavals that characterized Pakistan's politics were to touch her personally. Benazir's government was once again dismissed, charged with 'corruption, misrule and nepotism'. Benazir denied the charges, maintaining that they were politically motivated. However, her husband was charged with corruption and murder and imprisoned.

After a military coup in 1999, Benazir left Pakistan under fear of arrest. She now lives in the United Arab Emirates with her family, giving lectures and writing. She has an outstanding appeal against the accusations of corruption before the Supreme Court in Pakistan. In November 2004, Asif Ali Zardari was released from prison but rearrested a month later on further murder charges. Benazir is unlikely to return to Pakistan, for fear that she will not be allowed to leave the country again. An amendment to the Pakistani constitution now bars prime ministers from serving more than two terms, so, whatever the outcome of her appeal, she will never be eligible to resume her post as leader of her country.

Benazir Bhutto has said: 'I would like to be remembered for overturning a military dictatorship and heralding a world of democracy in Pakistan, for bringing in changes which could not be reversed which included an independent press and the move towards free markets... but above all I want to be remembered for what I did for women.' Unhappily it seems that for now at least her political legacy will continue to be compromised by the shadow of corruption.

Oprah Winfrey

Oprah Winfrey grew up in extreme poverty in Mississippi. Today she is a media entrepreneur who presents a TV show watched by millions of people in over 100 countries. She is the first woman in history to own and produce her own talk show, and the first African-American woman to become a billionaire.

'The big secret in life is that there is no big secret. Whatever your goal, you can get there if you're willing to work.'

BIOGRAPHY

Name:	Oprah Gail Winfrey
Lived:	29 January 1954 –
Place of birth:	Kosciusko, Mississippi
Nationality:	American
Famed as:	TV presenter, actress, producer

Oprah Winfrey was born to unmarried teenage parents in America's south in 1954. Her parents were a housemaid, Vernita Lee, and a soldier, Vernon Winfrey. Oprah was originally named 'Orpah', a name from the book of Ruth in the Bible. However, although this was on her birth certificate, when it came to writing and pronouncing her name, her family and neighbours usually transposed the 'r' and the 'p' and so she became known as Oprah.

Oprah was brought up by her grandmother on a farm with no indoor plumbing. A bright child, she was reading the Bible and reciting in church by the age of three. When she was six she moved to live with her mother in Milwaukee. This was far from being the improvement in life that she had hoped for. While there she was subjected to physical abuse and sexual molestation. She ran away when she was 13 and was sent to a juvenile detention home.

FACTFILE

- *The Oprah Winfrey Show* is watched by an estimated 30 million viewers a week in the United States and is broadcast internationally in 111 countries.

- Oprah has been named one of the 100 most influential people in the world by *Time* magazine.

- She has lived with businessman Steadman Graham for more than 20 years.

- In 2004, Oprah had to do jury service in a murder trial in Chicago, Illinois. The defendant was found guilty.

- As a publicity stunt, in September 2004 Oprah gave each of the 276 members of the audience of her live show a car – landing them all with a $7000 tax bill as a result.

At 14, Oprah was sent to live with her father in Nashville where she was given a strict upbringing. Vernon Winfrey insisted that she had a proper education – something for which she was later grateful. Of this time she says: 'As strict as he was, he had some concerns about me making the best of my life, and would not accept anything less than what he thought was my best.' Every week Oprah had to read a book and write a report about it. Reading helped her obtain a better education than she might otherwise have had. When she was in seventh grade her teacher noticed her reading over lunch and arranged a scholarship for her to a better school.

Oprah showed early signs of being a talented public performer. She was also extremely pretty and gained public attention through winning beauty contests. When she was only 17 she was hired to read the news on a local radio station. Following school, Oprah went to Tennessee State University and took a bachelor's degree in speech and performing arts. While there, she was given a job by a television company and became Nashville's first female, first black, TV news anchor person.

After graduating in 1976, Oprah worked as a co-anchor on the early evening news at Baltimore's WJZ-TV. However, news was not her forte, as she tended to become emotionally involved when delivering it. The company recognized her talent before

TIMELINE

Date	Oprah Winfrey	Related events
1954	Born in Kosciusko, Mississippi	
1955		Montgomery bus boycott 1955–56
1963		Rev Martin Luther King Jr speech *I Have a Dream*
1968	Moves to live with her father in Nashville	Shirley Chisholm becomes the first black American woman to be elected to the US Congress
1976	Moves to Baltimore to join WJZ-TV news as a co-anchor	Congressman Andrew Young becomes first African-American US ambassador to the United Nations
1983	WLS-TV's faltering morning talk show, *AM Chicago*, renamed *The Oprah Winfrey Show*	Alice Walker receives the Pulitzer Prize for *The Color Purple*
1985		Debut of the *Larry King Show*
1986	*The Oprah Winfrey Show* broadcast nationally Founds Harpo Productions	Martin Luther King Day first celebrated as a US national holiday
1991	Initiates National Child Protection Act and appears before Congress	Debut of the *Jerry Springer Show*
1996	Receives the George Foster Peabody Individual Achievement Award	Debut of the *Rosie O'Donnell Show*
2001	George W. Bush and Al Gore appear on her show	
2005	Personal worth estimated at $1.5 billion by *Forbes* magazine	

the camera, however, and made her the co-host of WJZ's local talk show. This turned out to be a niche that fitted her talents perfectly.

In 1983, she moved to Chicago where she took over as host of WLS-TV's low-rated half-hour morning talk show, *AM Chicago*. However, her presence unexpectedly made the show so successful that it was renamed *The Oprah Winfrey Show*, was expanded to an hour, and broadcast nationally in 1986. Oprah became famous for her daytime TV debates on controversial topics.

Initially *The Oprah Winfrey Show* was a traditional talk show, but by the 1990s Oprah had turned it into something different, a vehicle to look at major issues that she thought were directly relevant and important to women. She did a considerable amount of charity work, and used her show to feature people who were the victims of poverty or unfortunate accidents. On the show she also shared some of her own personal battles, including her struggle to lose 70 lbs in weight. Many women were able to identify with her ongoing problems in this area, possibly understanding the particular difficulties this brought her as somebody very much in the public eye. The show was to win her many awards, including three Emmys.

In 1985 Oprah had an entrée into acting when she was asked to appear in the film of Alice Walker's novel *The Color Purple*. Oprah was recommended to the director Steven Spielberg by record producer Quincy Jones, who had seen her programme on a hotel TV. However, Oprah was not an experienced actress and was initially terrified and intimidated by Spielberg. Gradually, mutual respect developed and her role was enlarged as her acting ability improved. Her performance was widely praised and in 1982 she was nominated for an Academy Award for Best Supporting Actress. Other acting roles followed, including a TV mini-series, *The Women of Brewster Place*, in 1989.

In the late 1990s, Oprah introduced the idea of a television book club on her show. The effect of this on book sales gave an indication of her extraordinary public influence: every book she selected immediately became a bestseller. She also introduced her audience to neglected classics. When she chose the John Steinbeck novel *East of Eden*, first published in 1952, it soared to the top of the book sales charts. A careless remark could have the same influence, to more damaging effect. When Oprah remarked that she would never eat a burger again, having run a feature on mad cow disease on her show, beef prices plummeted. She was sued for business disparagement by a group of Texan cattlemen but found not guilty.

Apart from her TV work, Oprah has started The Angel Network, an organization that raises millions of dollars a year for charities. The organization has helped to establish scholarships and schools, build youth centres and homes and support shelters for women. The Oprah Winfrey Foundation awards grants that support the education of women, children and families around the world. Its latest endeavour, a partnership with the South African Ministry of Education, is to build the Oprah Winfrey Leadership Academy for Girls, which is scheduled to open in 2007. Oprah has also published her own magazines: *O, The Oprah Magazine* and *O at Home*, as well as being a co-founder of a women's cable TV network. Having established her own production company, Harpo Productions – Oprah spelled backwards – she produced, among other projects, a screen adaptation of Toni Morrison's novel *Beloved*.

Oprah has a unique position in US popular culture and is widely idolized. She has the ability to motivate viewers to improve their own lives and the world around them, and to make them care about things she cares about. Some critics claim she stirs up misery in people's lives and argue that she is partisan, harder on the failings of the men she features on her show than the women. Whatever people's views of her shows, the power of Oprah's influence and her inspiration cannot be denied. She is a force for good through her charitable and campaigning activities, and a role model of how to overcome the obstacles of poverty and childhood maltreatment to achieve great things.

Madonna

Madonna is the richest female pop artist in the world. Her status as a cultural icon is, however, the result of more than just her musical output. Her flair for self-promotion through distinctive, often highly provocative images, has established her as an inspirational woman in control of her public persona, her career and her sexuality.

'I've never wanted to make the same record or do the same thing twice.'

BIOGRAPHY

Name:	Madonna Louise Veronica Ciccone
Lived:	16 August 1958 –
Place of birth:	Detroit, Michigan
Nationality:	American
Famed as:	Singer, actress, author, pop and fashion icon

Madonna Louise Veronica Ciccone, or 'Little Nonni', was born in Detroit in 1958, the third child and eldest daughter of Silvio Ciccone and Madonna Fortin, a devoutly Catholic couple. One of six children, Madonna was a notably articulate and vivacious child, but one who, according to her grandmother, 'liked attention from the family and she usually got it'. Her mother, who had been a talented dancer and great lover of classical music, died of breast cancer when Madonna was only five – a trauma that went on to affect Madonna deeply throughout her life.

Silvio Ciccone eventually remarried, but Madonna strongly disliked her stepmother and refused to call her mother. Her teenage years were troubled: her father was very strict and, as well as being heavily involved in bringing up her younger siblings and doing her share of household chores, Madonna was expected to do well at school. Although bright and an achiever academically, she was defiant and rebellious, but found an outlet for some of her energies in school drama and ballet, for which she showed real talent. On leaving school she studied dance at the University of Michigan, having gained a much sought-after scholarship.

FACTFILE

- Madonna is probably the richest female artist in the world. Her capital is estimated at over £235 million ($448 million).

- According to the *Guinness Book of World Records,* Madonna is the most successful female recording artist of all time, having sold over 250 million records – 75 million singles and 175 million albums.

- In the UK, Madonna is one of only two artists (the other is Kylie Minogue) ever to have a number one album and number one single in three different decades.

Encouraged by her dance teacher and mentor, Christopher Flynn, whom she idolized, Madonna left Michigan at 19 to become a dancer in New York. Once there she worked in various dance companies while supporting herself with a series of low-paid jobs and living a tough life in often squalid conditions. Teachers at that time noted her determination and self-belief, but although an extremely committed and talented dancer, it became clear that Madonna was too much of an individualist to fit in well as a dance troupe member.

After auditioning for a number of theatrical and musical roles, Madonna gained a part in a revue that took her to Paris. Here she met Dan Gilroy, a musician who became her boyfriend and encouraged her musical ambitions. On returning to New York she formed a pop/dance band with him called *The Breakfast Club*. Madonna initially played drums for the band, but went on to become the lead singer – a move that led to a split with Gilroy. She left the band in 1980 to form one of her own, *Emmy*, before going on to collaborate with another former boyfriend, Stephen Bray, in writing material for her to perform as a solo singer.

TIMELINE

Date	Madonna	Related events
1958	Born in Michigan	Jerry Lee Lewis records *Great Balls of Fire*
1976	Attends University of Michigan	
1983	*Holiday* released	
1984	First US no 1, *Like a Virgin* (6 weeks)	Tina Turner's *What's Love Got To Do With It?* US no 1 (3 weeks)
1985	Appears in *Desperately Seeking Susan* Marries Sean Penn	Live Aid concert in Wembley and Philadelphia
1989	Divorces Sean Penn *Like a Prayer* US and UK no 1	Janet Jackson *Miss You Much* US no 1 (4 weeks)
1990	*Vogue* US and UK no 1 *The Immaculate Collection* released	Sinéad O'Connor *Nothing Compares 2U* US no 1 (4 weeks)
1993	Sets up Maverick Records *Bedtime Stories* released	Whitney Houston *I Will Always Love You* US no 1
2000	Marries Guy Ritchie	Kylie Minogue's *Light Years* becomes her first Australian no 1 album
2003	*American Life* released Publishes *The English Roses*	
2005	Performs at Live8 in London Becomes face of Versace	Live8 benefit concerts held in all G8 member countries

Networking furiously, seizing every opportunity that came her way, Madonna managed to get a demo tape heard by a New York DJ and producer, Mark Kamins. As a result, at the age of 24, Madonna secured a record deal as a singer with Kamins' fledgling music company. Her first two singles were club and dance hits, and then in 1983 she released the highly memorable dance song *Holiday*, which became her first US top 40 hit, reaching number 16 in the chart. She also released her debut album, *Madonna*, and in 1984 had her first US number one, with the single *Like a Virgin*.

The album for which her number one hit was the title track propelled Madonna to international stardom. It was followed by *Material Girl* in 1985. These hugely popular albums, together with her appearance in the film *Desperately Seeking Susan*, imprinted Madonna's very individual image on public and, particularly, teenage minds. The previously struggling dancer was now an international celebrity with millions of record sales – due to a combination of raunchy videos, her powerful personality and her unique sound.

In 1985 Madonna married the actor Sean Penn. Their relationship, always a stormy one, attracted much publicity. Penn was known for his heavy drinking, wild behaviour and volatile response to the media. The marriage ended in 1989 when Madonna filed for divorce on the grounds of spousal abuse.

Changing her image yet again, Madonna released the album *Like a Prayer*, which was a turning point for her – the content was far more personal and emotional than any of her previous records. The *Like a Prayer* single caused controversy and the Vatican denounced it for its blasphemous mixture of eroticism and Catholic symbolism. Nonetheless, or perhaps helped by this, the single reached number one around the world and three further American top ten hits from the album followed.

Through the 1990s Madonna continued to cause controversy and to influence fashion. She popularized the idea of wearing underwear as outer wear and will forever be associated with the pink satin conical bra designed for her by Jean-Paul Gaultier. While continuing to produce highly successful albums, Madonna also guaranteed herself press and public attention by publishing *Sex*, a book containing erotic photographs of herself and other celebrities.

In the mid-1990s Madonna was keen to gain the title role in the film adaptation of Andrew Lloyd Weber's music *Evita*. She worked hard to make her voice suitable for the role, which she won. She received many positive reviews for her portrayal of Eva Perón – whose life in some ways paralleled her own – and won a Golden Globe Award for Best Actress. Having firmly established herself as a serious actress, Madonna now developed a more sophisticated musical style that mixed electronica, techno and hip-hop, and the record *Ray of Light*, produced by William Orbit, received critical acclaim.

Madonna became a mother in 1996 when she gave birth to a daughter, Lourdes. The father was Carlos Leon, her personal trainer, with whom she had a long-standing relationship. They later parted and Madonna did not marry again until 2000 when she became the wife of film-maker Guy Ritchie, with whom she had her second child, Rocco.

Following her marriage to Englishman Ritchie, Madonna settled in Great Britain and branched into writing children's books. Her first book, *The English Roses*, was published in 2003 and became the fastest-selling children's picture book of all time, in its first week selling only 220 copies fewer than J. K. Rowling's fifth Harry Potter novel, which also came out that year. Madonna is still a strong musical presence and was a main attraction in the Live8 concert in London in 2005. The diversity of her career was also illustrated by her becoming the 'face' of Versace.

Madonna's life is one of apparent paradox. From a strictly Catholic upbringing she has emerged as someone regularly prepared to outrage those with religious sensibilities. An astute businesswoman, she is also a devout follower of the Kaballah Judaic spiritual teachings. A heroine to some feminists, to other women she is an impediment to the feminist cause. Despite the enigma surrounding her real personality, there is no denying that through her exploits, Madonna has influenced the view women have of their sexuality and what they can achieve in life, as well as producing music that reflected the *zeitgeist* of the late twentieth century.

Diana, Princess of Wales

Diana, Princess of Wales was glamorous, approachable and universally admired for her high-profile involvement with AIDS issues and the international campaign against landmines. During the last years of her life she was the most famous, and most photographed, woman in the world.

'Don't call me an icon. I'm just a mother trying to help.'

BIOGRAPHY

Name:	Lady Diana Frances Spencer
Lived:	1 July 1961 – 31 August 1997
Place of birth:	Sandringham, England
Place of death:	Paris, France
Nationality:	British
Famed as:	Princess of Wales, patron of charities

Diana Spencer, the youngest daughter of Viscount and Viscountess Althorp, was born at Park House, Sandringham. Diana, her two older sisters and younger brother lived at Park House until the death of her grandfather, Earl Spencer, in 1975. Her father inherited the title and the family moved to the family seat at Althorp, Northamptonshire.

In 1974, Diana was sent to board at West Heath School in Kent. Not an academic child, she showed a flair for music and dancing and enjoyed domestic science. In 1977 she spent a few months at a finishing school in Switzerland, then returned to London where she worked as a nanny for an American couple and as a kindergarten teacher.

The Spencer family had been close to the British Royal Family for decades: Diana's maternal grandmother, the Dowager Lady Fermoy, was a longtime friend of Queen Elizabeth the Queen Mother. Prince Charles and Diana had met while she lived at Sandringham and Charles had briefly dated Diana's oldest sister, Lady Sarah Spencer. The Prince of Wales was unmarried and in his thirties. There was continuous public discussion about his duty to marry and provide an heir to the throne. However, his choice of partner was constrained by strict expectations. The future queen needed to have an aristocratic background, could not have been married before, or involved in another relationship, and must be a Protestant. Diana fulfilled all of these criteria and she and Charles were increasingly brought together by their respective families.

FACTFILE

- The title 'Princess Diana' was used widely but incorrectly by the public and media after Diana's marriage. This styling is only used by a woman who is a princess by birth.

- Diana was distantly related to Hollywood screen legend Humphrey Bogart through her American relations.

- Sales of Elton John's special version of *Candle in the Wind*, sung at Diana's funeral, raised £20 million for the Diana, Princess of Wales Memorial Fund.

Diana was 19 and Charles 32 when they married at St Paul's Cathedral in London on 29 July 1981, with around one billion people watching and listening worldwide. Diana was the first Englishwoman to marry an heir to the throne for 300 years and was now the most senior royal woman in the United Kingdom after the Queen and Queen Mother.

Diana was quickly pregnant and on 21 June 1982 gave birth to Prince William. She had begun to undertake official duties immediately after her wedding and from the very start her photograph was rarely off the front pages of the world's newspapers. Diana swiftly became the most popular member of the royal family. She was increasingly at ease in front of the photographers who pursued her ceaselessly on

TIMELINE

Date	Diana, Princess of Wales	Related events
1961	Born in Sandringham	
1974	Attends West Heath School, Kent	Charles becomes a Royal Naval helicoptor pilot
1977	Attends finishing school at Rougemont in Switzerland Meets Prince Charles	
1978	Works as a kindergarten teacher at the Young England School, Pimlico	
1981	Becomes engaged to Prince Charles	HM Queen asks newspapers to leave Diana alone
1982	Birth of Prince William	
1984	Birth of Prince Harry	
1992	Diana and Charles separate	HM Queen refers to 1992 as an 'annus horribilis' in her Christmas speech
1993	Announces her retirement from public life	HM Queen agrees to pay income and capital gains tax for first time
1994	Admits adultery in interview with BBC	Charles admits affair with Camilla Parker-Bowles in TV interview
1996	Diana and Prince Charles divorce	
1997	Dies in a car accident in Paris	
2005		Charles and Camilla Parker-Bowles marry

behalf of the world's media. As she moved into her twenties she grew into a beautiful and poised woman, who never looked less than stunning in formal or casual clothes. Her support was canvassed for countless organizations and events and she was president or patron of more than 100 charities. She publicized the plight of the homeless and disabled, children in need and people with HIV and AIDS. Her unaffected manner made people of all backgrounds feel comfortable with her.

On 15 September 1984, her second son Prince Harry was born. By this time, Diana and Charles were undertaking separate engagements and rumours that their marriage was in difficulties began to circulate. Charles resumed his relationship with Camilla Parker-Bowles, a previous lover, and Diana's name was linked with other men. Press speculation was frenzied and sustained by stories supplied by friends of both parties, which showed neither the Prince nor Diana in a positive light. On 9 December 1992, Charles and Diana separated and Diana announced that she would be reducing her public commitments to allow her to combine 'a meaningful public role with a more private life', although she continued to appear with the royal family on major occasions.

In 1993, Diana gave an infamous interview to a BBC journalist in which she spoke publicly about her unhappiness, her husband's adultery and the pressures of her public role. The repercussions of her decision to give the interview were far-reaching. No member of the royal family had spoken so openly before. Public opinion of Diana was polarized between supporters of her frankness and those who felt she had exposed the royal family unjustifiably.

On 28 August 1996, Charles and Diana divorced. They shared equal responsibility for the upbringing of their children, and Diana remained a member of the royal family. She was now known as Diana, Princess of Wales, and had a home at Kensington Palace, where her office was also based. After the divorce, Diana strove to protect her sons from the public scrutiny by which she felt herself to be increasingly victimized. She resigned from some charities and patronages and relinquished all service appointments with military units. She did, however, remain patron of Centrepoint – a charity for the homeless – the English National Ballet, the Leprosy Mission and the National AIDS Trust, and president of the Hospital for Sick Children and the Royal Marsden Hospital.

Diana was also an active campaigner for a ban on the manufacture and use of land mines. In 1997, she visited landmine projects in Angola and Bosnia where she met victims, visited sites and witnessed mine-clearing operations in the field. Her work and the publicity it generated gave a tremendous boost to the anti-landmine cause and brought worldwide attention to the effects of landmines on people's lives.

Throughout 1997, Diana had been seen repeatedly with Dodi Fayed, the son of Mohammed al Fayed, the owner of Harrods. They had holidayed together with her two sons and in August went together to Paris. On 30 August, the car in which they were travelling was involved in a high-speed accident in an underpass by the Seine. Dodi Fayed and the driver were killed instantly and Diana died shortly afterwards. Her bodyguard, the only person in the car to have been wearing a safety belt, survived.

Diana's funeral took place at Westminster Abbey on 6 September. More than one million floral tributes were laid outside Kensington Palace, making a sea of flowers, and three million people lined the route of the funeral cortège. Diana was buried on an island in a lake at Althorp. After the mourning subsided, there was a great deal of soul-searching. Her informal, empathetic image and huge popularity had revealed public distaste for the traditional values of the royal family, who now recognized the need for change. The media, too, reconsidered their conduct towards public figures – Diana's car had been speeding to avoid a pack of freelance photographers when it crashed. The British press voluntarily entered an agreement to leave Princes William and Harry alone during their school and university years. Huge sums of money poured in from the public and were donated to the Diana, Princess of Wales Memorial Fund, which continues to support work in the charitable fields with which she was most involved. The nation took to heart the words of her brother, Earl Spencer, at her funeral service: 'Of all the ironies about Diana, perhaps the greatest was this: a girl given the name of the ancient goddess of hunting was, in the end, the most hunted person of the modern age.'

Ellen MacArthur

Fearless, determined and heroic, Ellen MacArthur holds the world record for the fastest solo circumnavigation of the globe. During her voyage she battled hurricanes and extremes of fatigue and loneliness. However, asked what the worst part was, she replied, 'Getting off the boat at the finishing line.'

'It's good to be scared sometimes – it keeps me on my toes.'

BIOGRAPHY

Name:	Ellen Patricia MacArthur DBE
Lived:	8 July 1976 –
Place of birth:	Derbyshire, England
Nationality:	British
Famed as:	Long-distance yachtswoman and founder of the Ellen MacArthur Trust

In February 2005, Ellen MacArthur broke the world record for the fastest circumnavigation of the world in her yacht *B&Q/Castorama*. She was following in the tradition of pioneering British seafaring, which has fascinated the nation ever since Queen Elizabeth I knighted Sir Francis Drake when he returned from his round-the-world voyage. Drake completed the journey in three years in his flagship, the *Golden Hind*, with a crew of 50 men. In 1967, Sir Francis Chichester (1901–1972) sailed solo round the world in his ketch *Gipsy Moth IV* in nine months and one day, making one stop in Sydney, Australia. Queen Elizabeth II knighted him on his return, using the same sword that her ancestor used to knight Drake. In 1969, Robin Knox-Johnston became the first person to complete the voyage single-handed and non-stop, in just under six months. Ellen accomplished the feat 36 years later in less than 72 days. On her return, she was named a Dame of the British Empire, the equivalent of a knighthood.

FACTFILE

- For 71 days during her record-breaking voyage Ellen had no more than 20 minutes' sleep at a time, having to be on constant lookout day and night.

- Ellen beat the record set by the Frenchman Francis Joyon in 2004 by one day, eight hours, 35 minutes and 49 seconds.

- Ellen's boat is four times faster than Robin Knox-Johnston's, the first man to circumnavigate the globe non-stop and single-handed in 1969.

- Ellen's favourite expression is '*à donf*', French for 'go for it'. This is what her many French admirers call out to her during races.

Ellen was born and grew up in Derbyshire with her parents, Ken and Avril MacArthur, both teachers, and two brothers. At the age of four, Ellen was introduced to sailing by her aunt. She spent her spare time reading books about boats, including Arthur Ransome's *Swallows and Amazons*, and saved up her pocket money to buy her first boat, an eight-foot dinghy called *Thr'penny Bit*, when she was 13.

Ellen had initially wanted to be a vet but her school work was badly disrupted when she caught glandular fever. While she was recovering, she followed the progress of the Whitbread race on television and made up her mind to be a sailor. In 1994, Ellen made her debut in full-time yachting, working on a 60-foot yacht and teaching sailing to adults. She was awarded the Royal Yachting Association Instructor's ticket when she was still only 18. In 1995, Ellen won the Young Sailor of the Year award and sailed her 21-foot boat *Iduna* single-handed around Great Britain.

In 1996, Ellen made her first transatlantic crossing, leaving Newport, Rhode Island on her twentieth birthday. This was followed by successes in a number of transatlantic races, in larger boats and different classes. Ellen realized that if she was to continue to compete at this level, she would need the same support from sponsors that her male competitors routinely had. She managed to secure the

TIMELINE

Date	Ellen MacAurthur	Related events
1976	Born in Derbyshire, England	
1978		Naomi James, Krystyna Chojnowska-Liskiewicz and Brigitte Oudry sail around the world south of the Great Capes
1979		19 people die during the Fastnet Race
1989	Buys her first boat, *Thr'penny Bit*	Phillipe Jeantot develops the Vendée Globe race
1991		France's Isabelle Autissier circumnavigates the world
1994	Makes debut in full-time yachting	
1996	Makes first transatlantic passage	
1998	First in the Route du Rhum solo transatlantic race	Karen Thorndike becomes first American woman to sail solo around the world
1999	Yachtsman of the Year	
2001	Fastest female and youngest sailor to sail round the world Receives the MBE	Steve Fossett breaks transatlantic sailing record, smashing previous record by 44 hours
2003	Establishes EM Trust Broken mast ends Jules Verne round-the-world bid	
2004		Francis Joyon sets world record for solo non-stop circumnavigation
2005	Breaks Francis Joyon's world record Made a Dame of the British Empire	

£50,000 entrance fee for the Route du Rhum solo transatlantic race from St Malo to Guadeloupe from the Kingfisher Group. Ellen came first in a 50-foot monohull named after her sponsors. She completed the race in just over 20 days. Her achievement sealed her long-term association with Kingfisher.

In January 1999, Ellen won the Yachtsman of the Year award. Throughout the year she raced with French yachtsman Yves Parlier, with whom she won the Round Europe race on board the 60-foot *Aquitaine Innovations*. They finished in the top ten in the Fastnet race and the Transat Jacques Vabre two-handed transatlantic race from Le Havre to Salvador de Bahia, Brazil.

In early 2000, Ellen took delivery of the 60-foot monohull *Kingfisher* and in June sailed it in the Europe1 New Man STAR solo transatlantic race. She won, completing the crossing in 14 days, 23 hours and 11 minutes. She was the youngest ever winner of the race.

The year 2001 was a year of triumph. In February, Ellen became the fastest female and youngest sailor to compete in the solo non-stop Vendée Globe race. She came second. Her reports from the race were shown on national television and she became a household name. In December she became sailing world champion when she won the Fico-Lacoste World Championship. In the same month, she was runner-up in the BBC's Sports Personality of the Year award – second only to football hero David Beckham – and named the *Sunday Times* Woman of the Year. On 12 December, she received the MBE from the Queen at Buckingham Palace.

In 2002, Ellen announced her attempt to break the Jules Verne round-the-world record. Ellen began the voyage on 30 January 2003 on the 110-foot catamaran *Kingfisher*, with a crew of 14. Her record-breaking attempt failed on 23 February when the boat lost its mast 2000 miles from the Australian coast. In April, her sponsors announced that a new boat would be built for Ellen with the sole objective of breaking solo speed sailing records.

In the summer of 2000, Ellen had become involved with the French charity À chacun son cap (Everyone has a goal), accompanying a group of children suffering from cancer on a sailing trip. She described the time she spent with them as one of the best day's sailing she had ever had. She was determined to set up a similar organization in England and in 2003 launched the Ellen MacArthur Trust, which aims to support and empower children with cancer or leukaemia by introducing them to the joys of sailing on the sea. In Ellen's words, 'I have seen first-hand the joy and inspiration that time out on the water can give kids suffering from cancer and leukaemia – for the short time that they are at sea, they experience another life. It's a transformation for many of them. I love this work.'

Ellen began her next attempt at the round-the-world record on 28 November 2004 in the new 75-foot trimaran *B&Q/Castorama*. She set out from a point between Ushant and the Lizard in the Atlantic. During the voyage, she had to handle sails the weight of a car, stay up all night in storms, hang one-handed off a 90-foot high mast in churning seas, and negotiate hurricanes, icebergs and whales. Her strength, courage and competence were extraordinary. Apart from the physical fatigue, she also had to cope with great loneliness, 'times when you'd start spiralling downwards without really understanding why. You're tired, and a lot of little things pull you into that spiral, and before you know it, you're at rock bottom and there's no one to pull you out.' On 7 February 2005, Ellen broke the world record for the fastest solo circumnavigation of the globe, setting a new record time of 71 days, 14 hours, 189 minutes and 33 seconds.

Ellen returned to England on 8 February 2005, when she was immediately appointed a Dame of the British Empire in recognition of her achievement. At 28, she is the youngest woman to have received the honour. Once asked what motivated her to undertake her epic voyages, she replied: 'I often stand in the cockpit and stare out to sea, thinking I must be the luckiest person in the world to be seeing, feeling, smelling and touching all this.'

Index

Abolitionists
    Susan Brownell Anthony 66–9
    Elizabeth Cady Stanton 69
    Harriet Beecher Stowe 54–7
Academics
    Germaine Greer 175–7
Actresses
    Katharine Hepburn 118–21
    Jiang Qing (Madame Mao) 139
    Madonna 194–7
    Marilyn Monroe 158–61
    Eva Perón 147
    Oprah Winfrey 192–3
Albert, Prince 59–60
Al Fayed, Mohammed 201
Anthony, Susan Brownell 66–9
Anti-slavery campaigners
    see Abolitionists
Antony, Marc 8–9
Arden, Elizabeth 91
Asquith, Herbert 77
Austen, Jane 50–3
Authors
    Jane Austen 50–3
    Simone de Beauvoir 122–5
    Betty Friedan 153
    Germaine Greer 174–7
    Hildegard of Bingen 19–21
    Rosa Luxemburg 87
    Madonna 194–7
    Harriet Beecher Stowe 54–7
    Mary Wollstonecraft 46–9
    Virginia Woolf 98–101
Avedon, Richard 159
Aviators
    Amelia Earhart 110–13
    Amy Johnson 113

Becquerel, Antoine 79
Bernstein, Eduard 87
Bhutto, Benazir 186–9
Bhutto, Zulfikar Ali 187
Bloomsbury Group 99–101
Bogart, Humphrey 121
Boleyn, Anne 39
Boudicca 14–17
Bourke-White, Margaret 114–17

Caesar, Julius 7, 8, 15
Cassatt, Mary 70–3
**Catherine II Empress of Russia
(Catherine the Great)** 42–5
Catherine of Aragon 33, 39
Chanel, Coco 102–5
Charity work
    Diana, Princess of Wales 200–1
    Ellen MacArthur 205
    Helena Rubinstein 91, 93
Charles, Prince of Wales 199–201
Charles VI, King of France 27, 29
Charles VII, King of France 29
Chichester, Sir Francis 203

Christianity
    Hildegard of Bingen 18–21
    Joan of Arc 26–9
    Mary Magdalene 10–13
    Mother Teresa 126–9
Civil rights campaigners
    Rosa Parks 134–7
    Eleanor Roosevelt 109
    see also Abolitionists
Cleopatra 6–9
Columbus, Christopher 33
Conservationists
    Dian Fossey 166–9
    Germaine Greer 177
Corrigan, Mairead 178–81
Cosmetics
    Chanel perfumes 104–5
    Mary Quant 173
    Helena Rubinstein 90–3
Cults
    Mary Magdalene 11
Curie, Marie 78–81
Curie, Pierre 79–80

Dauphin 28–9
Davison, Emily 75
de Beauvoir, Simone 122–5
de Medici, Catherine 33–7
Degas, Edgar 72–3
Deng Xiaoping 141
DiMaggio, Joe 160–1
Diana, Princess of Wales 198–201
Diarists
    Anne Frank 162–5
    Queen Victoria 58–61
Disraeli, Benjamin 61
Drake, Sir Francis 203
Drug addiction
    Billie Holiday 145
    Marilyn Monroe 161

Earhart, Amelia 110–13
Economists
    Rosa Luxemburg 86–9
Edwards, Henrietta Muir 85
Eleanor of Aquitaine 22–5
Elizabeth I, Queen of England 38–41

Fashion designers
    Coco Chanel 103
    Mary Quant 170–3
Fayed, Dodi 201
Feminism
    Susan Brownell Anthony 66–9
    Jane Austen 52
    Simone de Beauvoir 122–5
    Eleanor of Aquitaine 25
    Betty Friedan 152–3
    Germaine Greer 175–7
    Mary Wollstonecraft 46–9
    Virginia Woolf 98–101
Ferdinand of Aragon 31–2

Film
    Cleopatra 9
    see also Actresses
Fonda, Henry 121
Fossey, Dian 166–9
Frank, Anne 162–5
Friedan, Betty 150–3
Fuller, Sarah 96

Gladstone, William 61
Goodman, Benny 143–4
Gorbachev, Mikhail 157
Greer, Germaine 174–7
Gurieli, Princess *see* Rubinstein, Helena
Gurieli-Tchkonia, Artchil 93

Hammond, John 144–5
Heath, Edward 155
Henri II, King of France 35
Henri III, King of France 37
Henry II, King of England 24–5
Henry IV, King of Spain 31
Henry V, King of England 27–9
Henry VIII, King of England 39
Hepburn, Katharine 105, 118–21
Hildegard of Bingen 18–21
Hodgkin, Dorothy 130–3
Hogarth Press 100–1
Holiday, Billie 142–5
Hua Guofeng 141
Hughes, Howard 121
Human rights campaigners
    Eleanor Roosevelt 106–9
    see also Abolitionists

Isabella I of Spain 30–3

Jiang Qing (Madame Mao) 138–41
Joan of Arc 26–9
Jogiches, Leo 87–8
Johnson, Amy 113
Journalists
    Margaret Bourke-White 114–17
    Betty Friedan 150–3
    Germaine Greer 174–7

Kautsky, Karl 88–9
Keller, Helen 94–7
King, Billie Jean 182–5
King, Larry 183, 185
King, Martin Luther 136–7
Knox-Johnston, Robin 203

Lagerfeld, Karl 105
Lawyers
    Emily Murphy 82–5
Leakey, Louis 167
Lenin, Vladimir 87
Liebknecht, Karl 89
Lincoln, Abraham 57
Louis VII, King of France 23–4
Luxemburg, Rosa 86–9

MacArthur, Ellen 202–5
Madonna 194–7
Mao, Madame (Jiang Qing) 138–41
Mao Zedong 139–41
Mary Magdalene 10–13
Mary Queen of Scots 40–1
Mary Tudor, Queen of England 33, 39–40
McClung, Nellie Mooney 85
McKinney, Louise Crummy 85
Medicine
    Catherine the Great 45
    Marie Curie 78–81
    Dorothy Hodgkin 130
    Florence Nightingale 62–5
    Mary Seacole 65
Melbourne, Lord 59
Miller, Arthur 161
Missionaries of Charity 128–9
Monroe, Marilyn 158–61
Mother Teresa 126–9
Murphy, Emily 82–5
Music
    Hildegard of Bingen 21
    Billie Holiday 142–5
    Madonna 194–7

Nightingale, Florence 62–5
Nobel Prize
    Mairead Corrigan 179
    Marie Curie 80–1
    Dorothy Hodgkin 133
    Mother Teresa 128
    Betty Williams 179
Nuns
    Hildegard of Bingen 18–21
Nursing
    Florence Nightingale 62–5
    Mary Seacole 65

Painters
    Mary Cassatt 70–3
Palmerston, Lord 60
Pankhurst, Adela 75, 77
Pankhurst, Christabel 75, 77
Pankhurst, Emmeline 74–7
Pankhurst, Sylvia 75, 77
Parker-Bowles, Camilla 200
Parks, Rosa 134–7
Parlby, Irene Marryat 85
Patrons of the arts
    Catherine de Medici 37
    Catherine the Great 45
    Helena Rubinstein 91
Peace campaigners
    Mairead Corrigan 178–81
    Dorothy Hodgkin 133
    Betty Williams 178–81
Peel, Sir Robert 60
Perón, Eva 146–9
Perón, Juan 147–9
Philosophers
    Simone de Beauvoir 122–5

Photographers
    Margaret Bourke-White 114–17
Pilots
    Amelia Earhart 110–13
    Amy Johnson 113
Politics
    Ancient Egyptians 7–9
    Benazir Bhutto 186–9
    Jiang Qing (Madame Mao) 138–41
    Rosa Luxemburg 86–9
    Eva Perón 146–9
    Romans 7–9
    Margaret Thatcher 154–7

Quant, Mary 170–3
Queens
    Boudicca 14–17
    Cleopatra 6–9
    Eleanor of Aquitaine 22–5
    Elizabeth I 38–41
    Isabella I of Spain 30–3
    Queen Victoria 58–61

Reagan, Ronald 157
Richard I, King of England 25
Ritchie, Guy 197
Romans 7–9, 15–17
Roosevelt, Eleanor 106–9
Roosevelt, President Franklin D. 107–9
Roosevelt, President Theodore 69
Rubinstein, Helena 90–3
Russell, Lord 60

Saints
    Hildegard of Bingen 21
    Joan of Arc 26–9
    Mary Magdalene 10–13
Sartre, Jean-Paul 123
Scientists
    Marie Curie 78–81
    Dorothy Hodgkin 130–3
Seacole, Mary 65
Spanish Inquisition 32
Sport
    Billie Jean King 182–5
    Ellen MacArthur 202–5
Stanton, Elizabeth Cady 67, 69
Stowe, Harriet Beecher 54–7
Strange Fruit 144
Suffrage campaigners
    Susan Brownell Anthony 66–9
    Mary Cassatt 73
    Emily Murphy 83
    Emmeline Pankhurst 74–7
    Elizabeth Cady Stanton 67, 69
Suicide
    Cleopatra 9
    Jiang Qing (Madame Mao) 141
    Marilyn Monroe 158–61
    Virginia Woolf 101
Sullivan, Anne Mansfield 95–7
Suu Kyi, Aung San 181

Thatcher, Denis 155
Thatcher, Margaret 154–7
Titus, Edward 92
Tracy, Spencer 121
TV presenters
    Oprah Winfrey 190–3
Twain, Mark 57

Uncle Tom's Cabin 56–7

Victoria, Queen of England 58–61
Visions
    Hildegard of Bingen 19–21
    Joan of Arc 29

West, Rebecca 75–6
Williams, Betty 178–81
Wilson, Cairine 83
Wilson, Teddy 144
Winfrey, Oprah 190–3
Witchcraft
    Joan of Arc 29
Wollstonecraft, Mary 46–9
Women's rights
    Susan Brownell Anthony 66–9
    Benazir Bhutto 189
    Henrietta Muir Edwards 85
    Famous Five 82–5
    Billie Jean King 184–5
    Nellie Mooney McClung 85
    Louise Crummy McKinney 85
    Emily Murphy 82–5
    Emmeline Pankhurst 74–7
    Irene Marryat Parlby 85
    Eva Perón 149
    Eleanor Roosevelt 109
    Elizabeth Cady Stanton 67, 69
    Mary Wollstonecraft 46–9
    see also Suffrage campaigners
Woolf, Leonard 100–1
Woolf, Virginia 98–101

Yachtswomen
    Ellen MacArthur 202–5
Young, Lester 144–5

Zardari, Asif Ali 188–9
Zoologists
    Dian Fossey 166–9